About the editors

Sita Venkateswar is Director, International, in the College of Humanities and Social Sciences and senior lecturer in the social anthropology programme at Massey University. Her ethnography *Development and Ethnocide: Colonial Practices in the Andaman Islands* is based on her PhD fieldwork in the Andaman Islands from 1989 to 1992. She has since been involved in research on child labour in Nepal and poverty and grassroots democracy in Kolkata, India. She is currently involved in exploring indigenous politics related to climate change as well as questions of displacement and belonging in relation to refugee resettlement in New Zealand and Europe. Email: s.venkateswar@massey.ac.nz

Emma Hughes spent several years living in Egypt and working with women's rights groups in Egypt and East Africa, where she was involved with development and advocacy projects. In New Zealand she worked first for the Centre for Indigenous Governance and Development at Massey University, and currently works as a research adviser. As a visiting research scholar at the American University in Cairo during 2008 she returned to Egypt to research the Nubian case. Email: e.l.hughes@massey.ac.nz

THE POLITICS OF INDIGENEITY

dialogues and reflections on indigenous activism

edited by Sita Venkateswar and Emma Hughes

Zed Books
LONDON | NEW YORK

The Politics of Indigeneity: dialogues and reflections on indigenous activism was first published in 2011 by Zed Books Ltd, 7 Cynthia Street, London N1 9JF, UK and Room 400, 175 Fifth Avenue, New York, NY 10010, USA

www.zedbooks.co.uk

Editorial copyright © Sita Venkateswar and Emma Hughes 2011
Copyright in this collection © Zed Books 2011

The rights of Sita Venkateswar and Emma Hughes to be identified as the editors of this work have been asserted by them in accordance with the Copyright, Designs and Patents Act, 1988.

FSC
www.fsc.org
MIX
Paper from responsible sources
FSC® C013604

Set in OurType Arnhem and Futura Bold by Ewan Smith, London
Index: ed.emery@thefreeuniversity.net
Cover designed by www.alice-marwick.co.uk
Printed and bound by CPI Group (UK) Ltd, Croydon, CR0 4YY

Distributed in the USA exclusively by Palgrave Macmillan, a division of St Martin's Press, LLC, 175 Fifth Avenue, New York, NY 10010, USA

A catalogue record for this book is available from the British Library
Library of Congress Cataloging in Publication Data available

ISBN 978 1 78032 121 9 hb
ISBN 978 1 78032 120 2 pb

Contents

Figures and table

Figures

Table

Abbreviations

CKGR	Central Kalahari Game Reserve
CPA	Comprehensive Peace Agreement (Sudan)
FAO	Food and Agriculture Organization
ILO	International Labour Organization
INGO	international non-governmental organization
IPO	indigenous peoples' organization
IWGIA	International Work Group for Indigenous Affairs
NGO	non-governmental organization
NHRC	National Human Rights Commission (Thailand)
NIF	National Islamic Front (Sudan)
REDD	Reducing Emissions from Deforestation and Forest Development
SI	Survival International
UNAP	Unión de Nativos Ayoreo de Paraguay (Union of Native Ayoreo of Paraguay)
UNDP	UN Development Programme
UNPFII	UN Permanent Forum on Indigenous Issues
WCC	World Conservation Congress
WHO	World Health Organization
WIPCE	World Indigenous Peoples Conference on Education

Additional materials

Selected audio files, including some interviews featured in the book, are available for free download from Indigenous Portal www.indigenousportal.com.

As a long-term project, we hope to add to this with various additional materials – including previously unpublished transcripts, articles, discussions, podcasts, further reading suggestions etc. – aimed at students, researchers, activists and readers interested in these issues. The website also contains a wealth of news, information and documents, with which to provide guidance to states, indigenous peoples, UN agencies, non-governmental organisations, the private sector and academics interested in using new technologies to improve communications and the quality of life for indigenous peoples around the world.

The Indigenous Portal is a focal point online created by indigenous peoples for indigenous peoples. The Portal is a place to share, with indigenous perspectives, cultures, history as well as indigenous aspirations for the future, in a way that supports the work of the global indigenous community. At the heart of this vision is respect for the dignity and human rights of all indigenous peoples as articulated by the United Nations Declaration on the Rights of Indigenous Peoples.

Indigenous Portal is an outcome of the World Summit on the Information Society (WSIS), a United Nations sponsored summit about information and communication which ultimately resulted in a Declaration and Plan of Action of the Global Forum of Indigenous Peoples and the Information Society. The portal project is administered by the Indigenous Portal Board and supported by the Swiss Development Agency and Incomindios.

'A portal is much more than a web interface. It is a focal point where Indigenous content will be available from our peoples and other stakeholders. Our portal will allow us to share, with our own voices, our traditions, values, history and language as well as our aspirations for the future.' – Indigenous caucus statement @ WSIS

To the many indigenous activisms and the many
more indigenous peoples inhabiting this earth:

We salute you!

Introduction

JITA VENKATESWAR, EMMA HUGHES,
CHRISTOPHER KIDD, JUSTIN KENRICK,
BENNO GLAUSER, HINE WAITERE,
KATHARINE MCKINNON, SIMRON JIT SINGH

This edited volume concurrently explores the notion of indigeneity and indigenous activism in different parts of the world and the strategic ways in which that concept intersects with the local, national and international imperatives of those identifying themselves as indigenous within the current global political conjuncture. As critical interlocutors, the contributors to this collection engage in dialogue with indigenous spokespersons and activists and with each other, to reflect on and envision possible indigenous futures.

Through such a process, the authors in this collection consider some of the key insights from their individual contributions to go on to presage the possibilities for what we want to identify as 'second wave indigeneity'[1] as the conclusion to this multifaceted engagement with indigeneity and indigenous activism. The concept of second-wave indigeneity[2] emerged when Manuhuia Barcham, a Māori academic who was based in Massey University during the early stages of this project, coined the phrase to characterize an enabling moment in international indigenous politics, which looked to the future in the wake of the UN Declaration on the Rights of Indigenous Peoples. Such a phrase embraces the wisdom garnered from the other major social movements of the last few decades, namely feminism and the politics of identity, marked by a subaltern claiming of rights.

Each contribution is reflective of the varied contours that are likely to inflect and shape such an emergent concept: whether in the deliberately performative indigeneity suggested by Judith Butler's work, as the 'invocation of an identity for the purposes of political resistance to a hegemonic threat of erasure or marginalisation' (Butler and Scott 1992: 109);[3] or through a process of accommodation based on a relational understanding of indigeneity as conceptualized by Rose. The quote below suggests that indigeneity is an identity that is continually in flux and is determined not by some original state of purity but by the relationships between peoples:

[O]ne of the most basic of all human questions: who are you? This is not a question that can be answered with a name nor can it be answered satisfactorily in words. Rather, the question requires qualitative demonstrations. Answers emerge in the lived experience of relationships developed in shared time and place. Ultimately, answers are a sharing of perceptions, attitudes, experiences, and, I think, compassion. (Rose 2009 [1992]: 26)

Indigeneity is, then, 'a process; a series of encounters; a structure of power; a set of relationships; a matter of becoming, in short, and not a fixed state of being', as de la Cadena and Starn (2007: 11) note in their edited volume. Benno Glauser emphasizes in this volume that indigeneity alludes to a set of relationships between people and what has come to be understood as 'nature', an 'identity not [...] responding to the question "*who*" but [...] responding to the question "*how*" a distinctively specific and different way to conceive identity and to "be in the world"' (p. 40). The concept of identity here appears as 'way of being'. Or, as Kenrick and Lewis suggest, indigenous identity represents only one side of a relationship, 'the side which has been dispossessed ... and "indigenous rights" describes a strategy for resisting dispossession that employs a language understood by those wielding power' (Kenrick and Lewis 2004a: 263).

The African Commission for Human and Peoples' Rights (ACHPR) defines indigeneity from a rights-based perspective, one that is of particular relevance to many peoples across Africa and Asia:

'Indigenous peoples' has come to have connotations and meanings that are much wider than the question of 'who came first'. It is today a term and a global movement fighting for rights and justice for those particular groups who have been left on the margins of development and who are perceived negatively by dominating mainstream development paradigms, whose cultures and ways of life are subject to discrimination and contempt and whose very existence is under threat of extinction. (ACHPR and IWGIA 2005: 86)

Francesca Merlan's (2009) paper with its wide-ranging debate in the leading disciplinary journal *Current Anthropology* disentangles the liberal origins of the international indigenous movement from the ways in which indigeneity is constituted in various parts of the world. Without a doubt, its publication is likely to arouse heated discussions, with ripples felt beyond the domains of mere academic exchange.

The indigeneities that are revealed in this collection are as alert to the challenges posed to indigenous aspirations by the neoliberal agenda of nation-states and their concerns with sovereignty. These manifestations of indigeneity are also deeply embedded in spiritual connections with the landscape in which they are situated, yet simultaneously maintain both a strategic and a pragmatic stance in the responses to climate change, carbon offsets or the geopolitics of the Kyoto Protocol and emissions trade. While being cognizant of the incommensurabilities inherent in a discussion of such a broad cross-section of peoples, the different expressions and displays signalled above can be linked by a move towards 'naming and claiming'[4] as the shared thread woven through all the chapters in the volume.

It is a significant moment to undertake such a project. The passage of the UN Declaration on the Rights of Indigenous Peoples in 2007 after almost twenty-five years in the drafting process articulates the aspirations of indigenous groups worldwide. As a wide-ranging and often contentious process of consultation and dialogue on the rights and aspirations of indigenous peoples across the world, the passage of the Declaration marks the collective achievement of indigenous activists, international non-governmental organizations (INGOs), nation-states and the United Nations (UN).[5] The negative votes cast at the time against the Declaration by the bloc of settler nations, the United States, Canada, Australia and New Zealand, though not unanticipated, emphasized the challenges that the Declaration poses despite its non-binding authority. But the recent changes in political regimes in all these nations, with their accompanying shift in positions regarding the Declaration, bode well for future processes pertaining to indigenous claims at these locations and their impact globally.[6]

Many challenges were manifest throughout the process and are highlighted by two controversies, one during the drafting process and the other within academia. In a provocative report submitted in 1999, the former UN Special Rapporteur Miguel Alfonso Martinez claimed that indigenous identity should be reserved to those continents that were the sites of organized European colonization and settlement. According to this view, indigenous status could not be applied within the post-colonial contexts of Asia and Africa, unsurprisingly triggering widespread outrage within African and Asian indigenous circles.

Contentions within UN processes are paralleled in the heated and increasingly acrimonious exchanges sparked within academic anthropological forums by Adam Kuper's (2003) call to discard the notion of 'indigenous peoples' because it referred to 'essentialist, romantic and discredited ideas within anthropology (Barnard 2004), marking a point of intersection between academic debates and international indigenous politics. Questions about indigeneity remain of enduring interest within anthropology and academia in general, as evidenced by the volume of writing on the subject,[7] the flurry of recent publications and journal articles (Castaneda 2009; Trigger and Dalley 2010; Poirier 2010), and the range of positions articulated within those discussions as well as within this volume regarding what constitutes indigeneity, and how it should or can be conceptualized.

Many of the commentators involved in the Kuper furore pointed to the fact that indigeneity as a concept and a global movement existed in the world regardless of any academic decisions within the discipline of anthropology that challenge the notion. But neither can the discipline claim innocence or neutrality regarding what eventuates for indigenous peoples across the world when crucial decisions are made about their rights, their lives and livelihoods that refer to semantic quibbles within the discipline. Ideas and concepts within the discipline of anthropology acquire political resonance and currency that dissolve notional boundaries between the realm of academia and global politics.

More entrenched, however, are the barriers that have been erected between different regions of the world, which are the lasting consequences of European colonialism, most notably the division between the anglophone and the hispanophone parts of the world, which are not easy to surmount. 'Although over the years I have met dozens of indigenous peoples from Latin America,' remarks Teanau Tuiono, reflecting on his numerous encounters at international gatherings, 'I only keep in close contact with the ones who can also speak English. Indigenous peoples who are bilingual or multilingual in the four common languages of communication (English, French, Spanish and Russian) are crucial bridges and links between peoples. Non-indigenous groups who have this capability are crucial in enabling us to connect the dots and I'm thinking about groups like DOCIP[8] (Indigenous Peoples' Centre for Documentation, Research and Information), a non-indigenous organization which does support work for indigenous peoples at the UN' (p. 236).

The combination of dialogues, reflections and analysis in this multidisciplinary[9] collection explores the complexities of indigencity and indigenous activism in diverse regions of the world, including Africa, Asia, South America and Oceania, to explore the global/local political space that they inhabit in the twenty-first century. It has confronted the challenges of engaging in dialogue across regions, domains *and languages* and surmounted the logistical difficulties involved in such a feat. An unforeseen consequence of the challenges posed by such a venture is the attrition that has occurred among the original list of contributors, who were unable to follow through with convening discussion forums in their regions in accordance with the timeline for this project. The final list of contributors and regions is based on a combination of serendipity and known contacts in a particular part of the world, as well as those who could commit to the *longue durée* of such a project. The collection does not intend to be exhaustive in its treatment of indigeneity across the world, but is mostly focused on those regions which have an explicit indigenous, activist presence, i.e. groups that are politically articulate and engage with local, national and international processes without the mediation of well-intentioned others acting *for* them. This has meant that although the expertise of one of the editors was in the Andaman Islands, with her own activism on *behalf* of the islanders, that region could not be included because of the absence of an indigenous activist presence in that group of islands. The Nicobar group of islands, the islands farther south of the Andaman Islands, especially the central Nicobar Islands, does have a history of indigenous activism, which has been addressed in this collection.

Each contributor is grounded within a specific context to explore how indigeneity and indigenous activism are shaped by that context and the ways in which they intersect with local, national and global domains, to articulate a vision of a future. Most chapters have an unusual dual structure, consisting of a wide-ranging dialogue with indigenous spokespersons and activists, followed by a reflective essay that considers the main threads of the dialogues and muses on the key issues of each context. This is, in turn, followed by a brief commentary by one or more contributors. Such a structure enables the contributors to straddle the realms of academia and indigenous activism to collaboratively envision a collective future and the diverse trajectories towards realizing such a vision.

A notable feature of this project is its emphasis on the dialogic and the several orders in which that has been constructed and embedded

5

processually at every stage of its development. This has involved more than the forums convened by each contributor, to address the questions raised in this collection with indigenous activists and spokespersons, some of whom are also contributing authors to this project. It has also meant finding ways to make that process visible in the writing and presentation of each section, in rendering the dialogue visible as an essential element within the final publication. As alluded to already, this discursive attribute is also maintained *between* the contributors, who are included as external interlocutors responding to the first order of discussions convened by each contributor. This is manifest in the commentaries at the end of each chapter, whereby a contributor responds to a discussion convened elsewhere, as an interlocutor speaking from the perspective of the context that is familiar to them, followed by a reply to the commentary by the author of that chapter.

Such a process has been enabled by the online technologies available in the form of a Google group site created for this project. It has provided ready access to various resources for everyone involved in this project, the sharing of pertinent information, audio recordings and podcasts, videos on YouTube, news features and, most importantly, each contributor's transcripts of the discussions that they convened. Technology also enabled the incorporation of a mosaic of perspectives into this project, elicited from indigenous participants at various international forums during the course of 2008/09.

To maintain a degree of cohesiveness to the collection as a whole, the contributors were asked to utilize four key overarching questions/ themes when conducting their discussions. The questions served as the starting point for discussions but were also reframed in response to the specificities of each context, as made evident in many of the chapters.[10] The framing questions are:

1 What constitutes indigeneity in the area where you work?
2 What are the politics of indigeneity in this area?
3 What is the vision for the future? (Related questions that emerge from this are: what are the steps towards realizing such a vision, and/or the obstacles that get in the way of such a realization?)
4 What role do local indigenous organizations and international indigenous organizations play in this process?

As previously mentioned, all the sections include a commentator who, except in the Aotearoa/New Zealand chapter,[11] is also a contributor to a different section of the book. Here, too, contributors are asked to address the following set of questions:

1 What are the points of connection and divergence between the perspectives presented in this discussion and the ones that you have convened?
2 What are the lessons to be learned from this context?

The final concluding section consists of a brief dialogue between two contributors, Hine Waitere and Sita Venkateswar, followed by a series of reflections involving all the contributors to this collection. As the contributors finished their individual chapters and approached the end of the project, they were asked to address the final question:

1 Is it possible to discern an emergent second-wave indigeneity from this context? Is this merely an academic mirage? If not, what are the ways in which such a concept can be given shape and form?

The questions addressed for the book connected with larger processes in Thailand and Aotearoa, becoming imbricated in ongoing indigenous political processes at those locations. Those currents have in turn shaped the project, enriching and extending collaborative ways of engagement despite the longer time frame necessary for completion of the book project.

This collection, therefore, presents a unique set of discursive narratives which attempt to straddle and thereby bridge often conflicting domains of indigenous politics and activism, drawing on indigenous experiences from 'old' and 'new' world, Fourth World settler and post-colonial perspectives. Section One, broadly entitled 'Settler', articulates perspectives drawn from the Ayoreo of Paraguay and the Māori of Aotearoa/New Zealand. Section Two, entitled 'Post-colonial', then shifts to the very different post-colonial geopolitical context of the Batwa of Uganda and then the Nubians of Egypt and Sudan. Adding complexity to the broadly entitled 'Post-colonial' are the indigenous groups in the highlands of northern Thailand, followed by the post-tsunami[12] context of the Nicobar Islands. Section Three is cast somewhat differently from the others, in that, rather than focusing on the experiences of one group in particular, it shifts its attention to the experiences of two leading international indigenous rights organizations (Survival International and the International Work Group for Indigenous Affairs). This section also includes discussions with spokespersons from the United Nations

7

Permanent Forum on Indigenous Issues. The chapters in this volume thus span the globe, weaving together regions, perspectives and voices not ordinarily heard or brought together in quite this fashion.

These introductory comments are followed by an invocation from Ibegua, an Ayoreo woman, elicited by Benno Glauser from Paraguay, on an occasion which he describes as 'listening to the voice of the collective body of an indigenous people, the Ayoreo, in an instance in which this body communicates itself to its members, in the traditional fashion of a vision coming to a chosen individual'. Glauser explains that 'the vision came to her as she was sleeping, and it is a powerful expression – although of a different kind – on the subject of indigeneity and the future, depicting what is going to happen in the future to the Ayoreo. As a warning, it stresses the essential role which being indigenous and being Ayoreo can play in this future while drawing attention to the role of dreaming and having visions as an expression of the collective subconscious.' Ibegua's lament and her foreboding in the invocation are answered in the concluding section of this volume by the naming, claiming and envisioning of second-wave indigeneity by each contributor. With the profound gift of accommodation[13] which bravely offers an affirmation of mutuality to the non-indigenous, second-wave indigeneity envisions an integrated, collective future in which both the indigenous and the non-indigenous have equal stakes, while also acknowledging the incommensurability of indigenous lives as it is currently manifested in different reaches of the globe.[14]

In Chapter 1, Glauser's subsequent dialogue with Ayoreo leaders Mateo and Aquino explores how they came to understand their own indigeneity, after having been contacted and taken out of the forests by force in the wave of 'ethnic cleansing' led by missionaries during the 1960s. The ways in which Mateo and Aquino presently view the future of their own people and other indigenous peoples that they know add substance to Ibegua's apprehensions, and are also reflected in Chupon's presentiment regarding the post-tsunami conjuncture to the Nicobarese lifeworld. Both Glauser's and Chupon's (hence also Simron Jit Singh's) meditations on 'being indigenous' draw attention to a lifeworld that is under severe threat, a radically incommensurable way of being that incorporates a spiritual connection to both the living and the non-living that an impoverished conceptual vocabulary attempts to contain within the expression 'nature'.

Incommensurability is writ large as we shift from the Ayoreo to the fiery, 'pull-no-punches' politically articulate Māori activisms in Chapter 2. As a contribution to indigenous writing, the issues addressed throughout this chapter reiterate the wider framework of self-determination, decolonization and social justice. Elizabeth Allen traces the lineage of the unfinished project of colonialism in Aoteroa/New Zealand, rendered violently visible most recently in the 'Terrorism Raids' of October 2007, while Hine Waitere and other participants provide insight into the complex array of forces that impact on indigenous peoples as they attempt to live indigenous lives governed by indigenous principles and practices. Unlike in the other chapters in the volume, the contributing authors, activists/spokespersons/participants and commentator are all *tangata whenua*,[15] 'variously of different *iwi*[16] [...] [academics], those who hold government positions, some are lawyers, others are involved in community education, such as family violence prevention and women's refuge. Still more are involved in unions, sheep shearing and gardening ... irrespective of their social and geographic location they are all involved in activism in one form or another' (p. 50–1), thereby conferring a distinctive edge to this section and to the collection as a whole.

Comparing notes with a hereditary chief from Guyana at an international forum, commentator Teanau Tuiono notes the impressive achievements of Māori in the area of language and culture as perceived by other indigenous participants at that forum. Tuiono does not regard the Treaty of Waitangi as a contributing factor to that realization and is somewhat dismissive of the Treaty settlement processes currently under way in Aotearoa/New Zealand in terms of the larger objective of *tino rangatiratanga*.[17] However, elsewhere in other Fourth World contexts, such as Paraguay or Australia, the mere existence of such a treaty with its potential for marshalling claims and seeking reparation is a point of envy. Incommensurability rears up again as we attempt to juxtapose the 'co-terminous heterotemporalities' (Chakrabarty 2007) that Tuiono, too, registers in his comparison of the situation of the Penan in Borneo with the 'privileges' of indigeneity within a 'well-off' Western nation-state such as Aotearoa/New Zealand.

As alluded to earlier, former UN Special Rapporteur Miguel Alfonso Martinez and others in both academic and the public domains have questioned the application of the concept of indigeneity, and indigenous peoples' rights in particular, in the post-colonial African and Asian contexts. Under discussion has been the question of whether indigeneity is premised on a category that is not relevant in the same way in the post-independent African and Asian contexts. According to this argument, *all* Africans and Asians are considered indigenous in relation to European colonization, and decolonization is considered to have been a process of liberating these continents from colonialism. Against this, we have argued that the internal colonization under way by nationalist elites in the post-colonial context of Africa and Asia extends European colonialism's diktat on the one appropriate form of social organization, which forces all others to fit the mould cast by them.

Experience from different societies across Africa and Asia has shown that the use of ideas of indigenous peoples' rights derived from international forums and processes fits with local experience and meanings. This is both in the sense that hunter-gatherers and former hunter-gatherers are seen as distinctly indigenous by their neighbours and themselves, and also because these people occupy the same marginalized position relative to dominant society as those considered indigenous elsewhere in the world. Thus the situations in central, north-east and southern parts of Africa, and in northern Thailand, as articulated in the 'Post-colonial' section, which encompasses different regions in Africa and Asia, forces us to rethink the term indigenous in a relational as opposed to a categorical way. This enables us to reconsider our understanding of indigeneity in these contexts, as well as draw on the experiences of indigeneity from elsewhere – for instance, as articulated by the Ayoreo in Paraguay. In this way, we highlight the processes of disempowerment and discrimination which work their way down into people's quotidian lives, but which nevertheless possess the strategic potential for building alliances that extend their way out from indigenous peoples' practices and perspectives. Thus incommensurabilities across settler contexts can offer linkages *between* settler and post-colonial locations.

Christopher Kidd and Justin Kenrick's Chapter 3 explores the implications of being indigenous in the Central African Batwa context. It does this through exploring Batwa experience of both discriminatory and equalizing processes, and through identifying how their claims to indigeneity are based in large part on a very real experience of conquest. Instead of understanding indigeneity as an exclusive category, they argue that it is better understood as one way in which these marginalized communities attempt to resist and reverse processes of enclosure and discrimination by reorienting the situation along an axis of inclusion and equality which both seeks to include others and insists on being included by others. These inclusive processes are central to such peoples' modes of production and their social organization. Kidd and Kenrick suggest that in order for the aspirations of Central Africa's indigenous peoples to be fulfilled, a re-evaluation of the social and political understanding of the role of alternative livelihood strategies and modes of production is needed. Such a re-evaluation, in the Central African context, would demand not only the acceptance of these alternative ways of experiencing, organizing and materially producing the world, but would also involve a re-evaluation of the dominant national and international ways of experiencing, organizing and materially producing the world. They are perhaps best characterized as the ongoing colonial project, a project which has at its centre the insistence that other lifeworlds should be made redundant.

The relationship of nation-state with indigenous peoples and indigeneity as a threat to the nationalist project of certain African states clearly parallels the Nubian experience depicted in Chapter 4. In Egypt, where Nubians are not acknowledged as a distinct group by the state, there is no entitlement to rights which would protect their culture, language, identity or lineage. The Egyptian government has perceived moves to recognize Nubians as a distinct people as a threat to national security: the threat of a separate political entity with its own language and history, which would extend across the border into Sudan. A call for autonomy was feared if a Nubian region could be easily demarcated. Parallels have been drawn with the perceived threat a defined Kurdish region posed to Iraq; the same nationalist anxiety is also visible in relation to the highland groups of Thailand. This fear, however, does not appear to have a strong basis in any material reality. As Emma Hughes's conversations with even the most committed activists reveal, they still regard themselves as Egyptian as well as Nubian: 'I am Egyptian; if I am not Egyptian then I am a relative of Egyptians for thousands of years.' In Sudan, the Nubians inhabiting the northernmost provinces of the country prevent the government from being able to extend a solid block of support for the Islamist regime from Khartoum through to Egypt, and the state has implemented various strategies to uproot the population, as Suad, interviewed in Sudan, describes.

As for the Batwa, Ayoreo or Māori,[18] a connection with the land has immense importance for Nubians, but this is expressed in different ways, and does not necessarily include a desire to live on the land. Many of the younger generations of Nubians who have grown up in cities outside of Nubia also wish to visit ancestral lands, but not to

11

return to live there, as does Fred in his discussions with Chris Kidd, when he refers to 'going to the forest' to visit. This remains a significant aspect of the maintenance of cultural continuity and the ability to assert an indigenous identity. It is clear, however, that whether or not an individual choice is made to live on the land, what remains important is entitlement to and ownership of the land by the community, as without this the connection to place becomes increasingly fragile.

The assertion of 'commonality represent[ing] unity in the face of oppression'[19] (p. 88) is another idea we are teasing out in this volume, and one that can be seen here to apply *within* indigenous peoples, as well as across. The relational nature of indigenous identity to other tribes as well as to the non-indigenous population has become visible through this process and is reflected on in further detail in both Kidd and Kendrick's chapter and Glauser's. It has a particular resonance in Sudan; as a society with five-hundred-plus ethnic groups, this must impact on the nature of our reflections on indigeneity and marginalized minorities.

A number of the issues raised in Hughes's interviews with Nubians in Sudan and Egypt will be recognizable as familiar concerns to indigenous communities displaced by the construction of large hydroelectric projects in other parts of the world: rights to land and water resources, housing, employment and education, and heritage preservation, particularly language. Suad Ibrahim Ahmed is from Sudanese Nubia and Ahmed Sokarno from Egyptian Nubia, and although both are seeking restitution of their rights, they now find themselves occupying quite different positions in their respective states: while Ahmed is struggling to retain the continuity of his culture, Suad is now once again engaged in a struggle for the very land her people inhabit. An exploration of the Nubian responses in each country to the erosion of their rights shows first how the experience of division and dislocation has in fact shaped and sustained Nubian identity on both sides of the border, and demonstrates how the politicization of identity is adopted as a tool to resist marginalization and reclaim rights.

Katharine McKinnon's Chapter 5 on indigenous groups of northern Thailand highlights the parallels between the various modes of internal colonization under way in Africa and in mainland South-East Asia, where the use of the term 'indigenous' is much contested, especially when used by organizations representing highland minority groups that straddle the borders between Thailand, Burma, Laos, Vietnam and

China. The use of 'indigenous' in reference to these minorities denotes a certain troubled relationship with the nation-state, and is a welcome alternative to the more derogatory use of 'tribal', but what does it mean (and what does it achieve) when used in the northern Thai context? Her discussion explores how concepts of indigeneity are being engaged by advocacy groups in their negotiations within and beyond nation-state boundaries. It reports back from a workshop convened by indigenous NGOs and village leaders in 2007 to discuss the applicability of the term indigenous for highland people. Participants gathered for one day in Chiang Mai, Thailand, to discuss what it means to be indigenous in the contemporary Thai context and how local indigenous peoples' organizations (IPOs) can engage better with international indigenous peoples' movements. Debate on the day centred on how to translate the term 'indigenous' into the local context and the Thai language. The importance of naming, who would be included or excluded, and how a name could create space for indigenous rights on a national agenda were some of the central issues. These conversations mark a new shift in a long struggle for the rights of highland peoples within the Thai state. By seeking recognition of their status as indigenous peoples, highlanders are building on the achievements of international indigenous activists worldwide, as well as forging a new path for themselves in the Thai context. Although the future remains uncertain, there is hope that this new strategy may at last push the Thai government to make space for highland people as valued and respected members of the nation, and perhaps even relinquish an unjust and inflexible vision of Thai nationality that has excluded highlanders for so long.

Simron Jit Singh leads us next to the Nicobar Islands in the Bay of Bengal in Chapter 6. His dialogue cum reflective essay is a piece of work inspired by recurrent discussions that took place between the author and the prominent Nicobarese leader Chupon over several years. The Nicobar Islands were devastated by the tsunami of 2004, which killed thousands of indigenous Nicobarese and completely destroyed their villages, material culture and economy. The humanitarian aid that followed did little to restore former life. Instead, the islands became a playground for donor-aid politics, rendering the Nicobarese more vulnerable than ever before, exposing them to the perils of an aid-dependent society and a complete restructuring of their sociocultural institutions. In a recent meeting with Chupon in Port Blair, the capital of the Andaman Islands, the fate and future of the indigenous

Nicobarese was discussed. In this encounter, Chupon bemoans the state of the present Nicobarese society and reflects on the future livelihood options that could possibly give a new shape to his society, for the better, while oscillating between despair and hope.

Shifting from the local political contexts of Indigenous activism, Chapter 7 is based on discussions with two international NGOs. Sita Venkateswar convened meetings with Stephen Corry of Survival International, Lola García-Alix and Jens Dahl of the International Work Group for Indigenous Affairs, and Ida Nicolaison, the Danish representative at the UN Permanent Forum. The wide-ranging dialogue that followed explored the experiences of these organizations in addressing indigenous issues and their strategies for the future following on from the Declaration. Venkateswar's analysis of the roles and influence of the INGOs in the wake of the same tsunami that Singh details draws on her experience of research and activism in the Andaman Islands,[20] to point to some of the crucial gaps in the intersection of INGOs with the local context: towards capacity-building in the Andaman Islands, which may have facilitated the emergence of politically adept grassroots indigenous activism. Venkateswar also draws on a mosaic of viewpoints garnered by Teanau Tuiono from participants at the May 2009 meeting of the UNPFII (United Nations Permanent Forum on Indigenous Issues) in New York, which enables us to comprehend the evolving indigenous activist political space as inflected by concerns around climate change.

The volume finally gathers all the threads of the preceding chapters to 'name and claim' the space for a second-wave indigeneity in a 'space-clearing gesture' (Appiah 1991), for something that is coming into being and is yet to fully become. Our concluding chapter is animated by an engagement with the contemporary conjuncture in a mode that is simultaneously descriptive, prescriptive and utopian. As a space pregnant with radical possibilities, second-wave indigeneity is also an affirmation of our mutuality which acknowledges that 'we are all here to stay' (Asch and Samson 2004: 261), and indigenous and non-indigenous alike have equal stakes in forging a meaningful relationship with each other as equal partners towards collective but varied futures.

We end this overview of the collection and begin the sections that follow by drawing on the wisdom that Deborah Bird Rose garnered from Hobbles, her Aboriginal teacher:

Hobbles says that we all [indigenous and settlers] own Australia now.

What he does not say, because for him it is so obvious, is that Europeans have already taken most of the country and ought therefore to be more equitable. They ought, in fact, to allow more opportunities for Aborigines to control land. His suggestion that Aborigines should have more land ... offers Europeans a form of accommodation. In more extensive narratives Hobbles says that the years during which people worked on cattle stations, offering their labour to pastoralists ... ought to be understood as an attempt at accommodation to which Europeans have yet to respond ... Hobbles has offered a set of profound gifts to a non-Aboriginal audience: an acceptance of the conditions of the past as the basis from which we will build our future; some means of transforming the wrongs of the past into more equitable relationships. (Rose 2009 [1992]: 196–7)

Invocation: What the spirit said to Ibegua Chiqueñoro[1]

TRANSLATED BY BENNO GLAUSER

I was fast asleep
In my dreams [it[2]] appeared and spoke to me as follows:
Ayorea, Ayorea! Wake up from your dreams right away!
How come you are in your bed and fast asleep! Get up!
Get up on your feet, right away
Look, look, look at the world
Look at the dwelling places of the other Ayoreo
Look at what I am pointing out to you
Do what I say and look at this

I tell you all that I saw in my dreams:
Look at the places I now point out to you
You must see what I am showing you
The ashes you see, the dust, this is the future
the new generations will live
Get up! Pay attention to what is happening in the world
It is a cloud of dust,[3] it is the future of the new generations
Your dream lasts, and you cannot wake up
Thus, this misty cloud you desperately want to stop
You cannot stop it

I wanted to stop it ...
I wanted to make it stop ...

It is hard to express
what I am being told[4]

I put myself in its way but
the foggy cloud pushed me aside
because it cannot be stopped
I wanted to protect our children
That is why I stepped in its way
Even though I would not succeed I wanted to protect them
But this thing was going in the direction of Asunción[5]

it went in the morning
But the spirit told me what it all meant:
If the children and youth stop being a cause of worry for their
  parents
If the young girls won't paint their faces,[6] the world of the Ayoreo
  will be saved
But I did not understand
Why our children do not pay attention any more to what we tell
  them
Our future will be much worse
That is what the spirit told me
They must stop painting themselves that way

It says about painting oneself ...
But I do not know
how to pronounce this word
My words do not come out well in my song

I looked at their daughters
and they were more and more painted
They cannot stop painting themselves[7]
and their Ayoreo faces remain dark
But this thing went in the direction of Asunción
That spirit left in the morning
This is it.

Ibegua Chiqueñoro is an Ayoreo woman living in the settlement of
Campo Loro in the northern Paraguayan Chaco. Ibegua's name means:
a plant stem that starts growing alongside another stem, quite close by.
She communicated her vision in April 2007, and explicitly stated that
it was important to make it known to non-Ayoreo and non-indigenous
people as well. Its publication can be viewed as a generous contribution
of the Ayoreo peoples to the readers of the present volume.

Credits

At Ibegua's request, her communication of the vision was recorded.
The recording session was conducted by Mateo Sobode Chiquenoi,
with the technical support of Miguel Angel Alarcón, from Iniciativa
Amotocodie. The translation from the Zamuco (Ayoreo) language into
Spanish is the result of long-lasting, very sensitive teamwork on the

part of Mateo Sobode Chiquenoi and Carlos Picanerai (both Ayoreo), the anthropologist Dr Volker von Bremen and Miguel Angel Alarcón. Translation into English and footnotes by Benno Glauser, who also prepared the material for the present publication.

ONE | Settler: South America and New Zealand

1 | Being indigenous: the concept of indigeneity, a conversation with two Ayoreo leaders

BENNO GLAUSER

Introduction

The following exploration is based on several interviews with the two Ayoreo leaders Mateo Sobode Chiquenoi and Aquino Aquiraoi Picanerai. The interviews[1] took place between January 2008 and October 2009.

Mateo is between fifty-five and sixty years old and today lives in a settlement called Campo Loro, a former mission station. He was born in the forests. At the age of about nine, he and his group were forced by missionaries to leave the forests and their territory. The missionaries said it was no longer their territory and they were all going to be killed if they stayed where they had always lived. This was in 1959. Mateo and his mother, along with other members of the group, were deported to the mission station. His mother literally lost her mind on the way, as they were transported on the back of a truck and were exposed to the frightening experience of the tree crowns flying past at unaccustomed speed high above them, for hours on end. She was never to recover her true self and died some time later. Meanwhile, Mateo's father, who had decided, along with other members of the group, to remain in the forests, died of measles within a matter of days, as a consequence of the short encounter with the missionaries. This is the beginning of Mateo's contact story. It is very similar to many others in the recent past within the Ayoreo realm. During his life since, Mateo has gone through the different stages of relationship with and dependence on the missionaries but eventually, like many others, has come to realize that the mission's proposals have never been and will never be compatible with being an Ayoreo. Between 2007 and 2009, he was president of UNAP – Unión de Nativos Ayoreo de Paraguay[2] – and particularly active in protecting the Ayoreo groups living in voluntary isolation. The other main field of action of UNAP is the recovery of the territories lost after the 'ethnic cleansing' by the missionaries. Mateo is also something like a spontaneous historian of the Ayoreo, and has also developed a capacity to oversee the collective past of his people, having reached a state of understanding and awareness of the collective

1.1 Ayoreo territory (*source*: Iniciativa Amotocodie/Miguel Angel Alarcón)

past and present which enables him to communicate about it in the form of meta-reflections and discourse.

Aquino is forty-three years old. He was president of UNAP (2003–07). He was also born in the forests, in a different region from Mateo and in a different local group. He was contacted when he was three years old and deported to the mission station. He often refers to tales and memories his mother, an exceptionally knowledgeable and far-sighted woman, had shared with him during his life. Like Mateo, Aquino is a militant defender of indigenous self-determination. He is well known for his clear opinions and his capacity to express them.

The Ayoreo, nomadic hunters and gatherers, became known to the external, non-indigenous world only sixty years ago. Then, white people (settlers, oil companies, farmers, etc.) found that their vast territory of some thirty-one million hectares,[3] spreading across the Gran Chaco in northern Paraguay and eastern Bolivia, had to be made 'safe'; thus, missionaries were brought and sent into the forests to make them free of 'the savages' – at that moment, non-indigenous society did not even know exactly with what indigenous people it was dealing. The 'ethnic cleansing' concluded with the deportation and imposed sedentarization of almost all Ayoreo local groups, with the exception of some six or seven groups (totalling 100–150 persons) presently living in voluntary isolation.

Methodology

The methodology applied to the present inquiry into indigeneity is one of the results of almost twenty years of my being near the Ayoreo, and of thousands of conversations whose experience is condensed in the clear conclusion that, in order to grasp and to start understanding the Ayoreo, it is far better just to be listening and waiting for knowledge, understanding and eventually meaning to appear, much as a hunter waits patiently for his prey, than to ask direct questions. If questions are asked at all, they serve to tentatively start, to motivate, to direct or redirect a conversation. Open, wide-ranging questions are better than precise ones, which leave only a narrow scope for answers.

The reason for this lies in a fact which is not new, but is not usually taken sufficiently into account: when talking to indigenous people, we communicate with a radically diverse realm, and one of its chief characteristics is its wholeness, its indivisibility. In the communication with this realm, two very different 'awarenesses' come to speak with each other, each from within its own paradigm. Paradigms are essentially incommensurable. The difficulties in the communication between these two specific paradigms arise, if we formulate it from the point of view of the characteristics of the non-indigenous realm, from the fact that our knowledge is fragmented, representing a fragmented world-view, and that we use abstractions in a way that reduces what is being talked about to an object. The Ayoreo discourse, in turn, always refers to an entire reality in its wholeness, and speaks about individual, concrete events, people, phenomena, very often using images which have a sensual quality that abstractions don't have.

Within such a frame, standard interview questions cannot reach across adequately: either they miss their aim and fall into empty space, or they hit but only create confusion. Frequently, they then prompt responses that try to adapt somehow to what was asked about and to what is intuitively perceived as the interviewer's own vision of things, inducing her/him to confirm what she/he had already believed in the first place. We often don't even realize that this happens, unless we remain sharply aware of the radical, paradigmatic diversity.

We need a methodology of listening without asking questions. In my personal experience, the initial mention of the subject matter, or else the posing of a highly open-scope question, prompts the surging, on the indigenous side, of associations.[4] They often appear without visible order, quite irrationally for us, and they can take the form of tales, images, anecdotes, jokes, sometimes myths. Sometimes there is no visible connection between them and the topic we had mentioned or asked about. As a consequence, very often there remains only our intuition as a cognitive device to link elements to each other in order to detect the meaning they convey once they are linked up, while the tools of our own non-indigenous rationality[5] fail.

Trusting our intuition is often difficult for us non-indigenous people; our life culture does not usually train us to do it or even discourages its use as a cognitive tool. Thus, using it can give us a sensation of walking on ice that may prove to be too thin for our weight. There is no guarantee. But indeed, through the use of intuition, the images appearing in an indigenous person's discourse can gradually facilitate our access to the knowledge we seek; they contain leads to an answer, and intuition can find these leads. A meaning starts to 'compose itself', and, in the Ayoreo realm, it is always a complete idea, a whole complete image, not an abstracted and marginalized fragment. This method, which is something like reading between lines and which obviously requires training and experience, goes beyond the scientific procedures commonly accepted by non-indigenous science. Its results, in our non-indigenous understanding, remain subjective, and as such could easily be disqualified. While writing this contribution, I have fought to be able to present a result acceptable also in non-indigenous, scientific methodological terms, until I recognized that this was an absurd pretension, precisely because the communication here occurs between the mentioned two radically, *paradigmatically* different realms. We discover that speaking to indigenous peoples forces us to abandon our own method, to abandon the safety of our own world, and it forces us specifically to reintroduce cognitive tools our life culture has long discarded: intuition, sensual qualities, 'the heart'. We also discover, or reconfirm, that even a method carries the genetic code of the life culture that generates it, and, if applied without awareness, will transform into a colonial tool and end up colonizing the world.

It is interesting to note that these methodological difficulties and considerations themselves also provide information about the concept we are investigating. As a consequence, and to share this highly demanding communication process, I have chosen the form of an alternation between interview quotes and short paragraphs of commentary/interpretation which render the results of my own cognitive process based on the conversation. This allows for the reader to 'listen' directly to, and to 'read into', what the Ayoreo say, with the additional possibility of comparing it to, and following, my own reading and its conductive thread.

Before ending this methodological part, two concepts need to be explained, as they play a prominent, even structuring, role in the content of what follows. On the one hand, there is a timeline that is implicitly present in the discourse of the two Ayoreo leaders; it goes from a time dating some 250 years ago to the present; associations, like images, tales, etc., jump back and forth between the various time stages as if it all were present time or happening simultaneously. The other concept needing explanation is explicit: it is the concept of 'contact' – already mentioned in the short life descriptions above – and it appears on the mentioned timeline, dividing it into a segment 'before contact' and a segment 'after contact'; the concept also appears in contact history. In all cases, it refers to a specific moment in a contact process beginning in the case of the Ayoreo shortly before 1960, when they started to be physically contacted by contact agents, usually missionaries, and subsequently were coerced to leave their territory and deported. It is the specific moment when their coherent cosmovision[6] collapses, as nothing makes sense any more. A change of paradigm occurs. When referring to indigenous peoples before this contact moment we speak about 'indigenous peoples in voluntary isolation'.[7] All other indigenous peoples underwent in one or the other way such a process. The fact that the Ayoreo went through it very, very recently – and in fact are still going through it – may give them, as informants for our inquiry, a somewhat special quality related to their close proximity to their original life in a different life paradigm, and to the fact that they still and explicitly struggle with trying to understand what has happened to them, and to come to terms with the non-indigenous world and life paradigm imposed on them.

The interview

BENNO: I am writing an article about what being Indigenous means ... What does 'indigenous' mean to you?

MATEO: We heard about that word, 'indigenous', for the first time in 1964. The white people used this word for the indigenous. It is a white people's word. Only much later I started to grasp its meaning, but not even today do I know exactly what it means ...

If somebody says [to me] 'you are indigenous', [then it] has little meaning to me. If I am asked [directly like that], I say 'yes' ... but the person asking does not know *what* indigenous I am. If he says: 'you are indigenous', well, I cannot deny, or say that I am a Paraguayan, or that I am a German, I have to say 'yes, I am indigenous' ... because I more or less know what he means [by that term], but in fact, I do have an origin, a name ... it is 'Ayoreo'.

[Mateo identifies the term as an external denomination, does not identify with it, and its exact meaning is not important to him. It is not a meaningful concept in the Ayoreo realm. It is a relational term given and defined by others. It does not even have a clear meaning for the Ayoreo. Mateo's collective identity has a name: Ayoreo.

Thus, the initial question leads back to the external people or non-indigenous who have created and started to use the term. Mateo's answer offers the non-indigenous interviewer a mirror: it is him/herself who has to answer the question about the meaning of 'indigenous', as well as possible further questions, such as 'What is the utility or function of the term for us?' and 'What are the possible consequences of the use of this term and concept for the Ayoreo – or in general for the people we call "indigenous" – themselves?' Before starting to answer such questions, however, and indeed also relate the answers to the very subject matter of the present publication and why its editors and contributors considered it relevant and important, the interviewer needs to continue listening to the Ayoreo as they emphatically state that, rather than indigenous, they are Ayoreo. What, then, is the meaning of 'Ayoreo'? And what about other peoples the non-indigenous call 'indigenous' but who are not Ayoreo?]

BENNO: You say you are Ayoreo, but the *cojñone*[8] call you 'indigenous', and they use the same word for other ethnic groups as well, like the Nivaklé, the Manjui, each one of these groups being entirely different ... does this make you feel bad, as if you were not recognized in your own right ...?

MATEO: No, it is not a problem. It even helps. I shall explain: [Normally] I prefer not to say too quickly that we are Ayoreo ... Because if the person said 'Are you an Ayoreo indigenous person?' ... well, then yes, if the person knows about [us] being Ayoreo, that can be a problem ... But it can also be a problem if he knows we are indigenous ...

BENNO: How come?

AQUINO: Because ... once, some time ago, I accompanied a big group of elders to get their identity cards, and I said to them, my people: 'There are a lot of strange people here in Asunción ... please, nobody of you say that we are indigenous ... because if we say we are, then the other people in their minds say: "the indigenous are ignorant! Do what you want, but any of you will be denied what he wants" ... But if somebody [already] knows, then one should answer "yes"'.

It would be better for that person to say 'people', it is better not to use 'indigenous' [but 'people' instead] ... it is then better to use softer terms, like 'people' ... because 'people' includes everybody, Americans, black people, red, brown, black ...

[For the Ayoreo, being identified as indigenous or as Ayoreo can have negative consequences: 'indigenous' is associated with ignorant; on the other hand, it may be added, many Paraguayans still regard the Ayoreo as being aggressive, belligerent, wild and violent warriors, referring to the time before contact (before 1960) when they were simply known as 'savages'. In both cases, 'indigenous' and 'Ayoreo', it is better for them to hide, if they can.]

BENNO: So, to say 'people' instead of 'indigenous' is a little bit like hiding ...?

AQUINO: Yes, yes. [It is] better to use a softer word ...

BENNO: I understand. But all the same you are proud to be Ayoreo ...

AQUINO: If anybody wants to know how we are, and ...

[It is to be noted that Aquino says '... wants to know *how* we are' ... It means that for him identity is not being something – responding

Glauser

to the question *'who'* – but being in a particular way – responding to the question *'how'*. We have here a distinctively specific and different way to conceive identity and to 'be in the world' ... The concept of identity here appears as a 'way of being'; likewise, the Guaraní use the term *'ore tekó'* (our [exclusive] way of being), nowadays translated as 'Guaraní culture', to refer to a collective identity.]

MATEO: ... what ethnic group we belong to ...

AQUINO: ... so we can say ... 'we are Ayoreo' ... and then the person can say: 'And what is your language' ... and we have a language ... and if the person wants to know more, then we tell more ... how many we are, what language, what culture. So we feel good being Ayoreo, but if there are many other people, one has to be very, very careful ... But there are cases when one has to say everything, in a meeting, in a meeting with people from other countries, or in a state institution ...

BENNO: A friend of mine recently took part in a parliamentary hearing on the new national law on languages which is in preparation. He went to testify that there are more than the prevalent languages Spanish and Guaraní, that there are others like an Enxet language, an Ayoreo language, and so forth ... and then, there are again the dialects in each language, the Ayoreo have the same language as the Chamacoco but they speak differently ... There is a tendency among non-indigenous people to overlook diversity and also to conceive all indigenous peoples as if they were all the same. As diversity is not being seen, neither is the wealth represented by diversity ...

AQUINO: It seems that the white people believe that we are an object ... Because, as an example ... if we see some thermos flasks, we say 'thermos flasks', but there are many ... there are thermos flasks of different brands, sizes ... So, the white people think that we are the same [as if we were thermos flasks[9]] ...

BENNO: An object?

AQUINO: Yes, an object. This is so, [it is] like [when] we speak of receptacle, but there are many receptacles, plastic, glass, even metal and so on ... So, they put a name on us, like an object ...

Or they think that we also are an animal ... For instance they say: 'we are going to hunt wild animals' ... there are many species of animals, but they just put a [common] name to all of them ... just as they say 'the indigenous peoples of Paraguay', they just put one name, instead of various, different names.

MATEO: The *cojñone* treat the Ayoreo like the chicoi plant[10] ... we are like the chicoi which grows in our territory. As long as it is there, it is a root full of water, even in the dry season. Then somebody takes it away and carries it somewhere else, and it will no longer live ... The *cojñone* treat the Ayoreo as if they were playing about with us, putting us here and there ...

[Both leaders here react not only to the white or non-indigenous people's tendency to mix any indigenous ethnic groups – or indeed 'nations', a term not yet accepted in Paraguay – together into an undifferentiated bunch. What they say goes farther: they share a perception which comes from their everyday experiences and feelings about the way they are being treated. The perception is that they are being treated like (abstract) objects, whose identities and characteristics can be generalized and, by way of generalization and abstraction, moved about, renamed, handled – 'manipulated' – with ease. It is an attitude which also extends to the discourse: 'being spoken of without care' ... What the leaders say points to the fact that the Ayoreo have been an object of non-indigenous (white) people's intentions and actions ever since being contacted (indeed, the contact initiative was always on the side of the non-indigenous, a fact which evoked an attitude of passivity on the Ayoreo side). In this way, not being recognized, seen and named as how they are is a problem – for instance, when government programmes do not care to respond to specific habits and needs. In general terms, ever since being contacted and forced into sedentarization and passivity, the Ayoreo have been subject to countless attempts and experiments by external groups (the contacting missionaries in the first place, later NGOs, government agencies, multilateral international projects) to provide them with an income and subsistence base, which have always failed because either they did not correspond to the Ayoreo culture and way of being, or the market changed. When a new attempt failed, the Ayoreo were often left to themselves without even being notified ... This is the background to Mateo's saying above that 'non-indigenous play with us as they please'.

Beyond, what the leaders say also expresses one of the already mentioned main differences between non-indigenous and indigenous perception and discourse: using abstraction and generalization versus using concrete, individualized and specific terms. Abstraction and generalization are 'diversity killers' in ways that well deserve to be elucidated.[11]

Glauser

Thus, the mentioned differences have deep, and also political, consequences for the handling, whether protective or not, of diversity, and relate directly to the environmental problems of today, as well as the lack of balance between genders in the non-indigenous world]

BENNO: Could you cease to be Ayoreo and become like somebody else?

AQUINO: On a recent journey up north to and within my ancestors' [and our group's] territory, we discovered and visited a region recently deforested by a Brazilian landowner in order to set up a large farm with thousands of cows. We spoke to him and told him that he and his farm were in our territory. He said as [an] answer that the time had come for us to have a different life and to become like white people ... because he thinks that we have to abandon our culture ... But: how could we possibly change? [becomes excited and angry] ... and how could we possibly enter [into] another culture? This is impossible, this is impossible ... we [are] like a plant, a plant of Palo Santo[12] cannot enter and convert into a white quebracho[13] ... this cannot be like that then ... Take an example: the Brazilians have their culture ... their habits ... and their traditions, I think they have them too ... [it is the] same with the Paraguayans ... [the] Paraguayans have their own language ... their own way of singing, their own culture ... and the same [is the case] with us ... the indigenous peoples, those who live in voluntary isolation ... [they] have their own tools, their own medications, their own singing, their own food ... all that traditional, natural food, let's say ... and one cannot say, gee, people in voluntary isolation, [they] must abandon this food ... this is very, very serious, if anybody says [you] must abandon this or enter into that ... so, I really did not like [his] speaking [like that], when somebody says no! The indigenous peoples have to abandon their culture ... because our culture is a traditional way of being ... from there we are born ... from there we commence our habit, culture, language, singing, [all] that we develop during our life ... this is our culture ...

[Aquino compares being Ayoreo to being a tree. It cannot change its particular, diverse way of being, its genetic code of growth, or its life plan. With this, he implicitly makes several statements. In the first place, 'being Ayoreo' refers to a collective individuality, and points to the fact that, for the Ayoreo, 'peoples' or 'nation' is not an abstract expression, but an indivisible entity instead; this is usually different for occidental, modern, non-indigenous societies, whose members tend to perceive themselves exclusively as individuals and as individual members of an abstract entity (state, country, nation). In the second place, there is a statement about cultural change or cultural transformation: it is not possible to become somebody else, neither as a person nor as an indigenous nation such as the Ayoreo (one can change, but only within the boundaries of one's own identity – on an individual or collective level). Finally, there is a critical statement directed at those who want to eliminate divergent ways of being in order to bring them into line with the rest and with their respective intentions and domination plans.

This raises the possibility of viewing being an Ayoreo – and maybe also being indigenous – as an expression in itself, an implicit denial of the tendency towards 'making everything the same' and the destruction of specificity, natural and cultural diversity and locality, nowadays linked to the globalization processes. Thus, 'being Ayoreo' potentially becomes a political standpoint and statement in our present world.]

BENNO: Many people think there is only one culture which is correct; they look down on other cultures and think that they should change … what do you think of that?

AQUINO: No … Everyone has their own culture and their own living … and their own [way of] developing their culture and habits … for instance, if you were a white [person], [you] cannot enter, convert into a black [person] … it already is your blood, your life, your [particular] way of living … So, the white [people] have to understand this at least … for example, a sun cannot convert into a moon … there is a very big difference … or a star [cannot] convert into a sun …

[Occidental, modern life culture preaches and proposes something like a capacity of maximum 'convertibility': the possibility that we can become almost whatever we want (and should follow what advertisements and propaganda suggest) … In contrast, the Ayoreo leaders stand here for a denial of such interchangeability and 'cultural mobility' …]

BENNO: What about the campesinos?[14] What do you think of the campesinos? … Are they indigenous?[15]

MATEO: No, they are white people.

AQUINO: They are well educated, as well. They have a good formation. That is noticeable in each person, they are well formed …

their leaders, their leadership ... So, [they] seem more powerful than all of us ... Yes! Because their ally sits in parliament. [It is] their ally more than ours. There is their ally ... [gives the name of a senator] ... Even the president himself, Lugo, is their ally.

[Aquino rejects the possibility of a closer association with the campesinos, but expresses admiration for what he conceives as their way of being powerful in modern non-indigenous society: to have a good education ('formation') ... and to have political allies in the state structure ...]

BENNO: For the campesinos, the notion of community is important, as well as that of '*ore valle*', a way of defining the physical, geographical place one belongs to most, although I don't know whether it means anything comparable to what you call your territory. Campesinos long for, and belong to, the '*valle*'. What about you, Mateo? Remember the time you sat in the bus terminal in Asunción, waiting, and how you rang me to say that you felt alone? Yet you were surrounded by crowds of people ... Was this also because you were far away from your territory ...?

MATEO: I feel good when I am in [my community] Campo Loro, because all my people are there. In the bus terminal I felt bad even though I was surrounded by crowds. They were not my people. [When being among white people] I still feel that I am an Ayoreo. But I also feel ill at ease, as I am from somewhere else, and surrounded by people who are not Ayoreo. [In those situations] I feel better when there are several of us, when it is possible to meet another Ayoreo and to speak together ... but still, I feel something which is not good at all ... I always think of [my people, my family] when I leave my community, it is impossible to forget my community and my people. When I'm far away, I always tell my son or any of my people, when I call them: 'My mind is with you, but you cannot see my mind.' My body is in Asunción, but my mind is in my community ... my mind is there.

I feel better when I am in our settlement, even when there are *cojñone* coming to visit us. I feel better then because the other Ayoreo are there too. It has to do with them, and [also] with the [physical] place.

BENNO: With being close to your territory?

MATEO: Yes. [When I am] in Campo Loro ... my mind is in Cerro León[16] ... When I travel in our territories I feel good, even better, because there is something ... something strong, something we feel when we are with our territories. Even if an Ayoreo is alone there, completely by himself, he still feels good. When I am farther north, inside our territory, I definitely feel a lot stronger.

Where we are today is a problem. They came and took our territory for themselves and today the Ayoreo territory is private property of the *cojñone*, as the *cojñone* say. The state says this as well. Now we are up against each other and confronted with the *cojñone*. On the other hand, there are the Ayoreo with all their life, force and way of being, which has to be as it is, because that is how it is. This is like a confrontation.

They lied to us when we were still in our territory and they came to speak about the evangelicals. They took us away. And we had no idea about the *cojñone*, and we had no idea how much one can suffer when living with evangelization ... Today, we Ayoreo eat pasta, sugar, bread, but this is not Ayoreo food, and one cannot be satisfied by it. This is why, nowadays, the Ayoreo elders say: 'Where are we going to buy our own food?' And: 'Here [where we are] one cannot find any of our food any more.' And then their bodies start becoming weak, and very quickly they turn into old people, men and women, because the food which is natural to them is missing.

[Having identified being with one's (Ayoreo) people as a necessary condition of Ayoreo well-being and 'being an Ayoreo', Mateo expresses the importance of being close to, and having physical presence, in one's (the Ayoreo) territory. He describes a feeling of strength conveyed by the territory, even if there are no other (Ayoreo) people around. Then he speaks about food, which is no surprise in the context of Ayoreo culture: I have often observed how the relation with the territory – once back there – immediately seemed to need to express itself by active communication; when travelling to their (lost, stolen) territories, the first thing Ayoreo do on arrival is disappear to hunt. Hunting and gathering seem like interacting and communicating, like saying 'are you still there?' and 'show me!' (with an animal, or a fruit). Eating the fruit of the territories is also an act of communication (the essence of the hunted animal or fruit passes to the person who eats it). The act of communication becomes a social act when observing the distribution rules for what has been hunted or recollected (see also Fischermann, forthcoming). Finally, let's remember also that parallel to their political organization, the Ayoreo peoples are divided into seven clans, the respective clan name being the surname (family name) of each and every existing Ayoreo anywhere. The members of each one of the seven clans share a common mythological origin as well as kinship ties, which comprise, for each clan, a series of animals, plants and natural phenomena in general, including, for example, meteorological conditions, as well as utilitarian objects and all man-made objects. In this way, the totality of the seven clans as a whole includes everything that exists and, in turn, everything that exists is a relative of the Ayoreo. Thus, for the Ayoreo, the fact of belonging to a clan, together with other beings of the world, provides a sense of strong union and solidarity. Being Ayoreo means being inserted in social relations which include everything existing in nature too. This becomes even clearer when Mateo adds:]

MATEO: We have a word, '*chomai*', it means 'one' ... there is one language we speak, all the Ayoreo, the same language. There is one [specific] clan [for] everyone [to] belong to. The territory is not the same for everyone, every local group [of Ayoreo] belongs to their mother's territory, but the word '*pachaminone*' stands for all the Ayoreo local group territories taken together as one ...

Therefore ... if I say 'Yes, I am indigenous' [it is as] if somebody asks 'have you got a culture [you belong to]' ... so I can answer 'yes, I have [a culture], I belong to a culture' ... because I am indigenous, I know my culture. I know my language, I know our clans. I know where my grandfather lived ...

[We have here some essential qualities which define 'being Ayoreo'. They can possibly be extrapolated also to 'being indigenous':

- having a territory, knowing it and needing it ... 'knowing where my grandfather lived' ('grandfather' means ancestors);
- having a life culture, belonging to a specific cultural way of being (like a tree in comparison to another tree of another species), and knowing one's culture;
- knowing one's language.

What draws the attention is the fact that 'knowing' (about one's territory, ancestors, life culture) seems essential to 'being Ayoreo'. On the other hand, 'knowing' does not necessarily refer to an explicit body of knowledge expressed in language; it also simply means something like 'internal, silent knowledge', or 'unaware' awareness.

Finally, the comparatively very strong relevance of the notion of territory seems to point to a quality which came up earlier: being attached to a 'place', which is defined both by physical and spiritual, intangible elements, puts a limitation on the scope of moving, or being moved about (like an object), and emphasizes on the other hand the concept of locality, or being local.]

AQUINO: Life is so complicated, difficult[17] for us [since] having been contacted by civilization. On the other hand, the uncontacted [Ayoreo] groups still living in voluntary isolation in the forests, they must be worrying a lot because of the destruction of the forests of their territory, but apart from that they must be quite happy as they keep having their life which permits them to be Ayoreo. In their life in the forests there is nothing they lack, they have all they need.

In turn, ourselves, who live with the white, there are many things we lack. The white people have destroyed all our powers, among them the power of our religion and the power of our shamans, who are our priests. With their prohibitions, the missionaries also broke the balance we had in the relationship between men and women.

[Another concept of power arises, contrasting with the concept of power associated with the campesinos in the non-indigenous realm and the possibility of succeeding in modern, non-indigenous society. In the Ayoreo realm, it is associated with religion, active spirituality embedded in everyday life, and the active presence of the shamans.

Deforestation, on the other hand, mentioned as presumably the chief factor of concern for the uncontacted Ayoreo groups in voluntary isolation, stands for more than what the non-indigenous view as loss of biodiversity and as risk factors for the planetary climate: the destruction and disappearance of the forest is the loss of an absolutely essential part of oneself.]

MATEO: First, they have taken us away from our lands, and then they have taken [from] us everything that makes us Ayoreo. The people in the forests, the uncontacted ones, they still have a lot of power. But we think it is the progressive deforestation which must worry them most.

Glauser

BENNO: Now, I would like to go back to the word *cojñón* you have used several times. You use it for a white, non-indigenous person. You call them *cojñone*. What does *cojñone* exactly mean?

MATEO: There is this story, the story of Namochai. It tells how the first *cojñone* were made

They took the bones of a dead person. [Apparently,] this person had been a white person. They put the bone in a mortar, and converted it into [like] powder. Then Namochai made a sculpture out of it again, and then, with a fan, he blew air on it in order to give it [life] breath ... then it started to move. But it was not an original white person any more, it was a mere copy, because it was made from another person.

So, being only a copy, it only had a little [bit of] brain, and very quickly forgets everything ... this is why today we say that the white people forget the thing they try to think and say. This is why they always put everything in writing, so they won't forget ... and thus they see something [written] and it comes back to their thinking ...

This story was told to me by one of our elders in Bolivia ... After that, when I came back here [to Paraguay], I started remembering this with our elders here, like Gahade and others ...

The person who did this has the name Namochai ... Namochai had several persons helping him ... it is a plant here, near by here too, the name is ... a cat, like a cat climbing ... its eyes were like the eyes of a German ...

AQUINO: Blue eyes!

MATEO: Yes! Blue. For this reason he had to pass the bones through a colander ... in order to clean them ... For that reason his eye is very ... like blue ... the powder of the bones had touched his eyes ...

BENNO: And who was Namochai? Was he an Ayoreo?

MATEO: It is not known whether he was an Ayoreo or some other animal ... Because before [our present time], all animals were still Ayoreo persons ... But nowadays, we don't use this [tale, myth] any more as before[18] ... nowadays, younger generations now ... do not use it as our ancestors did ... Namochai maybe was some sort of lizard, who climbs the plants ... a lizard who does not walk on the ground ...

And this lizard is he who took the bones, ground it and made a *cojñón* with it. [Says something in the Ayoreo language to Aquino and both laugh] ... All the young boys and girls who had listened to that elder [in Bolivia] telling this, said: 'Maybe yourself, you don't have too much wisdom, maybe yourself you only have half a brain!'

BENNO: Well, they say that because they already are from another generation ...

MATEO: Yes, yes ...

All this happened, because they liked the dead person – whose bone they ground and then used – a lot [and did not want to lose him]. That is why Namochai said: 'No, no, don't worry. I shall make an image, like a sculpture, a statue of the dead person ... then he will be alive again' ... So Namochai resurrected the dead *cojñón* again ... And as they say, he recovered the life but his mind was not good any more ...

The resurrected was called '*cojñón*' ... he became the first to be called *cojñón*.

[Namochai today is a mythical being and as such only described in myths. The Namochai story apparently is not told very often. It can be understood as follows: in the previous – mythical or prehistoric – time of the Ayoreo collective memory, Namochai, like all other phenomena of nature, was an Ayoreo, but his creating the first *cojñón* did not happen until later, in historic time; then Namochai no longer was an Ayoreo, but a blue eyed lizard instead, with the habit of climbing a plant whose name Mateo cannot remember at the moment. Was the person whom Namochai tried to recreate and bring back to life by using his bones, a blue-eyed person? Mateo says that Namochai himself has blue eyes like a German; frequently, in Ayoreo discourse, the qualities of one person or object appear associated with another person and object of the same context.[19] Apparently, Namochai's eye colour is related to the task he performs, in contact with the blue-eyed dead person, and in the attempt to re-create him he tries to free it from the blue-eyed quality or influence, which here may be associated with non-indigenous northern cultures and people.

According to this myth, the origin of white, non-indigenous people goes back to the time when a first group of them, who went to live with the Ayoreo, died. In our non-indigenous historiography, this happened in the eighteenth century, with the Jesuit mission San Ignacio Zamuco, which was installed in the northern Chaco and lasted for a little over twenty years, before being destroyed around 1740.[20] If we put the Namochai story or myth into that specific context, then we grasp that the white men living for a while with the Ayoreo seem to have been well liked, or at least considered a useful presence. They possibly brought advantages to the Ayoreo. In any case, Namochai became active

Glauser

on behalf of the Ayoreo, reshaping the bones of the dead into a new form which then receives the life breath, Christian themes related to creation – Eve from the bone of Adam, inspiration of life breath – and resurrection, seem to appear in the background, as if they were lending their images and conceptual vocabulary to the expression of present day retelling of the myth. The result is a re-created white person, but one who is deficient.]

BENNO: So the white person who had died, and whom the Ayoreo liked and did not want to lose, was not called *cojñón* yet?

MATEO: No, no. For that person, and until then, they did not say: 'he was a *cojñón*', they had another word: they called him '*amuama codedié*'. They did not say '*cojñón*' yet, that time, when that white person – whose bone they ground afterwards – had not died yet. The Ayoreo in that century called him '*amuama codedié*' ... Only afterwards, when he had died, they started using the word '*cojñón*' instead ... [It was only] from then on [that] we used the words that way ... saying of the white people 'they are *cojñone*' ...

BENNO: What does '*amuama codedié*' mean?

MATEO: It means a white person which is a little big, but not big like an authority, but his belly, like that [demonstrates], was very big ... fat, maybe like a giant ...

BENNO: So '*amuama codedié*' lived in that time centuries ago?

MATEO: Yes, and *cojñón* they only used for the person which was made as an image of the *amuama codedié* by Namochai ... Namochai knows those white persons, the *amuama codedié*, well ... They were persons, but not Ayoreo ... They were called '*dacode*' ... very big ... Nowadays we use the term *dacode* for a big grandmother ... who has a lot of life and who was born a long time ago and whose life never ends ...

Namochai did not manufacture the *amuama codedié*, he manufactured only their copy, which then the Ayoreo called *cojñón* ... I don't know how many years the *amuama codedié* had been dead when Namochai made their copy, using their bones in order for them not to be terminated, to recover and continue being there with the Ayoreo ... Thus, the *amuama codedié* were the *cojñone* of that time [centuries ago] ...

Another story about the first *cojñone* is from much later ... This was when the Ayoreo were still living in the forests ... there were missionaries who went to contact them in the very forests ... Indeed there was

1.2 Aquino Aquiraoi Picanerai

one missionary the Ayoreo had decided that they were going to kill ... and they wounded him ... and then they thought they had killed him ... but he had not died but came back ...

Because he fell into a ditch, and the Ayoreo [when they saw him falling] thought that they had killed him, because they had thrown the spear at him ... one of the Ayoreo men had thrown a spear at him, and also hit him with the mallet ... then the Salesian threw himself to the floor and the Ayoreo thought that they had already killed him. They did not go and check, because they were very frightened of him.

Then later, they said, he came back ... he was back in the mission station, and an Ayoreo spying on the mission station saw him ... And the wound he had had on the side of his chest, it was now on his arm, here [demonstrates] on the left arm ... they thought they had wounded him in the chest, here [demonstrates] ... So, among the Ayoreo, when hearing the spy's story, they said: 'No, it is him, he is the same person, but ... it can be that he changed his wound to another place ...'

After this happened, the Ayoreo were afraid of the *cojñone*, because ... [with Namochai] a *cojñón* had been made from another person, he had already been a dead person, and it is impossible to know about his origins. He has a different origin [from ours]. They resemble people but in fact are not. Like a ghost, a spectre. They ceased to be original persons, because they were made from another person.

Also, because of [what happened] that time [with the Salesian missionary], the Ayoreo thought that all *cojñone* were tricksters, like shamans, and that [therefore] they were able to cure an injury anywhere and [also] move it to some other place ... [They came to think] that they did not die easily.

1.3 Mateo Sobode Chiquenoi II

Conclusions

The present material gives leads to possible interpretations and allows conclusions on different levels. One of the first facts drawing my attention is my ending up in front of a mirror when the inquiry into the concept of 'indigeneity' leads back to my own realm, that of a non-indigenous person. The concept of 'indigeneity' has to be explored in the first place with the non-indigenous who created and who use it – independently of the fact that some indigenous peoples may now have adopted it for their own discourse.

Having left 'indigeneity' aside, I then try to explore something which is real and which I have in front of me, with the presence and testimony of the two interviewed leaders, something for which I have no other name than 'being Ayoreo'. Here, I receive images with a high charge of implicit information ('the Ayoreo are like Palo Santo trees which cannot possibly be or convert into quebracho trees ...').

What can be inferred and concluded from such images is that being Ayoreo is comparable to collectively being a tree species. Like a tree species, the Ayoreo collectively have their 'genetic code' and (implicit) 'growth plan', which, like any growth plan, has its scope but also its limits, which cannot be exceeded. This puts a limit on the potential of social and cultural change and also provides a potential for resistance to such change, as well as a positive potential for staying diverse, or, in other words, for keeping up diversity. Further, identity is a *way* of being (responding to the question *how*, rather than *who*). And being Ayoreo appears as something indivisible.

Other characteristics which come with being Ayoreo, which appear in the interview, are: feeling a strong communication with the territory;

being at one with the territory (implicit: relatedness; being related to everything, wholeness); knowing about it (in the sense of 'silent, internal knowledge' or 'unaware awareness'); having and using the (Ayoreo) powers: spiritual vitality and shamanism.

In another part of the interview, the definition of *'cojñón'* provides also an alternative definition of 'Ayoreo'; if a *cojñón* has only half a brain, then the Ayoreo have an entire brain. This indicates also that Ayoreo implicitly feel superior to non-indigenous people, even though present-day Ayoreo living precariously on the margins of non-indigenous society may actually internalize and express in their explicit attitude a feeling of inferiority ... but there is, farther down, a basic superiority. On the other hand, the definition of *cojñón*, as a side product of this inquiry, may be more than just a strange collection of concepts. We witness the genesis of an explicative myth which conveys to us elements about ourselves, the non-indigenous, and the characteristics attributed to us. If we are interested and take it seriously, it may allow for a glimpse of the cultural characteristics and history of non-indigenous people, viewed through the eyes of a collective 'other' who has a privileged quality of perception from the outside and from a different position within the history of humanity.

Finally, I would like to draw conclusions from yet another level of this interview: the level of the implicit attitude or standpoint of the two leaders, which may not be on the level of their awareness, but which communicates implicitly through what they say and also how they say it. Something like the answer to the question: what do I perceive and feel if I close my eyes and just listen to them? Indeed, in Mateo's and Aquino's answers and associations, an acting Ayoreo subject becomes visible, and it is worthwhile finding out what it is like and how it is.

In the leaders' answers, an Ayoreo 'observer' and 'commentator' comes through, a person who seems to be well centred in his/her realm and who seems to act with sovereignty and an already mentioned sense of superiority. It is somebody driven by curiosity and at the same time somebody who feels free enough to make conjectures and in the end to reach conclusions codified in myths about what becomes visible when inquiring into the conditions and powers of diverse beings belonging to other than the Ayoreo realm. The Ayoreo observer does not even shy away from experimenting with such beings (using as allies the powers of nature in the attempt to bring back to life the dead *amuama codedié*).

The Ayoreo observing the non-indigenous, although inspiring a sense of superiority which comes from the freedom and ease of his/ her traditional unconditioned ways of observation,[21] is not driven by an intention to dominate the other, diverse being. This gives him/her a great advantage as an observer: he/she is free in his/her curiosity to grasp what is there and also to admit defeat when their own capacity of understanding reaches its limits. The curiosity we find here when faced with 'the stranger' is severe, sober and pitiless in its characterization, beyond compassion. The non-indigenous, in contrast, as he comes as invader and seeks domination, submits the 'diverse other' with the help of the terms and concepts of his/her own realm and can therefore not reach any clear perception; he/she remains at the level of a prejudice. This is why we, the inquiring non-indigenous, bounce back on to ourselves.

Comment

Editor's note As elsewhere in this volume, the choice of commentator for a chapter is based on building bridges between arbitrary conceptual/ regional/historical categories such 'settler versus post-colonial', 'new world versus old world', 'anglophone versus hispanophone', etc. What we want to highlight here in the choice of Simron Singh as commentator for this section are the similarities in the content of the relationships between Simron and Chupon and between Benno and Mateo/Aquino, as well as the roles that those leaders play within their communities.

Simron Jit Singh

The text by Benno Glauser on his dialogue with two Ayoreo leaders raises a number of issues relevant to the discussion on 'indigeneity' and anthropological research in general. At the outset he reflects on the challenges of communication with his research subjects that emerge from the interaction of two differing 'paradigms' that are incommensurable. The Western paradigm is fragmented and abstracted; the other, that of the Ayoreo, signifies wholeness in a lived reality. In presenting his dialogue to a non-indigenous audience, Benno inserts at intervals his own interpretations of what the two leaders are saying, which further reveal the inherent contradictions in the two logics of communication. In some ways, the approach is rather similar to my own in the chapter 'Chupon's dilemma', where I use in-between narratives to reflect on my own feelings and interpretations of the ongoing dialogue with Chupon. Another similarity is that of a long, trustful relationship that the author has developed with the Ayoreo leaders which allows this open communication. While the two dialogues are initiated around different themes, they both indicate strongly what has been lost, whether it is the indigenous identity, as in the case of the Ayoreo, or livelihood and social stability, as in the case of the Nicobarese. These two aspects, I believe, are inseparable in the indigenous consciousness.

The reference to the 'contact' in the Ayoreo sequence of time is very similar to the 'tsunami' in the Nicobarese awareness. These events transformed their entire world, and with it a loss of meaning and of the capacities to deal with the new context. We find a feeling of helplessness with outsiders ruthlessly taking over their world and attempting to transform them with a power that is beyond theirs. In both instances, there is an inherent critique of not being understood by outsiders in terms of 'how' they live their life and express their culture and world of meaning, and being treated as 'objects' to further their own interests. Mateo and Aquino express their anger at the fact that they were forced to leave their lands, consume food that weakens their bodies and live a life alien to them. Chupon criticizes how the tsunami aid transformed Nicobarese society, corrupting leaders, creating internal conflicts and the introduction of agriculture without an understanding of the indigenous system of cultivation. In the Ayoreo case, the change was forced, unacceptable and challenged their sense of being in the world. However, with the Nicobarese, it is not so. Chupon bemoans the internal changes and how some Nicobarese even benefited from the situation to gain wealth and power. Hence, one wonders whether the 'collective identity' and 'genetic code' so emphasized by the Ayoreo leaders actually exist.

In terms of the discourse on indigeneity, the Ayoreo leaders do not actually associate themselves so passionately with the term 'indigenous' as with their being Ayoreo. However, they also do not deny the power it holds over them; whether it is a term to be avoided in public (since it evokes negative connotations of savagery and ignorance), or to be used to gain attention in their political and social struggle. They are aware that the term has been created by outsiders to label certain types of 'exotic' communities to justify imposing punitive or welfare measures on them, but that in present times the term has also become a tool to facilitate being heard since it is loaded with political meaning and the wrongs of a colonial past.

Reply

Simron's empathetic comment makes me feel that the worlds we interact with, the Ayoreo world, and the world of the Nicobarese, might be very different and very far away from each other, yet they have a lot to share and to exchange.

I imagine a lively conversation between Mateo and Aquino on one side, and Chupon on the other. Maybe they would not explicitly talk about the need to continue being Ayoreo, or Nicobarese, but they would tell each other stories about how they were and how they are, and it is these stories which would communicate the importance of holding on to one's own collective way of being. In Chupon's case, it is this, his culture of origin, which inspires him to seek a way forward for the Nicobarese, a way of changing without changing, a way to the future without losing themselves.

Acknowledgments

I wish to thank the Ayoreo leaders Mateo and Aquino for this conversation and for many others held along the way of our shared endeavours. They have helped to grasp, each from within his own world, and to express and contribute to the understanding of the fabric that unites all worlds.

2 | Beyond indigenous civilities: indigenous matters

MINE WAITERE AND ELIZABETH ALLEN

Kotahi te kowhao o te ngira e kuhuna ai te miro mā, te miro pāngo, me te miro whero.[1]

1 INDIGENOUS STRUGGLES
Elizabeth Allen[2]

Tu mai ra a Hikurangi, rere ana nga wai o Waiapu kia ora ai te iwi ko Ngati Porou. Karanga mai ra ko Te Awemapara Ngai Te Aowera mai i raro i te whakaruruhau o Kapohanga a Rangi ki Hiruharama. Whakatau mai ra te minenga ki te wharekai ko Tamatoa. Moe mai ra o tatou mate ki Huria. Kati, tuhi mai nei he uri o te whanau ko Hiroki.[3]

This chapter engages in the ongoing struggle to not only name and claim the space to canvass, think through and theorize (Smith 1999; Waitere 2008; Waitere and Johnston 2009) our diverse realities (Durie 1995), it also provides insight into the complex array of forces that impact on indigenous peoples as they attempt to live indigenous lives, governed by indigenous principles and practices.

As a contribution to indigenous writing, the social issues we address throughout this chapter lie within a wider framework of self-determination, decolonization and social justice. The legacy of British colonization informs the context in which we write. Hence, in order to gain an understanding of the relationship between the *tāngata whenua* (indigenous peoples of Aotearoa/New Zealand) and the state (the British Crown), one must have an insight into their history. Although it is not feasible to draw exact parallels between the past and the present, it is possible to demonstrate the continuation of a colonizing history and how it continues to inform policy and attitudes today.

Aotearoa/New Zealand became a British colony in 1840 with the signing of a treaty between the Crown and a number of Māori chiefs. There were in fact two different versions of this treaty, the Treaty of Waitangi, published in the English language, and Te Tiriti o Waitangi, published in the Māori language. The two versions of the treaty were not exact translations of each other, and these differences continue to be an area of great contention. The English version essentially stated that British intentions were to protect Māori interests from the encroaching British settlement, to provide for British settlement and establish a government to maintain peace and order. The Māori text, however, suggests that the Queen's core promises to Māori were to provide a government while securing tribal *rangatiratanga* (loosely translatable as autonomy or self-determination) and Māori landownership for as long as they wished to retain it.

The reality of the matter is that the Crown failed to recognize either version of the treaty, and within four years the colonial government had come to view the Treaty of Waitangi as 'highly inconvenient' (Moon and Biggs 2004: 390), noting that the Treaty should never had been created, that the natives could not understand it and that it was really just developed as a convenience to maintain peace at the time. The Select Committee then recommended that Māori land extend only to their villages, *pā*, burial grounds and cultivated lands, reclassifying all other lands as 'waste lands' to be vested in the Crown.

Between 1840 and 1860 the demographics of New Zealand changed drastically. The Pākehā population increased from approximately 2,000 to almost 200,000, while, owing largely to introduced diseases, the Māori population dropped from approximately 85,000 to less than 50 per cent of the total population. This dramatic shift of population created enormous pressure for land acquisition and the government decided to create laws to obtain it.[4] During this period numerous 'land wars' broke out between Māori and the Crown. After these wars a number of invasions and attacks were carried out by the 'Armed Constabulary' (established in 1867) and the New Zealand Police Force. This included the attacks on the remote and peaceful community of Parihaka, in 1881, and the peaceful community of Maungapohatu, in 1916.

During the early years of the twentieth century, Māori society and culture were at their lowest. Reduced population, racism and diminished resources led to a lack of Māori visibility and voice in relation to the nation's affairs. Some thought, even hoped, that as a people Māori would become extinct. It was during this period that a number of influential Māori leaders emerged, including Sir Apirana Ngata and Te Puea Hērangi. These leaders were passionate about the well-being of their people and were to prove to have a significant enduring effect on the generations to follow.

At the end of the Second World War a large number of Māori, in search of work, opted to move from their tribal and rural communities to the cities. This great urban shift had a detrimental impact on many of the urban-based Māori as they lost contact with their tribal communities and became increasingly influenced by Western institutions. However, during the late 1960s there was a growing awareness of colonization and its impact on the Māori people, and urban protest movements, such as Nga Tamatoa, shaped by radical action, challenged the state on issues regarding education, health, development, government policy, loss of land and culture. The following two decades, referred to as the Māori renaissance period, saw numerous Māori political activists rise up and protest against the ongoing land alienation, the status of Māori, and a number of other social ills, including racism, classism, sexism and homophobia.[5]

Even in the contemporary context where Māori experience diverse realities, many continue to assert their *rangatiratanga*. And it is because of this factor that both historically and contemporarily numerous encounters have occurred between the Crown (via the criminal justice system) and Māori. It is owing to the insistence of their right to *rangatiratanga* that the state has labelled them rebels, radical activists and now terrorists.

The ongoing struggle against colonization was manifested in October 2007 in what has been described as the 'State Terror Raids'.[6] As a direct response to the homeland security hype brought on by the September 11th attacks in the United States, one of America's global allies, the New Zealand government, created the 2002 Terrorism Suppression Act. In October 2007, under this frame of security and terror, more than three hundred police carried out dawn raids on a number of Māori and political activists throughout the country. An overwhelming majority of these people were Māori, the majority of these from the *iwi* of Tūhoe. In the case of Tūhoe the whole community of Rūātoki was targeted.[7] It was only in Rūātoki that people were forced out of their cars at gunpoint and photographed, where whole families were searched and held at gunpoint, with no potential for arrest, among an array of other human rights breaches.

Despite previous police invasions, land thefts, breaches of human rights and terrorism, the *iwi* of Tūhoe, who never signed the treaties, have always asserted their independence from the Crown. And to this very day they continue to assert their rights despite colonization and state violence that continues to frame our existence as indigenous in Aotearoa/New Zealand.

You put uncertainty in their eyes,
invaded their homes
and thoughts.

With your naming,
comes your
claiming.

Once your noble savages,
now your
global terrorists.

Your fears
and your fetishes
we continue to embody.[8]

2 INDIGENOUS CIVILITIES
Hine Waitere

Ka hoki nei au, ki te puku o te whenua, ko Tuwharetoa te iwi.
Ka piki ake au, ki te maunga tapu o Tauhara.
Patata atu ko te hapū Tute Mohuta
Na, kei raro iho reporepo ana te moana nui a Taupo-nui-a-Tia.
Ka huri taku mata ki te Tairawhiti, ko nga rehu ena o te waka Te Arawa.
Mauri ora koutou katoa.[9]

As we talk about Māori issues in relation to the parameters set by this text, we choose to enter the conversation in a customary way, by explicitly locating ourselves (who we are and where we come from) within the text. We do not choose to do this as a way of privileging our voices over those we have interviewed but, rather, by providing located and locatable voices we acknowledge, like those we are speaking to, that we also have a history that inhabits space on these pages. Invariably, in conscious and in unconscious ways, these histories, embodied and located, affect the telling of the tale. We also want to make explicit that in the attempt to make ourselves visible we are not only working to locate ourselves within the conversation, we are also working against assumptions that texts written by detached authors are inherently more neutral, objective, rational and (here's the kicker), therefore, somehow more universally applicable to all. Paradoxically, for some of our cultural peers, in providing an explanation for our introduction we have already slid outside the 'common sense' of Māori cultural practice. This serves to further mark the gradations of the terrain that we negotiate as we work to map the issues traversed here. The paradox is that academic convention requires us to operate in ways considered *less Māori*, *by Māori*, in order to talk about *things Māori* (linguistically and culturally) considered important in being *Māori* when speaking to *non-Māori*.

We have chosen to start with the paradox.

A response from the wilderness

Q: What constitutes indigeneity in the area where you work?

GARETH (PARTICIPANT): This question is problematic. I object to it being asked – non-indigenous people are never asked this question. The asking of it serves to make us prove or legitimize our existence. I would prefer to assume that it exists, it does not need to be proven, and then to address issues on those presumptions. Defining and justifying ourselves we are immediately on the back foot.

Q: So what are the politics of indigeneity in this area, then? (Aotearoa)

GARETH: This is like a book, a naïve question. It would be like saying: What's it like being Māori? I would cut and paste a history of Aotearoa since colonization.

Q: Is there a vision for the future?

GARETH: This question should be – what is the vision for the future? Sounds like a typical dumb non-indigenous question. All indigenous peoples have a vision for the future, the problem with the non-indigenous people is they are so removed from us they have to ask questions like – do you fellas have a vision?

The backstory: Gareth's challenge

It may seem hard to fathom but Gareth's responses made us laugh. We didn't laugh because it was a response to be taken or to be dismissed lightly; we laughed because the unashamedly unapologetic response was familiar to us in both tone and content. To be honest, our laughter was tinged with discomfort; after all, we were more used to providing this type of response than bearing the brunt of it being directed at us. Whatever the mix of emotions that underpinned our laughter, Gareth made us sit up and take stock of ourselves and the questions posed. We tried to quietly rationalize the questions we uncritically applied from the larger project. They were never intended to be pious abstractions or false platitudes, but just because this was not the intention didn't make them less so, certainly not in the context in which Gareth heard them. His response made us think about accountability and validity as we rethought the questions in relation to the people we were speaking to. Gareth made us think seriously about a number of contextual issues. We all knew that within the politics of indigeneity in Aotearoa/New Zealand adhering to normalized civilities is not a skill practised by many *tāngata whenua* activists. In fact, as Gareth would have seen it, there was no need to mind his 'manners' in the context in which he was speaking. As far as he was concerned he was talking to a friend, a fellow activist, a person whom he had stood beside shoulder to shoulder in protest lines. In other words he was speaking to the kind of person that you know well enough not to be governed by the polite protocols that one reserves for strangers. He was offering us a challenge; this was his *wero* to us.

Sitting at the kitchen table, we talked about the political and ethical issues raised by Gareth's initial response, and while participant responses are always important, in this chapter they felt particularly poignant, primarily because we weren't talking to others about the topics canvassed in this project; we intended talking to, with and through each other. We had invited *whānau* (family), friends, colleagues and our wider social networks into conversation. As indigenous researchers we understood that the participants that we talked to in the day were some of the same people we would be sleeping with that night, others we would be cooking for that afternoon, some we would be arguing with tomorrow and still more would be directing us on other occasions. So yes, the conversations were replete with subjectivities, power relations, gender dynamics and cultural norms, the likes of which exist when people talk to each other within and across communities.

Commonly, all those spoken to were Māori, variously of different *iwi*. Among the group were mothers, fathers, brothers, sisters, uncles, aunties, grandparents and grandchildren involved in a range of things to earn a living. Some of the group own suits, others sew their moccasins from the tops of wool fadges. There are those who hold government positions, some are lawyers, others are involved in community education, such as family violence prevention and women's refuge. Still more are involved in unions, sheep shearing and gardening. Given the diverse range of occupations it's not surprising that they experience different socio-economic realities and that they are geographically dispersed. Nevertheless, irrespective of their social and geographic location, they are all involved in activism in one form or another. As a group they are in your face, down to earth and generally engaged in activities that sit well outside the comfort zones of the vast majority of Pākehā New Zealanders, and, to be fair, beyond the comfort zone of some Māori too.

Realistically, then, the challenge expressed by Gareth could have come from any one of the participants; he just happened to be the person we spoke to first. What we were left with then was the question that shouted from the quieter spaces between Gareth's words – what were we going to do about the challenge?

As already stated, Teanau, Elizabeth and I (the convenors of the discussions), are also Māori. We too are of different *iwi*, one man and two women; we also have different day jobs. Somewhat divergent to the Māori sociotype, we, like many of those we have drawn into conversation, have been to university. We hold different degrees, and while Paul Holmes[10] would consider us 'clever darkies', our families simply see us for what we are, human; people with strengths and weaknesses, who, whether it be in the mundane day-to-day activities or the more grandiose public performances that we sometimes engage in, are simply people of this land, *tāngata whenua*, attempting to live principally as Māori in Aotearoa/New Zealand. The aspiration commonly shared by those we have talked to is the desire to live as Māori, not as the beneficiaries of paternalistic state benevolence but as the enactment of justice. As our conversation progressed and we worked to modify the questions, the tape was turned on and the roles of participant and researcher, interviewer and interviewee, collapsed into one.

As we work to canvass the questions engaged with in this volume we not only weave together the voices of six Māori activists from diverse backgrounds and interests with our own but also with the complicated and complicating issues embedded within Gareth's challenge, not least of which is the fact that Gareth has more difficulty attempting to identify any *apolitical* space far more than he does locating the politics of an indigenous reality.

As we commence the conversation the speakers in this chapter are acutely aware that there is no ideological *Terra Nullius*. The very nature of being *tāngata whenua* in a Fourth World context makes it difficult, if not impossible, to assume the luxury of vacuous spaces waiting to be filled by indigenous insight. There is no neutral acoustic where indigenous voices remain unmarked or unscathed by competing and often hostile voices. This is particularly evident in public domains, where the acoustic favours the voices of their colonizing counterparts. Gareth's ambivalent point of entry into the discussion is underpinned by an understanding that neither the conceptual focus that shape debates about, on, for or by indigenous peoples, nor the socio-historical context which provides the acoustic, will necessarily afford him a hearing. While the dissonances his responses evoke are locatable in a number of places, the first point of resistance is likely to occur out of his refusal to use the venerated, disconnected voice of the academy; a voice stripped of context, and disembodied. Gareth, like the others engaged in conversation here, insists instead on an inhabited response.

Ironically the dissonance these voices create occurs in a period when there is an increasing call for others to speak (Flower 2003, 2008; Cockburn and Hunter 1999; Jones and Jenkins 2004). The ambivalence that permeates Gareth's response pervades many of the conversations woven together in this chapter. They are voices infused with a double consciousness born of knowing that once one speaks then the struggle to be heard commences. The conversations here begin with the politics of naming. Typical of the Janused debate, Helen Potter, working in a government position, noted, 'The concept of indigeneity is routinely abused and used to promote certain agendas while simultaneously denying and pathologizing other claims.'

Although the tension Helen identifies is not new, its most recent incarnation has been through political aspirants publicly jockeying for leadership roles within different political parties. For example, when Don Brash, as leader of the National Party, made the claim that proactive policies to engage indigenous aspirations were forms of reverse racism, and that all race-based policies should be eradicated from government policies and practices, he did two things. First, by putting 'race' on the political agenda, he discovered a catalytic route to political popularity. Second, he rekindled debates that constructed Māori political claims as problematic and debilitating, obstructive of any form of shared national identity or cohesive society. Brash conveniently ignored or falsely assumed that unnamed, unqualified policies are somehow 'raceless', that they are located outside of social histories derived from and predicated on racial hierarchies that underpin the current inequities. Brash played on the popularly held assumption that Māori want preferential (rather than equitable) treatment. Helen goes on to explain the debilitating effects of amalgamating indigenous claims with all others and the impact it has on the context in which one works to self-define as she expands on her earlier comment,

> For detractors, indigeneity is often reframed as 'race' to place Māori in a 'special needs/privileged' category and to divorce our identity-based claims to land, language and *tino rangatiratanga* from our status as indigenous, First Nations people (rights affirmed in Te Tiriti o Waitangi) which makes them meaningless. This also allows claims of racial privilege to be made despite a material context of deprivation, poverty and institutional prejudice. In addition, the concept of race is often used to discredit those seen as mixed race and to thus disqualify the claims they are raising.

Moana Jackson, working in the legal field, identifies the need to use our own terms when working to self-define in ways that make sense to those who are being defined. He works to clarify the resistance towards the term, locating some of the problematic within colonial historiography. Like all social constructs, the term has been open to contestation and change; it is chequered history making its meaning unrecognizable, in intent, to Māori.

> If I have to use the word indigeneity then what I take it to mean is people who define themselves as *tāngata whenua*, as people who through history or culture define themselves as being of a particular place. The reason I have difficulty with the term indigeneity is because, while it was taken by *tāngata whenua* in the seventies, really in good faith, as an English word to use, it very quickly got co-opted by Pākehā people. So now we have a rather strange phenomenon in this country with Pākehā people now saying they are indigenous based on outlandish claims 'because they were born in Wainuiomata'. So for me, indigeneity and indigenous, if we have to use the term, then I use it to indicate people belonging of a particular land, but that doesn't mean belonging just because of the earth. It means belonging because of the very sense of belonging say in Māori terms, which holds layers of meanings. It doesn't just mean being born somewhere,

it means tracing who you are to the stories of the land, being able to read the land, creating your cosmogony from that land, creating your law from that land ... Colonizers can never be indigenous here because they live a culture that came from another land. Their history grew from another place. The law of their land is not the law of our land, so it's all of those things that are tied up in the word for me, but I, I find the term problematic because it has been co-opted.

One of the most significant tensions that underpin the debate surrounding acquired labels is that indigenous peoples are often called upon to rationalize or defend these ill-fitting terms and their clumsy fit with our world-views as if the lack of conceptual fit was of our making. In short we are asked to rationalize and name our existence in and through terms incapable of embracing an alternative epistemic and ontological view.

Furthermore, indigeneity is open for co-option in ways that *tāngata whenua* has never been. For example, while Moana's reference to being 'born in Wainuiomata' (a suburb of Wellington, our capital city) was a throwaway line used by a politician in the heat of a political debate, the co-option referred to is not limited to the quickfire banter of posturing politicians. The claim also exists in more calculated or considered writing. The most notable exists in the work of a respected New Zealand historian, Michael King (see *Being Pakeha Now*, 2004). In an interview conducted by Terry Locke, King was asked to talk about what he referred to as 'a second indigenous culture'. King's view was that the assumption that the word 'indigenous' could only be applied to Māori was problematic. King then went on to explain why he also applied the term 'indigenous' to Pākehā. He offered two reasons for this – one, because Pākehā culture, mainstream New Zealand culture, is no longer the same as its cultures of origin, which were non-indigenous; and two, because, in his view, a key element of indigenous as distinct from imported culture is its focus on the country and culture of occupation rather than the country or culture of origin. What is ignored in King's position is that all migrant groups experience gradations of cultural shift after leaving their countries of origin as they adapt to what he aptly identifies as the country of occupation.

In response to the types of claims made by King, Linda Tuhiwai Smith (1999), a Māori academic, notes that descendants of 'settlers' who lay claim to an 'indigenous' identity through their occupation and settlement of land over several generations, or simply through being born in that place, don't tend to show up at indigenous people's meetings, nor do they generally form alliances that support the self-determination of the people whose forebears once occupied the land they have 'tamed' and upon which they have 'settled'. Nor, she further suggests, do they actively struggle as a society for the survival of the indigenous languages, knowledges and/or cultures. She maintains that this is primarily because their linguistic and cultural homeland is somewhere else; their cultural loyalty is to some other place. Their power, their privilege, their history are all vested in their legacy as colonizers.

In the attempt to historicize and track the shifts in the struggle to name who, and what, we are in Aotearoa/New Zealand, the discussion with Moana turned to origins of language, overlaying etymology and points of contact.

> When colonizers came here and they saw *iwi* ... they had to find an English word for *iwi* so they came up with the word tribe. But *iwi* is not tribe. They chose tribe because it comes from the Latin *'tribus'*, which means the lowest class. Now if you want an English word that's close to *iwi* then the nearest English word is actually nation, because nation also comes from the Latin, which means birth, so we get words like natal, antenatal and postnatal, and if *iwi* means anything it's to do with birth, and so tribe to me is always a good example of how you can't actually get an exact equivalent, particularly if languages are deliberately being misread.

One of the fundamental points being made is that language does not sit outside the political will of its users. Moana's claim that the interrelationship between *iwi* and nation provides a better fit than *iwi* and tribe is based on an understanding that *iwi* are made up of smaller collective units called *hapū*, both of which, like nation, connote connectedness, pregnancy, expectant growth. Like Moana, a number of the speakers similarly acknowledge the regressive tensions inherent in using the colonial term while also recognizing its utility internationally, particularly among groups that have been colonized by Britain. Di Grennell of Amokura (Family Violence Prevention Consortium) asserts:

> ... it's a controversial term, particularly if it's applied to us, rather than applied by us. There may be instances in which identity is mobile and fluid depending on the alliances that we want to make.

So often when Māori use the term indigenous it's a way of creating or speaking to alliances with other First Nations people or peoples of the land, as we would refer to ourselves. So to speak of ourselves as *tāngata whenua*, it is obviously our choice, but having travelled in Canada, Australia and the USA, frequently, in order to communicate effectively with other *tāngata whenua* then it is important to be able to use language that will establish connection and sometimes that's indigenous or indigeneity. Others will speak of themselves as First Nations, some will use aboriginal, others will use native and [with] some of those terms we have varying degrees of comfort because they carry different kinds of weighting and different kinds of histories. So to assert our status as *tāngata whenua* is obviously our primary choice but in different environments we can use and work with the term indigenous where it enables us to establish alliances.

In reference to these connections with other indigenous peoples, Moana also makes the comment that

... I think [these connections are] really invaluable, just because at a very basic level it says to our people you're not alone. The struggle you have is shared by other people. Now that is not cause for celebration that so many people are getting screwed but it is I think a reassurance for us that because if you know you're not alone then the struggle's actually easier. I always think that those exchanges are two way, they're beneficial, we can learn from them and hopefully they can learn from us. I certainly know that a lot of what I've learned has been shaped by my time with other indigenous peoples. And I think ... that in spite of the immense differences, all of the indigenous peoples I've met also share many commonalities. Often they have a very similar cosmogony, quite similar views towards the land and so on, so there's that symmetry and then just the history of the last five hundred years, a shared oppression really.

Both Moana and Di have highlighted the benefit of the term 'indigenous peoples' as a tool for enabling the collective voices of indigenous peoples to be expressed strategically in the international arena. Nevertheless, while the term has also enabled communities and people to develop a network in which to learn, share, plan, organize and struggle collectively for indigenous peoples' rights on the global fronts, it has also had its limitations, particularly when working beyond English-speaking peoples. A couple of the participants raise this point as they reflect on the decade and a half of political activity that underpinned the development and ratification of the Declaration of Indigenous Rights. In the mid-1980s Moana took part in a number of preliminary meetings before the working group that drafted the Declaration of Indigenous Rights was established in Geneva. During our conversations he reflected on the discussions that took place around the name indigenous, during this period:

> We had long discussions about what we should call ourselves because there were *tāngata whenua* from all over the world who spoke different languages, so how should we define ourselves? We couldn't get agreement. Someone came up quite early on with indigenous peoples but we couldn't get agreement because indigenous *pueblo*, the Spanish version, actually doesn't mean the same as indigenous peoples, so even in using the different colonizing languages you couldn't get a similarity of meaning, but each group of people were really clear in their own language who they were and defined indigeneity, if you like, without a problem in their own *reo* [language]. But in the language of the colonizers, whether it was English or Spanish or Portuguese or French or Belgian or whatever, it's actually really hard to encapsulate what all that means ... if I can, I try not to use indigeneity as a marker of who the people of the land are, I'll use the term indigenous peoples as a collective for *tāngata whenua*, but I'd prefer to use, if I know or can find out, the words that the people themselves use. Certainly the *tāngata whenua* throughout the States and Canada and South America and Australia and so on name themselves in their own language with words that mean the people of the land, so they have a very similar sort of construct, I think.

Smith notes that the final 's' in 'indigenous peoples' has been advocated quite vigorously by indigenous activists because of the need to recognize the diversity within the collective indigenous people. It is also used, she notes, as a way of recognizing that there are real differences between different indigenous peoples. As if the issue of naming were not complicated enough within binaries that ring-fence discussions around *this is their language, their name for us* (and therefore problematic), *and this is our language* (and therefore fine), Smith is signalling a more complicated tension showing how colonial constructs have also bled into indigenous languages, refracting the debates in multiple ways.

To be clear, while the discussion so far has been about the difficulties surrounding the adoption of colonial names imposed through the promotion of colonial languages, linguistic borders were not enough to stem the flow of colonial ideology. As laid out elsewhere (G. H. Smith 1992; Durie 1998; Waitere-Ang 1998), group and individual names, both formal and informal, carry with them a store of past and present history Personal names, for example – though not always – serve as indicators of basic group identity. Two group names commonly used as ethnic markers in Aotearoa/New Zealand are Māori and Pākehā. The origin of the terms 'Māori' and 'Pākehā' as we currently use them – as identifiers of groups of people – is in itself derived from a historical context arising from inter-group relations between early Europeans and diverse tribal groups. The term 'Māori' provided the means to collectively name a group of heterogeneous tribal peoples by colonial groups that were beginning to arrive in Aotearoa/New Zealand. L. Smith (1992) maintains that although both 'Māori' and 'Pākehā' as group names are of Māori linguistic origin, their attendant socio-historic meanings are best understood within colonial discourse. She further asserts that although the word Māori is of 'Māori vernacular it is a Colonial construct that is as political in nature as is the ideological construct race' (p. 35). Durie (1998) notes,

> Before European contact, the word Māori simply meant normal
> or usual. There was no concept of a Māori identity in the sense of
> cultural similarities. Instead, the distinguishing features, which
> demarcated groups, were mainly attributable to tribal affiliations and
> the natural environment. ... In that sense, identity reflected historical,
> social and geographic characteristics. (p. 53)

Thus in the late eighteenth and early nineteenth centuries, with the arrival of Europeans, the word Pākehā emerged as a new word (to identify Europeans) and the term 'Māori' (which pre-existed contact) took on new meaning. Where once it referred to the notion of 'normality' or 'purity' as in *wai Māori* (pure water), it was adopted by the British to refer to *tāngata whenua* as a racial category (Department of Labour 1985). Durie (1998) suggests that the stark contrast between the culture of the newcomers and the culture of *iwi* provided the rationale for emphasizing commonalities across *tāngata whenua* (tribal groups) rather than reiterating their commonly understood uniqueness. 'Even then it was an identity more obvious to the newcomers, and in truth largely determined by them, rather than a true reflection of any sense of homogeneity on the part of Māori people' (p. 53).

Earlier in the debate, Rangihau (1975) had argued that the notion of *Māoritanga* (one universal set of cultural practices encompassing all Māori) was (and is) problematic because it obscures the rich variation evident across *iwi*. For Rangihau it was his *Tuhoetanga* (cultural characteristics specific to the Tuhoe tribe) which delineated his identity, providing the cultural characteristics, history and territorial specificities of ethnic identity. While collapsing diverse groups into one within colonial discourse was problematic, he argued, there were political motives afoot in homogenizing heterogeneous groups, '... because if you cannot divide and rule, then for tribal people all you can do is unite them and rule. Because then they lose everything by losing their own tribal histories and traditions that give them their identity' (p. 233).

The political tension alluded to by Rangihau was created, as he sees it, through the (re)categorization and (re)classification of *iwi* into universalized Māori constructs as a way of claiming authority over *iwi* Māori, as over many indigenous peoples, becoming the basis upon which many early botanists and fledgling anthropologists sought to make their careers through the 'discovery' of strange and exotic cultures residing in 'uncharted' territories. From many written accounts indigenous groups were commonly constructed as passively waiting in 'unnamed' territories to be discovered, to be named and claimed through systems of classification and categorization unfamiliar to them (Waitere-Ang 1998). At the point of discovery within colonial binaries identity markers vacillated from savage, uncivilized, heathen, cannibal to qualifications of the nobler, but nevertheless still savage, kind.

What I am trying to do here is to locate our current conversations within a context that not only signals the global but which also situates the detectable tenor of ambivalence outside the 'flawed' character of individuals (and yes, I am also aware that in the constant need to qualify and justify the conversation I expose my own). The struggle is to find an acoustic for dialogue that is capable of equal treatment when speaking across difference. Ambivalence is grounded within what Radhakrishnan (2003) calls a double consciousness and Bhabha (1994) a double vision, neither of which is solely cynical. Rather, both writers, cognizant of the progressive and regressive tenets encased within the ambivalent, ask under what social conditions does ambivalence provide a productive space of articulation. In fact the discussions held showed much more than a simple bifurcation; the voices speak to what Bhabha describes as a consciousness that continues to split.

Bringing Radhakrishnan (2003) and Bhabha (1994) into conversation with those we spoke to helps tease out an ambivalence that is on the one hand marked by an aversion to speaking (the cynic), particularly in contexts where indigenous voices, too often, fall on the deaf ears of their colonial counterparts, and on the other by a discussion that also indicates a form of resistance mediated by the need to speak in order to establish different modes of dialogue. The dissonant voices mark a more complicated space than simply signalling the pulling away from something, as in the simplistic refusal to speak, because such end points also mark the commencement, or, as Radhakrishnan (2003) would put it, the presencing, of something else. The 'something else' for this group indicates a place where being Māori within Aotearoa/ New Zealand is taken for granted. Such a space is predicated on an indigenous politics that seeks more productive modes of engagement. Radhakrishnan argues that the alternative plains of interaction mark the difference between speaking *for oneself* and the position most preferred by the participants, where indigenous claims are located *within oneself*. The former marks the space where speaking for self occurs within the logocentric paradigms of the dominant while the latter shifts to a plain of interaction where one not only speaks for oneself but does so through indigenous epistemic and ontological frames of reference.

Reclamation of the discursive terrain: shifting across two different plains of interaction

Looking more closely at the splits expressed in conversations shows more than a double consciousness; for these organic intellectuals (Gramsci 1971) the continuous splitting Bhabha (1994) speaks of occurs as I see it across at least five different plains of interaction. The conversations show a consciousness cognizant of

1 how the colonial centre sees itself (epistemically and ontologically);
2 how that same centre sees its indigenous other (individually and collectively), often as the despised other;
3 how *tāngata whenua* sees them/us (also *tāngata whenua*) as activists and/or academics in the academy;
4 how *tāngata whenua* sees their colonial counterpart; and
5 how *tāngata whenua* see themselves (epistemically and onto- logically).

Each plain offers a different array of subject positions that presuppose different modes of interaction. The first and second plains are predicated on a view of indigenous as other. While these plains are most likely to mark sites of distraction for indigenous peoples they offer the places of most comfort for their dominant counterparts. They are the spaces where indigenous subject positions are constituted around pathologies regarding what is 'lacking', the 'gaps' and 'absences' according to dominant structuring devices. The third plain marks the complex pivot upon which ambivalence teeters: a space where one is potentially, but not necessarily, held suspect by both dominant and indigenous groups. This plain not only marks the emergence of something else; it also marks a different presencing for our colonial counterparts too. The plain is Janused. It simultaneously indicates potential assimilation and movement away from customary ways of knowing, while also indicating another very different potential in the opportunity to harness dominant ideologies in the service of indigenous hopes and aspirations. In this plain of interaction indigenous scholars represent a threat to the status quo and entrenched orthodoxy which has the potential to expose the subterfuge of liberal rhetoric; revealing in our presence the academy's ambivalence towards its indigenous other in the moment of institutional anxiety about loss of power and control.

The fourth and fifth sites demarcate the spaces where the productive commencement of something else is most likely to occur. The politics of indigeneity on these plains of engagement are not only likely to be expressed from *for itself* positions but also to be expressed *in itself*. It is a space where dominance begins to unravel and break down, where indigeneity in colonizing contexts marks the transitional points where, in the eyes of our colonial counterparts, at least according to Bhabha (1994), the colonized mimic becomes menace. While the space beyond the counter-narrative appeals to those here, the socially constructed nature of the acoustic is at its poorest. The positions are menacing because they are sites of engagement that by and large reside in territories uncharted by the dominant; knowing here thus resides beyond their authoritative control. Thus, marking the space where indigenous agency is at its strongest simultaneously marks where the discourse and discursive practices associated with multiculturalism unravel and break down. In other words, when the indigenous community sees itself on its own terms within its own epistemic and ontological frameworks located within its own regime of truth, colonial hegemony becomes destabilized, evoking anxiety for the dominant. Radhakrishnan (2003) suggests it is 'the powerful moment when the for-itself of identity is in addition transformed to an in-itself that can be acknowledged and respected by other identities' (pp. 18–19).

The reclamation of language and the imaginative space – claiming a right to the future

Anchoring the conversation back in Gareth's challenge, one of the fundamental points being made is that the ambivalence expressed here is not the sign of the problematic other; rather that the colonial encounter is already marked by ambivalence – 'the task is to politicize this "given ambivalence" and produce it agentially' (Radhakrishnan 2003: 2). These speakers unequivocally and unapologetically enact their agency, which constitutes their menace, making as it does the politics of indigeneity transparent both as a discourse and as a set of discursive practices infused with both progressive and regressive tenets.

When we broached the subject of indigeneity the responses fell into a number of categories. One was to do with the power to name our world. The position articulated here is that being *tāngata whenua* has integrity in and of itself. The logic of binarism permeates the struggle for us to better invest our energy in the talking forward about what is or might be, rather than talking back or positioning ourselves in terms of what we are not – that is, cognizant of our own sense of making mechanisms with the conceptual tools to name, claim and think about the world from an indigenous location. One of the differences is found somewhere between being able to speak forward without the constant qualification found in the need to talk back. Realistically this chapter sutures together the two positions, where ambivalence constantly attempts to ameliorate the two; one of needing to talk back while also finding the space to talk forward. Ironically the centre finds this position difficult even at a juncture in its own history where diversity is being purportedly not only acknowledged but also embraced, because it marks the point at which multicultural discourse in the West breaks down – these voices simultaneously constitute the frayed and fraying edges where the indigenous body, as part of the multicultural other, claims its own agency and chooses to speak for itself within itself.

In the spirit of speaking both for and in itself, those we talked to claim the imaginative space where they lay bare their projections, hopes, aspirations and challenges as they look to the future.

3 VISIONS FOR THE FUTURE
Hine Waitere and Elizabeth Allen

Ko tou rourou, me tāku rourou, ka ora ai te iwi! [11]

The final section of this chapter is based on the interview responses to the question concerning visions for the future.

Moana Jackson's response

To get our land back. Well, to bring colonization to an end, I guess, in the broadest sense, 'cause one of the greatest lies that the colonization perpetuates in this country is that it's actually ended, but when you're trying to pin Pākehā down and say, well, when did it end, they actually can't tell you. They come up along when we died at Gallipoli, they have this weird romantic perception that being killed in a battle marks nationhood or something, or else they're getting more weird and say, oh, it was when the 1905 All Blacks went and beat the English in England at rugby. That marked the end of colonization. If you're a lawyer you say, oh, it was in 1907 when New Zealand became a dominion and so on. The fact is, of course, it hasn't, hasn't ended, so the first vision is to bring about its end, and for me that involves a number of things. I think it's a, it's a journey really, that I think our people are already on. I think it's an unstoppable journey.

... For me it will end when three or four things actually happen, because what I've got is a very simple definition of colonization. It's actually a culture in my view, there is a culture of colonization so the colonization is a learned behaviour and western Europe after Columbus, I mean colonization is as old as humankind, but after Columbus it became a culture, that is western Europe learned to colonize as a way of life. It became normalized, it became natural, and they created a whole design for living that was based around dispossessing innocent people, and so the aim of that culture then was to take away the lives, the lands and the power of innocent people. So for colonization to end, those three things have to end so our people have to stop dying in the numbers and the way that we have died. We have to become a well people again, it seems to me, and that means not just not having as much diabetes or whatever as we have but actually being well as a whole and complete Māori, and so if you look at the things that it seems to me make a people well, it is getting to a stage again where our language again is the first language of this land, in practical terms, not

63

just in historical terms, so that our kids grow up or our *mokopuna* grow up speaking *reo* as their first language again, that we reclaim our faith, because one of the worst things that colonization does, and it usually does this through a monotheistic religion, is that it destroys the faith that people should have in themselves and it makes you believe that you are only whole if you have faith in someone else, and some other system, so we make our people well by restoring faith. We get our land back and I mean that literally, all of our land. I don't mean by that that we drive every non-Māori person into the sea, because we actually promised them in the Treaty they could come, but you change who the land belongs to, or who belongs to the land, and that's why I really like the Bolivian constitution because it does return that first basic right to the Mother Earth, and so if you have an individual property right and you use that right to abuse the earth then you lose that right, so we return the land to Mother Earth and then we return the first right of belonging to our people so that where, for example, now the people who live in this city pay rates on their land to the City Council, when we get the land back they'll pay it to us. They'll pay it to the *iwi* and the *hapū* of that area so you return the land, so you don't drive everyone off their quarter-acre sections but you say instead of paying rates now to the Palmerston North City Council, you will pay it to the *iwi*. So you shift to whom the land belongs, that's the second thing, and the third thing is you return the first right to make decisions to our people, and you do that through, I used to call it constitutional change, but Pākehā people talk about that now so I don't like that phrase any more, 'cause when they talk about constitutional change all they talk about is, say, becoming a republic, but that's not what I talk about so I now use the term constitutional transformation. That is you actually transform the constitution and a constitution often frightens our people, the word, but to me a constitution is just the *kawa*, the rules that a people make to govern themselves, so the *kawa* of the *marae* is the constitution of that *marae*, so when you go on that *marae* you know the rules within the borders of that place, and so for me our land is our *marae* and we should set again the *kawa* and so I draw a distinction between what I call a concept of power, which Pākehā call sovereignty but which our people call *mana*, or *rangatiratanga*, and then the fight of power which is the institutions where the power is exercised. And for Pākehā that's parliament ... sovereignty came from France ... parliament came from London. So they don't grow from this land and in the end that *kawa* only has legitimacy if it comes from the land to which it belongs, so the *kawa* of Tainui has no legitimacy in Kahungungu because it doesn't come from Kahungungu, and so we need to find or refind a *kawa* that comes from this land, and that's what I mean by constitutional transformation. And if it is a *tika* constitution, if it's right, if it's just, then there's a place for everyone within it as a concept of power because the *kawa* of the *marae* has a place for everyone. That's what the *pōwhiri*'s about, allowing the *manuhiri* a place, but these are the rules, yes, you are welcome, but these are the rules. And so *mana* as a concept of power has all that idea, and then the trick is to translate that into a site of power for the twenty-first century, and it won't be parliament ... Pākehā can keep their parliament for them. I'm prepared to be generous but I don't think the parliament should be for us, because it's not ours. If they want to keep that for them that's fine, but Ani Mikaere uses this neat phrase that *tikanga* is the first law of the land and so if they have their parliament then that will be subject to the first law of the land, and that's just a universal human condition that colonization ignores, so that if someone from England travels to France, they automatically accept the first law of France, they accept the jurisdiction of France, so all I'm suggesting is we say to Pākehā, well, you've come here, after 160 years you need to accept the jurisdiction of this place, and if you don't then you can go, you can leave.

Helen Te Hira's response

Not one vision. Do I need to make a grand statement here? How about we get back to liking and enjoying each other as people. Seems to me like our earth, a whole lot of people need healing. It's hard to write these words without a whole vision of people rolling their eyes, but I'm not proposing that it be just the one person at a time thing. 'Cause in a way that is depoliticizing. I'm talking about a vision where people can think for themselves and we learn to keep working together collectively on the basis that your struggle is my struggle. In a way the values of our *tūpuna* offer solutions to racism, and classism, so easy to fall into, values of *manaaki* and *whanaungatanga*, for example, *aroha ki te tāngata*. Something I regain by staying in contact with indigenous struggles of people in [the] Third World is memory of strong collectivism, and that's one of most precious tools our *tūpuna* left us, a model to survival and reaching our greatest potential. [The d]ominant model pushed for development and for 'success' has become commodified and

65

corporatized. [We n]eed to keep talking about where we are being led and having the role of young and old in steering the vision, not just those who have degrees or [are] old in years but not in struggle. If I could summarize all of the above to answer the vision question, I'm pretty sure they are there in our *whakataukī*, in the *mahi he* and *pai* of our *tūpuna*, for us to learn and do something with.

Helen Potter's response

The vision is definitely about strengthening a recognition of *whakapapa*, of the importance of being indigenous, of what it means to be *tāngata whenua*. A strong sense of identity as a collective, whether as *whānau*, *hapū*, *marae*, community, *iwi*, Māori, Polynesian, Pacific peoples, etc., means a strong political voice to articulate for political change, justice, for authority over ourselves, our lands and resources, our images and identity, the constitutional form of the nation, our relationships with others, and so on.

The obstacles are also identity related – namely a continuing and pervasive colonization which calls us deficient, backward, as needing 'special' help because we're never quite enough; a not-quite-humanness which sometimes becomes internalized so that we think we can't determine ourselves without someone else's blueprint, that the world is now too advanced and complex for our *tikanga* to have relevance and meaning in our lives, that our time has passed and we've got to give up being Māori to 'get ahead' and be participants in the modern world.

This view is endemic and pervades many of the 'wins' we've etched out: e.g. the context of Treaty settlements which requires *iwi* to first become corporate entities to receive settlement monies; *kōhanga reo*, *kura kaupapa*, *wānanga* being required to submit to Crown standards, monitoring and curriculum requirements for funding and legitimacy; family group conferences controlled by courts; an indigenous television station which is increasingly required to appeal to a Pākehā mainstream audience to secure ratings, approval and funding.

These are all attacks on our very identity as we're always being asked to give way. It can become difficult to challenge these wins as wins; to articulate that more needs to be done and can be done – when we're being told that the 'problem' is now resolved, that this is a good deal and stop being negative or obstructive, that we're really very lucky (to be given part-human rights).

Kane Te Manakura's response

Global indigenous revolution!!! (This is just my vision, I can't speak for any organization or my *iwi/hapū*!) Either that or modern 'civilization' will force *Papatūānuku* to roll over in anger, meaning no more people indigenous and non ID alike.

In my lifetime I'd like to see the Tuhoe nation come together and negotiate a separate state for us based around the Urewera National Park – or [at] the very least an autonomous region similar to Nunavut. But more important than changing our constitutional relationship with the colonizer is our people relearning a practical, everyday self-determination. I'm talking having independent food production, independent education, etc. We rely on the government and corporations to provide us with food, money and other resources far too much. Even without political autonomy we could still grow enough *kai* so that none of our *tamariki* need to go the McDonald's or the supermarket.

I want to think about this question inter-generationally. I know a lot of brothas and sistas in the movement in Aotearoa, and also Australia and the US, who are impatient for revolutionary change. Lot of them want to take up the gun and lead the people to freedom, to glory, etc., etc. I am wary of these people – don't get me wrong; being a student of history I know well that the powerful never relinquish their power without a struggle. So I know in order for Māori to take up their responsibilities as *kaitiaki* we will need to engage in armed struggle at some point.

But I think that we as a people are not ready for it. Too many of our people are sleeping, comfortable in their oppression. I think if we who recognize the need for change work our arses off doing the grunt work – education, consciousness-raising, organizing, etc., then maybe our *mokopuna* will be in a position to embark upon armed struggle, and then maybe the *mokopuna* of our *mokopuna* will achieve our *tino rangatiratanga*.

My vision for my own life is largely one of reclamation – I am the third generation in my *whānau* that grew up out of the tribal homeland with no experience of Tuhoetanga. So my life's *mahi* is to reclaim my 'Tuhoeness' so that my *tamariki* will be able to stand tall as members of the *iwi* and never have to question who they are and where they are from.

The vision for my life in the TR (self-determination) movement is dedicated to education, consciousness-raising and organizing. It's humble and humbling *mahi* for real.

I'm very interested in the idea of sustainable, permanent *noho whenua*. I do a lot of work on sustainable food production, tool-making and waste management. One day when I am much older and wiser I'd like to share these skills with Māori communities so that they can just move on to their *whenua* that has been stolen and reoccupy it permanently. I have seen how effective temporary *noho whenua* [is], and how it brings *whānau* and *hapū* together, and I'd love to help people live like that on a permanent basis, and in keeping with *kaitiakitanga*.

Ian Takarangi's response

My vision for the future is to bring up my future children in a society that allows for the right to live in such a way that I can choose if I wish to, walk the lands my forefathers walked, drink from the springs my forefathers drank from, gather food from the places my forefathers gathered from, teach my children and their children what my father taught me, worship whom I choose to worship, and believe what I believe to be the truth. Our role at a grassroots level would be to share the vision and raise the awareness. Inspire others to want to get involved and make a difference for a better future for our children. Speak the truth, at all times. Be as transparent as possible, and do not allow personal agendas to lead you. Be POSITIVE! Never allow any room for negative influences. Stay tight! Always take care of the inner circle. If we can implement these basic fundamentals in our organizations at a grassroots level, it will duplicate out into the bigger organizations we become a part of.

Comment

Editor's note: This commentary section provides the opportunity for an exchange between Avril Bell and Teanau Tuiono, who were also participants in the Aotearoa/New Zealand component of the project. Both Avril's and Teanau's comments on and responses to the preceding chapter and to each other draw on comparisons with other indigenous contexts elsewhere in the world. This enables the discussion to render visible (audible?) contrasts and attributes that may otherwise remain muted.

Avril Bell

Hine and Elizabeth's chapter foregrounds Māori struggles against colonizing power as their participants talk about being indigenous in

Aotearoa today and their visions for indigenous futures. Gareth's objection to being asked to define indigeneity precisely pinpoints and resists the colonial demand for indigenous self-disclosure and transparency. I was reminded recently of an article that appeared in a popular New Zealand monthly, *North and South*, in 2003. The title of the article, 'What is Māori? Who is Pakeha?', says it all; the 'what' that counts or doesn't count as Māori is constantly a subject of debate in which Pākehā/white New Zealanders feel qualified to participate. As one of those non-indigenous New Zealanders, I don't want to take part in that debate. Any study of colonialism soon highlights the crucial role played by the colonizers' usurpation of the right to define. Further, the authors of and contributors to this chapter point to the difficulties of translating terms from one language to another, and hence concepts from one culture to another. A culture cannot be learnt from a book. Cultures must be lived, and as someone who doesn't 'live Māori' I have no experiential base from which to comment on what the contributors to this piece have to say about being Māori/Māori being.

'Living Māori' is of course precisely what colonization has sought to destroy and, even as it has failed, has certainly made very difficult. I am drawn to Moana Jackson's indigenous/*tāngata whenua* distinction. To the extent that indigeneity refers to the state of being colonized it is a relational term, implying that 'after' colonialism indigeneity would disappear also. But as Moana and others also point out, being indigenous is not just about resisting colonization. It is also about survival as peoples with distinct ways of life and world-views that pre-existed colonialism and continue under it. In *te reo Māori*, '*tāngata whenua*' signifies that indigenous difference in Aotearoa – or actually indigenous normality against colonial/Pākehā difference. Indigenous people everywhere have similar names for themselves; names that signify not only their belonging but the importance of the relationships between people and the natural world that are central to their ways of life, religious beliefs and world-views. In that respect there is a stubborn non-colonizable core to the notion of *tāngata whenua*. It can be destroyed but it can't be owned/controlled/colonized. It refers precisely to the persistence of the indigenous '*longue durée*' (Clifford 2001) evident here in Hine and Elizabeth's opening *mihi*.

Reply: Teanau Tuiono

Ko Ngai Takoto, Ngapuhi, Ngati Toki, Ngati Ingatu nga iwi, Ko Areaora me Poroti nga papakainga, Ko Enuamanu me Te Taitokerau nga whenua tipuna[12]

For me, as someone active in the *tino rangatiratanga* movement, I believe that the concept itself is intrinsically linked to land, culture and territory. About ten years ago we were using this definition to define what that meant for us:

There are many different meanings for *tino rangatiratanga* and the concept itself is part of a rich and ongoing debate in Māori society. The word '*tino*' is an intensifier and the word '*rangatiratanga*' broadly speaking relates to the exercise of 'chieftainship'. Its closest English translation is self-determination – although many also refer to it as 'absolute sovereignty' or Māori independence. Such a concept embraces the spiritual link Māori have with *Papatuanuku* (Earth Mother) and is a part of the international drive by indigenous peoples for self-determination.

To further add to this idea of *rangatiratanga*, it is made up of a word called *rangatira*; the closest (but not quite right) translation of this is chief. *Rangatira* itself is made up of two words, *ranga*, short for *raranga*, and *tira*. So a *rangatira* is seen to be someone who *raranga* (weaves) the *tira* (group of people). So it is not an absolute right to boss people but more a role that someone plays in bringing together and acknowledging the collective will of the people.

I had an interesting conversation a few months ago with Damon Corrie, a hereditary chief from Guyana, during which we compared notes about where we thought our people were at. He was impressed with what was happening with language and culture in Aotearoa, and I was impressed that on their 'reserve' the state had no power and the police could not arrest people, and importantly by the amount of control they exercised over their territory. At the same meeting I spent time with representatives of the Navajo government; the Navajo nation is the size of Ireland but operating as a nation within a nation. There are examples everywhere, from the Saami with the Saami parliament to Nunavut with the Inuit. Then you have the reservation system, and the interesting example of the Kuna and Panama (I have a good friend there who has talked to me about this arrangement they have: en.wikipedia. org/wiki/Kuna_%28people%29[13]) and other arrangements such as, for example, the one that Bouganville has with PNG.

If you look at all these examples there are common themes. I probably don't have them all but they relate to land, culture, possibly language. Land and culture are crucial elements for me; if you don't have those two at least then you don't have self-determination.

Here in Aotearoa I think we do the culture and language thing very well, more so than a lot of indigenous peoples. What I think we are seriously lacking is territorial control over a specific geographical area. So for me *tino rangatiratanga/Mana Motuhake* is yet to be realized here in Aotearoa.

I see the treaty settlement process as a distraction in that context. There have been entire books written on the subject so I won't dwell on it, but for me the litmus test with treaty settlements is whether they have improved the lot of Māori in the lower socio-economic bracket. There are lawyers who are doing OK, and I think that is fine, people have bills to pay and kids to feed, and I know a lot of these lawyers, if it was working I'd be all for it. I don't think of it as a step in the direction of self-determination/*tino rangatiratanga*.

Just to illustrate with another conversation I had with a friend of mine, who is a lawyer for her tribal *runanga*, who will remain nameless. She commented that often people in the *hapū* would attack the *runanga* and call it oppressive and so forth. My response was that the problem is that many of these tribal corporations are using the tribal names, which is misleading, because the tribe itself is actually the people, not the charitable trust or incorporated society set up to manage assets, or the company set up to manage the asset base. This is where people are coming unstuck, because regardless of whether you name the company after the tribe, at its very heart it is still a company or charitable trust or incorporated society or whatever other legal construct they might be using, and those structures will always be what they were originally designed to do. Companies will make profits and those profits will be better spent on a smaller number of people. Those things need to be clear in Māori society, and the problem is they are not, and they get mixed up with the rhetoric of self-determination, but I think they fall short on actually being self-determination.

Reply: Avril Bell

Teanau concisely pinpoints the key different bases necessary for indigenous self-determination – land, culture, language – along with a viable economic base. And it was great to have his translation and explanation of the term '*tino rangatiratanga*'. I love the concept of the *rangatira* as someone who 'weaves' the people together.

My question, arising out of a very brief visit to North America, relates to different possibilities for the link between land and indigenous sovereignty. At first glance the sovereignty provided by a reservation or reserve system might seem like something Māori should/could aspire to in Aotearoa. However, if you have self-governing territory you have to be very clear about how you define membership. That doesn't have to be resolved in harshly exclusionist ways (see Chapter 1 of Garroutte 2004 for an overview; also see Part I of Lawrence 2004), but it often is, as in the Kahnawake Mohawk reserve in Canada that has recently evicted twenty-six non-Mohawk tribal members, breaking up families in the process (see www.theglobeandmail.com/news/national/non-natives-evicted-from-mohawk-reserve/article1468533/[14]). I agree with Teanau that land is important – not just as places to live and bases for economic action, but also the *traditional* lands of the people, where stories reside in the landforms as the basis for community identity. But my puzzling over the land/sovereignty connection is really about what forms of governance are needed to support indigenous sovereignty. And what are the prices to be paid for them?

I wonder whether New Zealand has done quite well in terms of cultural and linguistic sovereignty precisely *because* of the national reach of Māori sovereignty claims? I worry that a reservation-type system would result in the Māori world becoming a set of territorial enclaves, leaving the rest of the country to do as they wish and to ignore any wider Māori interests as something they should deal with 'over there' on their lands. Are Māori, in some ways, better served by holding to the position that all of New Zealand is Māori land, that New Zealand society generally should be the territorial site of Māori sovereignty? But maybe these things don't need to be either/ors. Maybe Māori can aspire to both distinct, reserve-type lands and nationwide sovereignty.

Conclusion

We, Elizabeth and I, have worked to provide a multivocal dialogue with indigenous groups and individuals that has included friends, acquaintances, colleagues and in some instances *whānau*, about indigenous issues that are grounded in the material realities of *tāngata whenua* and their quotidian lives in Aotearoa/New Zealand. The gritty materiality of the conversations no doubt will abrade at times. In fact we started with our own abrasion, choosing to see Gareth's initial response as a challenge to us as much as to non-indigenous peoples. What it served to do was to shake us from any false sense of complacency. The voices are not abstract and should not be read as being simply of vague theoretical interest. We want to acknowledge and thank them all. We entered the conversation with a third writer, Teanau, who remained with us throughout the project in heart and mind and appears at the end in his exchange with a Pākehā colleague, Avril Bell. The contents of the conversations shared were not begun in this chapter, nor will they end with the drop of the last full stop at the end of the final sentence. As we draw this chapter to a close, for those invested in the politics of indigeneity in Aotearoa/New Zealand, it is simply a pause, a reflective moment in a conversation that is a long way from finished.

We entered into this dialogue in a customary way with our *pepeha*; we choose to exit it in the same vein, in the agentic position of not only speaking *for* ourselves but importantly *in ourselves*.

Mihi whakamutunga[15]

'*E kore e piri te uku ki te rino.*'
Clay will never stick to steel.

Glossary

Aroha ki te tāngata	Respect for others, empathy
Hapū	Sub-tribe
Iwi	Nation
Kai	Food
Kaitiaki	Custodian/guardian
Kawa	Māori protocol/customs
Kōhanga reo	Māori language nest; Māori pre-school education
Kura kaupapa	Māori schooling
Mahi	Work
Mana	Prestige/status
Mana motuhake	Autonomy
Manaaki	Support/protect
Manuhiri	Guest
Marae	Māori meeting house
Mokopuna	Grandchildren
Noho whenua	Reoccupation
Pā	Fort
Pai	Good, excellent

Pākehā	New Zealander of European descent
Papatūānuku	Mother Earth
Pōwhiri	Welcome ceremony
Rangatiratanga	Loosely translatable as autonomy or self-determination
Reo	Language
Tamariki	Children
Tāngata whenua	People of the land
Tika	Correct
Tikanga	Correct procedures/customs
Tuhoetanga	Cultural characteristics specific to the Tuhoe tribe
Tūpuna	Female ancestor
Wānanga	Māori tertiary institute
Wero	Challenge
Whakapapa	Genealogy
Whakataukī	Proverb
Whānau	Family
Whanaungatanga	Relationship, sense of connection
Whenua	Land

Acknowledgements

I would like to acknowledge Hina and Te Hinemoa, and all of those terrorized by Operation 8. – Elizabeth Allen

I want to thank each of the contributors to this chapter who gave selflessly of their time and energy. *Ka nui te mihi kia koutou katoa.* – Hine Waitere

TWO | **Post-colonial: Africa and Asia**

3 | Mapping everyday practices as rights of resistance: indigenous peoples in Central Africa

CHRISTOPHER KIDD AND JUSTIN KENRICK

Introduction

This chapter will focus on Central Africa by specifically highlighting the experiences of the former hunting and gathering Batwa people of south-west Uganda. Historically, the Batwa were forest-dwelling hunter-gatherer people living within the high-altitude forests in the Great Lakes region of Africa. The Batwa are widely regarded by their neighbours and historians as the first inhabitants of the region, who were later joined by incoming farmers and pastoralists approximately one thousand years ago. Today, the Batwa are still living in Rwanda, Burundi, Uganda and eastern Democratic Republic of Congo. In each of these countries the Batwa exist as a minority ethnic group living among the largely Bahutu and Batutsi populations. Slightly more than 6,700 Batwa live within the present state boundaries of Uganda, with approximately half living in the south-west region of Uganda. The Batwa in this region are the former inhabitants of Bwindi, Mgahinga and Echuya forests, which comprise the final forested remnants of their ancestral territories. Recently, however, they have suffered evictions and exclusions from these forests, primarily as a consequence of the creation of protected areas. As a result of this exclusion from their ancestral forests, the majority of Batwa suffer severe isolation, discrimination and socio-political exclusion. The Batwa's customary rights to land have not been recognized in Uganda and they have received little or no compensation for their losses, resulting in a situation whereby almost half of Batwa remain landless and virtually all live in absolute poverty. Almost half of the Batwa continue to squat on others' land while working for their non-Batwa masters in bonded labour agreements. Those who live on land that has been donated by charities still continue to suffer poorer levels of healthcare, education and employment than their ethnic neighbours.

In order to map out 'indigeneity' in this context we will have to map out responses from not just indigenous peoples but also from the non-indigenous partners in the indigenous experience. We begin this chapter by detailing and providing analysis of two interviews carried

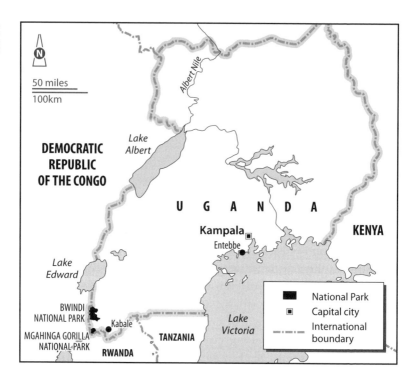

3.1 Batwa ancestral territories: map of Uganda showing the remaining forests in south-west Uganda that were once the Batwa's ancestral homes. Upon their eviction from these protected areas, and without any resettlement programme from the government, the Batwa were left landless on the edges of these protected areas where many of them continue to stay.

out with indigenous rights activists in Uganda. In Part Two we move on to an analysis of state responses to indigeneity in sub-Saharan Africa and offer some explanations for why indigeneity may be so hard to accept in the African context. Finally, in Part Three of this chapter, we provide a fresh and optimistic way to understand indigenous peoples' use of indigenous identity by drawing on examples from Australia and Central Africa to show that rather than inciting confrontation (as many African governments fear), indigeneity can actually be a tool of accommodation that seeks to build bridges instead of deepening divisions.

1 INDIGENEITY AS LIVED EXPERIENCE
Interview 1

The interview is between Chris Kidd and Fred, the chairperson of a Batwa-run organization that seeks to advocate on behalf of its fellow

Batwa. Despite coming from a remote community near the border with Rwanda, Fred has travelled to Europe and West Africa in the two years he has been chairperson to attend conferences and workshops. Fred's responses are in Rukiga, his native language, and translation into English is provided by a member of Fred's organization

In the Batwa's language Urufumbira, the concept of indigenous is translated as *abasangwa* (the people found) *butaka* (on the land). (For a discussion of *umusangwa butaka* among the Batwa in Rwanda, see Adamczyk 2011.)

CHRIS: What do you understand *abasangwa butaka* [indigenous] to mean?

FRED: I feel that IP is the first occupant of that land where they are found.

C: Who are those people in Uganda?

F: Those people in Uganda are the Batwa.

C: If the Batwa are indigenous, apart from being first on the land, are there any other attributes that are special to the Batwa as indigenous people?

F: [Not clear about the question] Yes, we have Gatwa, Gatutsi and Gahutu.

[While Muhutu refers to a single Hutu person and Bahutu refers to the Hutu people, Gahutu is the name of the progenitor of the Hutu people. In creation stories the Batwa, Bahutu and Batutsi progenitors are represented by Gatwa, Gahutu and Gatutsi.]

C: What makes the Batwa different from these other Gahutu and Gatutsi? Is the only difference that they were the first to be there?

F: The only difference from Gatwa, Gahutu and Gatutsi is that Gatwa stayed in the forest whereas Gatutsi when he came he was a person with the cattle, and when Gahutu came also following the Gatutsi he was a peasant. So Gatwa never did all that. Gatwa stayed in the forest. He did not think of doing what Gatutsi and Gahutu were doing.

['Peasant' is used by the translator to refer to a farmer in this instance. The Batutsi are stereotypically cattle keepers, the Bahutu farmers, and the Batwa hunter-gatherers.]

C: Do the Gahutu and the Gatutsi accept that the Batwa were the first on the land?

F: Yes. If that Gatutsi and Gahutu can follow, what was there? The

Gatwa was the first occupant. Yes, if Gahutu and Gatutsi knew they found us on the land there is no reason why they can't believe that Gatwa was the first occupant.

C: Is it true that in the stories of creation that the Bahutu and Batutsi have, most of those stories suggest that the Bahutu, Batutsi and Batwa were all created together at the same time?

F: Gatwa, Gatutsi and Gahutu originated from one man but Gatwa was the leader. Gatwa stayed all the time in the forest. When Gatutsi and Gahutu joined hands for them they had to prosper and they achieved a lot. As a result they took over the leadership of the Gatwa. Gatwa was actually the original person to be leading while in the forest.

[The insinuation here is that while all the brothers stayed in the forest their relationship remained equal but that at some point Gahutu and Gatutsi left the forest and 'joined hands'. This positions the forest as a realm of egalitarian relations and the non-forest world as a realm of discrimination. It also provides an astute explanation of the present predicament of the three peoples; while Gahutu and Gatutsi joined hands to arrive at their current 'developed position' in society, they left the Batwa behind in the 'undeveloped' margins of society.]

C: If the Batwa were the first on the land, why has the government not respected their land rights if they were the first on the land?

F: 'Cause of ignorance. Batwa are ignorant.

[In this and other sections of the interview, Fred uses language which suggests that he is blaming the Batwa for their current situation through describing them as lazy or ignorant. His attitudes can be seen to mirror those very same attitudes which are levelled at the Batwa by external groups who blame the Batwa and what is seen to be Batwa culture for their perceived backwardness. On some levels this may indeed be true given the Batwa receive a range of narratives that are imposed on them and that urge them to become educated, developed, sedentary, agricultural and Christian. These narratives are imposed on the Batwa by the government, aid agencies, development organizations, missionaries and their local neighbours, so it is no surprise that given such a tirade of narratives the Batwa often adopt these narratives as their own.

However, this is not just a case of impoverished and passive Batwa participants, and the comments from Fred can also be read as an empowered call to arms to his fellow Batwa. These imposed narratives which blame the Batwa for being ignorant may be understood as being about the imposing groups not taking responsibility for the impact they are having on the Batwa, enabling them to ignore the role that the structural forces, from which they benefit, play in disempowering the Batwa. However, for Fred, blaming the Batwa is about taking responsibility, about getting Batwa to see their responsibility for re-creating the situation and for finding a way out of it. In such a situation the most empowering step may be to take responsibility. In the tone of his comments, Fred is showing his frustration at the Batwa's failure to take full advantage of the few opportunities that are offered to them, and he is demanding that the Batwa stop replicating the situation they have been placed in.]

c: What are the Batwa ignorant of?

f: They are not educated, they do not mind to follow up their rights, not knowing themselves, not understanding themselves.

c: Does the government then take advantage of the Batwa?

f: Yes.

c: Given that you are the chairman of the Batwa organization, what is your vision for the future of the Batwa people?

f: What I see is that since they have well-wishers, donors and friends, in the future Batwa will be different people like Bahutu.

[The demand by Fred for his people to be 'like Bahutu' may have more than one interpretation. On one level this can be read in a similar light to Batwa describing themselves and their communities as ignorant and backward. Given the narratives that are imposed on them – which range from them being described as ignorant and undeveloped by the state to savage and dirty by their ethnic neighbours – it is no wonder that many seek to claim that they are not like other Batwa and more like those who discriminate against them (see Adamczyk 2011; Leonhardt 2006; Namara 2007: 22–3).

On the other hand, when Fred envisions a future for the Batwa in which they are more like the Bahutu, he is also making a statement that refers to the current inequality between the two groups, and he is hoping that one day the Batwa will be regarded as equal to their neighbours – whether by their neighbours, the government or other external groups that currently discriminate against the Batwa.

In many ways the first context suggests a process of assimilation whereby the explicit and implicit characteristics of the Batwa are replaced by the characteristics of the dominant ethnic groups. In this scenario the Batwa have no ability to let any particular characteristics remain as all are replaced. The second scenario, however, suggests a much more equitable process of integration, whereby the Batwa are not demanding the retention of their perceived cultural characteristics but instead are demanding control of how their culture changes and adapts in present and future contexts.]

C: When you say you want the Batwa to be like Bahutu, what do you mean?

F: After eviction, Batwa were really unhappy and were not listening to anyone. Today they can now listen to what a good person is advising them to do. So that listening is also a step forward, that there are good things in the future, like when you tell a Mutwa to do this today he or she does it, like agriculture, they go and do agriculture. In that listening and doing the agriculture there is a chance of getting food whereby you can no longer now depend on someone or beg instead, by having listened you are now doing things on your own. Secondly, if there is any injustice, a Mutwa now because of listening knows where to go for that injustice done to him. If you keep on listening like that and there are more good people coming to help them like there is now, in the future they could even have surplus food for them whereby even the Hutu can buy from them. Then they will have equality in that manner.

C: If we look forward to that day when the Batwa have the same opportunities as the Hutu, will there still be things which are particular to the Batwa and not the same as the Hutu? When they both have the same opportunities will there still be some things which are special to the Batwa which are not available to the Hutu? If the Batwa are to have the same opportunities as the Hutu to live the same lives will the Batwa still be interested in the forest?

F: If there is opportunity that equality prevails, you get everything that like the other group are getting, then I don't see why the people would want to go to the forest.

C: But there are still some members of Batwa Organization who want to go to the forest and get the things from there, to visit their ancestors.

F: Yes, true. Among ourselves there are those who want to visit the forest, yes, it is true, because we need to practise our culture and visit the ancestral lands, but we feel we should visit and come back and we don't stay actually inside there. One thing is that if we have those activities we were talking of, equality outside the forest, we will be having land, animals, goats in particular and food, then what remains is for us to go there and do our cultural practices that we don't lose them. But we don't look at what's there and look to grab it.

[This apparent contradiction between not wanting to go to the forest and needing to practise their culture in the forest is most probably a mistranslation or a misinterpretation by the translator of the intent of the question. When the term 'go to the forest' is used this implies going to live in the forest, in contrast to visiting the forest to maintain cultural practices. Most Batwa do not want to reside ('go') in the forest but do want to visit the forest to maintain their relationship with it.]

C: In this future that you see for the Batwa, where you see equality, do you see the forest as always being important to the Batwa?

F: Yes, Batwa can still be attached to the forest because of their culture but the forest is not only good for the Batwa. It is good for everyone because within the forest is where we get air, is where we get the rains, and some food also, so people should learn how to take care of the forest and not particularly for the Batwa but for the good of everyone.

[This response may be influenced by his recent trip to the Convention on Biological Diversity – Convention of Parties (CBD-COP) in Bonn, Germany, as well as the Batwa's inclusionary attitudes towards the ownership and management of their ancestral forests – see later sections of this chapter.]

C: This vision for the future. What steps do the Batwa need to take for them to reach that vision of the future?

F: The Batwa should live in harmony with other people. Batwa should be able to listen and act. Batwa, if they are given any chance, they should use it, they shouldn't be given things and throw them here and throw them there, that way you cannot prosper. So you need to listen and act wisely.

C: But what about other people, not just the Batwa?

F: Other tribes or other people are advanced already. For them they listen and act, for us Batwa we have not reached that. Other tribes and other people are on top of the Batwa, the Tutsi and the Hutu, whereas the Twa are still here so probably if the Hutu and the Batwa can work together then maybe everyone will be on the same level.

c: What is stopping them being on the same level?

F: Other tribes have enough experience like taking the children to school. In that case they are [more] intelligent than those people who have not been to school, the Batwa. Whenever the Hutu and Tutsi produce a child they have the target of saying they take that child to school whereas the Twa haven't started that. The newborn are like their parents.

c: What is stopping the Batwa taking their children to school?

F: Because parents never went to school they have never thought of taking their children to school, they probably think maybe they will never live again in the forest or a forest can be somewhere coming up and then they think they will have the chance [to go back to the forest]. They have never bothered to send their children to school.

c: What role does Batwa Organization have in helping achieve that vision for the Batwa?

F: If Batwa Organization is strengthened, has much strength, the vision is good, we are heading somewhere. One thing we have, children who are at school, we have adult literacy, we are practising agriculture, all those are good things going on, then we have a strategic plan which goes up to five years, 2012, that one if it is followed then things will be good in the future.

c: You were in Bonn at the CBD this year?

F: Yes.

c: What is the value of these international meetings to the Batwa?

F: It is very good, one thing is the Batwa will be known worldwide. There is the chance that if people were not knowing, they will now be known worldwide. The governments will also understand the Batwa are suffering. When you who participate in the meeting when you come back home you tell them you presented what is happening and they will know they are being represented. Another good thing is that while we were in those meetings our governments from our own countries were also there so when you talk they know the problems you have because for them they are on top and they don't know those people at the grass roots are having the problems. So when you who went to the workshop talk people will know those problems and other governments will share your talk. They will have listened to you and your problems will have been heard.

[This response is typical of many sub-Saharan indigenous peoples who believe that they are in their situation because those in power are ignorant of their situation and who place their hope in the belief that once they are aware of their situation the powerful will help peoples like the Batwa. While this attitude may be naive and not reflect the reality that many indigenous peoples are maintained in their marginalized position by those in power, in the light of later discussions in this chapter it is also a very astute analysis. Those who maintain their positions in power through the destruction of peoples and lands that they are interconnected with and dependent upon could only continue such destructive ways, which will lead to their own destruction, through ignorance of the outcome of their actions. Fred's analysis is both astute and filled with hope that the destruction will end through the simple act of listening to each other and responding to each other's stories (Rose 2009 [1992]: 234).]

C: Is there anything you would like to add or ask?

F: I don't think I have anything to add generally but I have a question. Thanks for talking to us. What we are trying to discuss or talk, suppose there is a chance that these things [the vision] are in place but the Batwa fail to implement them. What is your advice so that these things are implemented?

C: [long pause] My advice, when I think of all that, I am not a Mutwa, I am an outsider. So all I can do is try and help and make sure those opportunities are in place, I cannot decide for the Batwa what they then do with those opportunities. My advice to the Batwa, and my advice is personal, is just to be strong, to always be fighting and always be ready – if those opportunities are there, be ready to take them. To always be strong, not to be divided, to try and work together and not work against each other and then always to have hope and to believe, I think the most important thing is to believe that the vision you have, if you work hard enough and if other people allow you those opportunities, that future can be yours. If you do not believe and you do not have hope then I think you will never be able to achieve those things.

F: It is good to have hope and belief, if someone gives you a chance, an opportunity, then you should have that hope and belief and work hard. But if someone wants to help me, and I just fold my hands, that means that person will not be able to help me because I am just getting away from him or her. So the best way to do it: Batwa in all the communities where they are should be told what to do and have hope

85

and trust that things one day will be fine if they all work hard and have that hope.

Interview 2

Beatrice is the project coordinator for the Batwa organization that Fred is the chairperson of. While the organization is composed of and managed by the Batwa, owing to low literacy levels it is in part staffed by a secretariat of non-Batwa workers who manage the day-to-day running of the organization. Beatrice is one of these workers and has supported the Batwa for over ten years.

c: What word do you use to mean indigenous when you are talking to the Batwa?

B: *Abasanga butaka.*

c: What does that mean?

B: Indigenous peoples.

c: But translate that for me.

B: The ones that others found on the ground, the people that were there before others, that is *abasangwa butaka*, *butaka* is land or soil, *abasangwa*, those who were found, like for example if you find me here, I am the first person before you.

c: Is that the most important part of being indigenous for the Batwa, that they were first?

B: No, they were there first and when you came you found them, maybe you came and found them while others who came before you had also found them there, that is the meaning. Because it doesn't say they came before you, everyone who came found them there.

[There are two main components to this idea of *abasangwa butaka*. First, the term should be understood to describe a relationship and not a people. The phrase talks about being 'found' and to be found demands that there are two different parties, one to find, and one to be found. This raises another issue, which is that the term *abasangwa butaka* also implies that the relationship is unequal. Indigenous people are not described as the finders but are instead passive and described as the one found by others. This is almost identical to the word Batwa, which is the name the Batwa call themselves by but is actually a non-Batwa word that was used by Bantu peoples to describe them. It is thought that the word has historically meant 'those who were found' or 'the others' and was used by Bantu peoples to describe the people they encountered when they migrated through Africa (Jeffreys 1946, 1953; Schadeberg 1999). Secondly, the term *abasangwa butaka* also suggests that indigenous is not about being found at a certain moment but that they have always been found by everyone who has come after. In essence they are then the first to be found and therefore the first on the land, before others arrived.]

C: When you speak to the Batwa about *abasangwa butaka*, what do you think that means for them, what does it mean to be indigenous?

B: Now, I answer you according to how I talk to them?

C: How you think – when they see themselves as indigenous peoples, what do you think they mean?

B: They mean one, I can say they mean the same culture, they mean the people with knowledge, better knowledge on the biodiversity, for example, better than I do. Have the relationship with some of the, eh [pause], if I come straight, with the animals, for example, they have [a better] relationship with them than I do, they have [a longer] story than I do, more than any other non-Mutwa could be having in my region. And, they know the herbal medicines, medicinal plants, you can be talking to them in a minute, the moment they are used to you and you complain on any pain, where you are feeling pain, in a minute they will tell you let me come and they give you medicine. So I take them as people with knowledge who are knowledgeable on these medicines and their culture is very unique in the sense that there are those [animals] that they don't eat or that they have the culture which is still so important for them that most of us we are trying to forget, put aside. However much they are poor but they are having that relationship to their fellow members, they don't tend to forget their fellow members, however much at any stage they are than most of us, as we can be having among our people. For example, if they meet, if they take time or if they don't know you but they happen to meet you they will say this is our tribe. So if they meet from Uganda, they meet the Rwandese [Batwa] as the first time, they will really understand each other and really identify that this is my friend.

C: Is that different from the other tribes [Bahutu, Batutsi]?

B: Fine, yes, to me, maybe to others it may be different, but to me if other tribes, it happens a lot if you are well off, then the rest you can bypass and you leave your [people behind].

C: But why do you think the Batwa have more unity, are stronger together than other people?

B: I don't know, maybe this is the way they are created or their culture.

C: Is it because they have been attacked, they have been under pressure for so long by other people that they have been forced to stick together?

[During the 2008 World Conservation Congress (WCC) Beatrice and I were watching a video about potato farming communities in the Peruvian Andes. During this video Beatrice made the comment that 'the difference is language, everything else is the same'. She was suggesting that the communities in the video were very similar to the Batwa communities she works with. At first my reaction was that this was a romantic and essentialized idea and that any similarities were only skin deep, they were both potato farmers, etc. However, I have since considered whether this assertion of the similarity between the two peoples might actually be an expression of relief: relief in the realization that there are others in very similar situations. When most IP are surrounded by non-IP who discriminate against them, maybe the assertion of commonality represents unity in the face of oppression.]

B: I really can't tell the reason why but for me I think as God created us differently that is the talent that God gave the Batwa.

C: Now this, what it means to be indigenous in Uganda for the Batwa, is this different from the indigenous peoples that you have seen here?

B: Me, I haven't seen any difference completely apart from the language.

C: So, but there are two elements, you are saying they experience some of the same culture, the food, the weapons, the clothes, but also that they share the same situation.

B: Now, that is on the side of being discriminated, being evicted, they suffer the same problems.

C: Now surely there must be differences, do you see differences between the indigenous peoples?

B: Well, I can say yes, but the differences are [fewer] than the common.

C: So what are the differences?

B: The differences are the languages are different, the behaviour may not be the same.

C: What do you mean by behaviour?

B: Like, some may be smokers, others may not, some may be drunkards, some may not.

C: But then what about all these arguments at the caucus? One group of our indigenous people were saying one thing, one group were saying the other thing, there was Africa's indigenous people

[Prior to the WCC, the indigenous peoples' caucus had a strategy and planning meeting which we both attended. At this caucus meeting there was political wrangling between groups of indigenous peoples from different parts of the world. These wrangles revolved around what was the best strategy to use to lobby for recognition of the rights of indigenous peoples.]

B: OK, fine, the level maybe, that is brought by the level of the standards, the Latin Americans for example have reached a level where they can sit with the ministers and discuss and others, others in Asia or wherever are working, if you are to take the example of this lady from Kenya, the one you have been meeting, she has been staff of Kenya Wildlife Service so do you think the way she can push on her points it's the way the other one who doesn't have any representative at the government level would do that? Definitely they have to be different. And the Kunas [Central America] have reached the level of really having the same beer with the minister or whoever and discuss. The environmental staff who would be either a Kuna person from a Kuna area ... so the way he understands the things is not the way the Batwa views will be heard by [Ugandan government staff]. You need to have that sort of backing and that is why meetings like that you saw some are saying this, some are saying that, it is because the level of things, for us we want to move slowly and start with the lower things, for them they want to reach the fifth stage, yet even for us the number one stage we haven't achieved it. We are saying yes, let's move slowly, we agree [with] the government on this and they also agree with us on this, for them they are saying no no no no no let's rush. So it's because where they are today and where others are today.

C: Can we go back to the Batwa in Uganda? What do you think are the problems that specifically come to the Batwa as indigenous people?

B: What do I think?

C: Do they face specific problems for being indigenous people? That other people don't face.

B: Come again, do they face these problems because they are Batwa?

C: Yes.

B: No, they are not facing the problems because they are Batwa. To me the Batwa are a tribe. So if they are to face the problems because they are Batwa, the Bahutu and the Batutsi will also face, but they are facing the problem because they are poor and this poverty was originating and brought by the eviction from the forest. So they are facing the problems because they lost their ancestral lands, they don't have any start-up completely which they can call a base. They need a base to reach somewhere. You need to give them a project while they are having somewhere there. They cannot achieve from anything when they are scattered. So that is one of the reasons they are facing all of these problems. Their children can achieve from university education but because they are poor, and don't have the homes, their children cannot achieve anything from education so [...] society remains poor. Because they don't have anyone who is working through education to earn something.

C: What, then, is the future for the Batwa?

B: The future for the Batwa. I would think that the future for the Batwa is to keep lobbying, pushing things to the government, to see how the government can resettle them and compensate them for their losses. That's one of the things that can be done. Then another thing is we can say that we can answer what is the future of the Batwa. The international community can keep lobbying them to see that they can come and help the Batwa to overcome the challenges they are in.

C: That is what can be done for the Batwa, what is the future, what do you think they will become in fifty years' time?

B: If the situation remains like this the future may be bad, but I am saying that the future for the Batwa it's to keep sensitizing for them to speak out and say these are the problems we are facing because of this and now we want this.

C: And if those problems are answered what will become of the Batwa?

B: They will become educated to their children, their children may become employed. The Batwa will also work as people who can help in these forests maybe and the life becomes OK if they are to be answered.

C: Now, a Hutu has land, he has a job, enough food for the family, his children go to school, you also have a Mutwa who has enough land, he has a job, his children are going to school, is there any difference? Is the Mutwa still a Mutwa or has he become a Hutu?

B: If they are educated to the level of the non-Batwa they will remain a Mutwa.

C: What keeps them the Batwa?

B: It's their tribe. It's their tribe that keeps them Batwa. Today a Muhutu is a graduate, does the Bahutu go away? The Bahutu remains on him. He may not be a Mutwa but he will be Chris, but Chris being a Mutwa, the word is sort of abusive, *wagitwawe*, they are calling Batwa as the name because they are poor, but the moment they are educated, the moment they have some houses, they will be John, they will be Kazungu, but not be *Chakazungu*, Kazungu at this stage is not *Kazungu* as Kazungu. Some of them abuse them in a way that they call them *Chakazungu* as if it is an animal.

C: *Cha* means what?

B: It is an abusive word that one can use if, for example …

C: *Chachris*?

B: Yes, it's abusive word, so if he or she is educated they will remain Chris, the Batwa will only come in when you are presenting your passport, when you are talking about your tribe […].

C: Will the Batwa still be part of the forest, will they still want to be part of the forest?

B: Why not, I think they will?

C: Because that is their history, that is where they are from?

B: To me I think still they will maintain that attachment to the forest, however much you are educated, this, for example if I show this example of Vicky, she is at the United Nations Permanent Forum as chairman of the indigenous peoples [Vicky Tauli-Corpuz – chairperson of the UN Permanent Forum on Indigenous Issues]. Has that one removed her from being an indigenous person which is attached to the forest of the Philippines? I do think that however much you are, it depends on the way on how you introduce yourself, on how you take yourself. If, for example, I am [Beatrice] from the Batwa group, however much I study even up to PhD I cannot forget that originally my grandfather used to live in Mgahinga/Bwindi, so it will depend on how they will take themselves. We may not predict today, some people say that in Rwanda there are those who are educated and working with the president and they don't want to call themselves Batwa. Is this the same as Uganda, we don't know, we have never heard about this, but to me if they are educated really, that education cannot take them away from that historical background.

c: One last question and then we can finish. Do you think it is better, because of the problems of the Batwa, to understand the Batwa as marginalized minorities or indigenous people?

b: Marginalized minorities?

c: Is it better to understand them as people without land, who don't have education or healthcare, or is it better, do you think it will help them more, if they are understood as indigenous people who have special relationships to the land? Which can be more effective?

b: I think both but I think the indigenous people sound more strong at the international level and which the Batwa are too much attached to because the indigenous people have that connection to their ancestral land which the Batwa are, the minorities fine, there are these areas that can address minorities, but then the indigenous peoples [is more applicable to] people that can claim [to be] from Bwindi and Mgahinga. If we are talking about minorities there are so many in Uganda [so its use] may not bring much case.

2 INDIGENEITY AS SUBVERSION

The difficulty in acceptance

In 2002 at a workshop in Uganda I (Chris) witnessed an argument taking place between two participants. The viewpoint of one participant, the Ugandan programme officer for a Batwa development programme, was that the Batwa were not a uniquely indigenous people. He reasoned that as all Africans were black, and equally colonized by Europeans, they could all claim to be 'indigenous'. The other participant, a Ugandan human rights lawyer, argued against this by suggesting that the Batwa were uniquely 'indigenous' based on international definitions. His argument, however, failed to persuade the programme officer. If it is accepted that indigenous people are best understood as people who are dominated by colonizers then this definition can lead a number of people, including the programme officer, to conclude that all African populations are indigenous. More recently, one attorney in Uganda provided the following legal opinion:

> There is no doubt that if you consider the cases of North and Southern America or North and Southern Africa, you can directly draw the dichotomy between migrant populations and indigenous populations ... Examples are the red Indians of North and Southern America *vis-à-vis* the Caucasian migrants that occupied these lands later ... In case

of the Interlucustrine Bantu of East, Central and Southern Africa as well as their Luo counterparts, their migrations within the area are more theoretical or academic as they were moving, if at all, within the same region ... It is therefore not possible to talk of indigenous peoples and migrants in this context. This title will for all intents and purposes mean a technical fatal blow to the Batwa case if they continue to refer to themselves as indigenous peoples. Their right may derive from other entitlements but not by being the indigenous of the areas in question. (Personal communication, 2009)

Indeed, Article 10 of the constitution of Uganda states that any group existing and residing within the borders of Uganda before 1926 is indigenous (Republic of Uganda 1995). In Botswana, home of over half of all San peoples of Africa, the government 'refused to participate in the 1993–2003 UN Decade of the Indigenous people, on the grounds that in their country *everyone* was indigenous' (Lee 2006: 459; emphasis in original). But this is too simplistic a model of African population dynamics and fails to recognize the internal colonization that Africa has faced. When this internal colonization is taken into account it may be more accurate to understand indigenous peoples in Africa as being not just indigenous but as being the 'Original Colonized Society'. This highlights the tension that the application of concepts such as 'indigeneity' can uncover, particularly in the African context, where 'indigenous' can be applied on different levels within the same situation.

It is important to understand the implications of indigeneity not only for indigenous peoples but also for those positioned as non-indigenous. In the African context the use of terms such as 'indigenous peoples' becomes problematic (Barnard 2002; Kenrick and Lewis 2004b; Saugestad 2001a) to a point where indigenous identity becomes 'inconvenient' for those who foreground their identity by it, since, if those with power recognize the realities that the term 'indigenous' points to, the subsequent changes required would be 'inconvenient' for the powerful (Saugestad 2001b).

McIntosh rightly states that 'in colonial and successor states [indigenous status] is intimately linked with the struggle by formerly self-governing groups for land rights and self-determination, as well as claims for restitution, reparations and compensation for loss of life and liberty' (McIntosh et al. 2002: 23). This is a much simpler process when an oppressor group and an oppressed group are clearly identified, as is the case in Australia. In African contexts, however, indigenous peoples are often asserting their rights in relation to those who have identified themselves as 'indigenous' against one-time colonial oppressors.

The assertion of an indigenous identity by ethnic groups may be seen by current African governments as a demand for those governments to deny the status they originally used and to reclassify themselves as non-indigenous. In some situations governments may even feel that the assertion of indigenous status by others is tantamount to having to accept that they have become the very thing they once opposed, the 'colonials'. The political ramifications of this perceived demand by indigenous peoples show very clearly why some African governments are in no hurry to acknowledge the indigenous status of certain ethnic groups in their countries. They may see themselves as being required to devolve some of their powers to such groups (or as having to rethink the relationship between 'post-colonial' governance and all those in whose name they supposedly govern) and this helps to explain why the African members of the UN Human Rights Council spent years trying to stall the adoption of the UN Draft Declaration on the Rights of Indigenous Peoples. In 2006 the Namibian representative, speaking on behalf of the African group of countries at the Third Committee of the United Nations' General Assembly, opposed the adoption of the draft declaration. He said, '... some of the provisions of the draft declaration contradict the national constitutions of a number of African countries and therefore these countries are unable to adopt the declaration in its present form' (Indigenous Peoples Caucus 2006). During this same session of the General Assembly the Botswana delegate was reported as saying,

> The [draft declaration] suggested that certain groups had the right to claim to be the sole indigenous peoples of specific regions of a sovereign Republic ... Further, it gave blanket recognition to the right of regional, ethnic and tribal groups, in general, to full political and economic self-determination ... The Declaration should clearly balance the rights of a group or tribe versus the rights of a nation as a whole. (United Nations 2006)

Having so recently gained their independence from European colonializers, it may be that many governments are concerned that in accepting indigenous peoples' rights they place question marks against their own political authority, since that was exactly what they demanded of the colonial powers in their own struggle. Mohamed Salih even suggests that African governments create this fear purposely: '[indigenous peoples] have been used as a scapegoat to cement a bankrupt and disintegrating political society looking for far-fetched legitimacy by creating an enemy image looming from the periphery and striving to hijack political power from the centre' (Mohamed Salih 1993: 272).

Additionally, 'the denial of "indigenous rights" by southern African governments is justified broadly by reference to nation building and the need to pursue an explicitly non-ethnic form of nationalism' (Geschiere 2005; see also Leonhardt 2006; Pelican 2009; Suzman 2001: 285). This strategy is underpinned by the acknowledgement that 'if African states are to take their rightful place in the world, progressive Africans believe, tribalism must be destroyed' (Clay 1985). In this process indigenous peoples can be seen as subversive and dangerous since their identification as 'indigenous' can be interpreted as challenging the image of the unified nation, an image that is largely the product of dominant elites (see Rosengren 2002: 25; Saugestad 2000: 211). It is this definition of the nation-state, created by the dominant elites, which Friedman describes:

> [The nation-state] is represented as a closed unit, whose population is homogenous and whose mode of functioning is dominated by boundedness itself, by territoriality, and thus, by exclusion ... for this metaphor to work the nation state has first to be reduced to a cultural totality ... When this notion is culturalized it suddenly implies total cultural homogenization, i.e. the formation of identical subjects. (Friedman 2002: 25)

Moving briefly outside of Africa to Asia, a comment from the former prime minister of Malaysia is revealing in its portrayal of a dominant elite's political representation of indigenous communities within its borders. He is quoted as saying, 'nowhere are [indigenous peoples] regarded as the definitive people of the country concerned. The definitive people are those who set up the first governments ... Malays have always been the definitive people of the Malay Peninsula' (Gomes 2004: 10). This interpretation of Malayan politics has no room whatsoever for the history of the indigenous Orang Asli people. This example mirrors historical discourses, from Australia and Canada, over the legal doctrine of *terra nullius*, which proposed in law that indigenous peoples' lands were unoccupied because the indigenous peoples were too 'primitive' to have political or legal rights that required recognition by the colonizing power (Asch and Samson 2004: 167). As Buchan and Heath write, in Australia 'The state of nature and civil society were not merely alternatives or opposites, but indexes of social progress away from savagery – understood as an absence of state and society – and towards state-governed civilization' (2006: 12). In these contexts indigenous peoples were simply too 'savage' to have the capacity to form any kind of civil governance and as a result could hold no claims to sovereignty over their own lands.

Can it then be said that indigenous peoples in Africa, by collectively asserting their indigenous identity in public forums, are actually questioning the imagined idea of nationhood created by national leaders? Certainly in Malaysia, the nation-state has gone as far as creating laws that '[prohibit] public discussion of the issue of indigenous status ... [as it] ... is considered seditious' (Gomes 2004: 10). Barnard goes farther; he states that the ethnic identities of foraging people are framed in opposition to non-foraging peoples' identities within nation-states, and suggests that foragers' identities are inherently antagonistic towards dominant state identities (Barnard 2002: 18). In Botswana, attempts by Survival International to assert the Gana and Gwi Bushmen's 'indigenous' status were viewed as unwanted interference by the government because, according to Suzman, 'such sentiments are felt particularly acutely in post-colonies attempting to assert an indigenous – for want of a better word – national identity forged on an indigenous ethical code' (2002: 5) In turn, this assertion by Survival International on behalf of the Bushmen was seen as little more than an 'unfounded attack by a malevolent foreign force on their national integrity' (ibid.: 5). If this is the case, then indigenous peoples and the NGOs that represent them are, in the eyes of nation-states, inadvertently positing themselves outside of the state and becoming what Ramos describes as 'internal outsiders' (in Conklin 2002: 1053). As a result, this may be one of the ways used by political leaders to justify their failure to provide the services and benefits of living inside a nation-state to these marginalized groups.

It is clear that the resistance to indigeneity in Africa goes beyond claims of precedence in residence and the dispute over resources that such a claim might entail. In Africa such a claim to indigenous identity asks dominant sections of society to do more than relinquish control. It asks nation-states to reassess the very identity they have constructed for themselves, the values they base such an identity on, and the way they respond to other citizens whose values and identity are seen to be different.

A legitimate alternative

The dominant national image is of an Africa in a rush to become 'civilized', 'developed' and 'First World' in order to become accepted by the West and to '"leap across the centuries" to the Western present' (Argyrou 2005: 33). As Suzman notes of Botswanan elites: they had a 'strong sense of themselves as having progressed from a state of primitive penury to modern affluence' (2002: 3). But as Argyrou has noted, 'Acceptance by native elites of the ideology of progress involved a fundamental contradiction. It was both a recognition of European superiority and an affirmation, however grudgingly, of the inferiority of one's own culture' (2005: 22). He suggests,

> The 'developed man' ... had no doubt about what 'man' could do in the long run with the use of science and technology. The trick was to get the 'undeveloped man' to believe in the same thing and act accordingly. Such was the trick. 'Undeveloped' nations were economically backward precisely because they were 'traditional'. They lived the past in the present and reproduced it over the centuries with little or no change. (Ibid.: 28)

By maintaining what has been perceived to be a 'traditional' way of life, indigenous peoples are seen to stand in sharp contrast to this race for development. Where this dialectical view of the relationship between tradition and modernity exists, the dominant group is forced into understanding indigenous peoples in one of two ways. Indigenous communities are either backward, and their demands have no legitimacy, or their belief in alternative livelihood strategies means that the dominant ideology of modernity may not be the only answer. Those holding to the dominant ideology will not accept a challenge to its validity, so automatically assume any opposing ideology must be illegitimate. This process of denial is made crystal clear in comments made by the then vice-president and future president, of Botswana: 'How can you have a stone-age creature continue to exist in the time of computers? If the Bushmen want to survive, they must change, otherwise, like the dodo they will perish' (in Suzman 2001: 286).

Dominant Western ideology has for centuries enforced the belief that

Africans are wild and uncivilized and has sought to validate this through a particular understanding of their relationship to nature. In their rush to disprove the West's perception of Africans, African governments today paradoxically perpetuate this essentialist identity by acknowledging it and condemning as backward indigenous peoples' culture and the particular livelihood strategies and relationships to the land these embody. If nothing else, the dominant ideology is threatened by the very presence of indigenous peoples' modes of production. As a result, the only way it can exist alongside it (since in many cases it has failed to destroy it) is to class it as inferior and on the verge of extinction. In this way, until the dominant ideology adapts to accept difference, indigenous culture will always be seen as sufficient for nothing more than a money-generating yet somehow shameful tourist curiosity, or simply as something to be eradicated through dispossession and the denial of basic human rights.

For these reasons, asking governments in many African states to acknowledge the term 'indigenous' is actually asking them to fundamentally question and reconsider a dominant ideology that portrayed itself as bringing development for all but which has more often simply entrenched and deepened inequality within nation-states. This could go some way to explaining the reluctance of those holding state power to commit to the process of acknowledging indigenous peoples' rights within their own countries. Rather than this negating indigenous peoples' right to seek justice, it highlights why they are so often met with hostility by such governments. Saugestad goes farther when she says,

> ... most [African] national governments ignore, reject or are downright antagonistic to the very concept. Why then use this concept as a political argument? Why challenge a sceptical government with the use of a controversial term, if perhaps a term like 'marginalised minority' may be used to single out the most deprived section of a population equally well? (Saugestad 2001a: 309)

In sub-Saharan African contexts, might it be more useful to base debates on equality for indigenous peoples around concepts of 'human rights' instead of 'indigenous rights'? In the eyes of sub-Saharan African governments, this difference in how rights are framed could signify a difference between divisiveness and something 'more in tune with the rhetoric of nation building' (Suzman 2001: 293), since this concept of nationhood is a major stumbling block to the acceptance of 'indigenous' identity. However, while this approach may seem to be more appropriate for achieving social and economic equality for indigenous communities, acknowledging groups' marginality has not tended to lead to social and economic equality, and it is also unclear how a rhetoric of individual human rights could bring about a paradigm shift that involved acknowledging alternative ways of relating to the world, and so enabled a questioning of state ideologies that have deepened inequality. As Saugestad suggests, a response to indigenous peoples' rights which neglects their specific cultural context would lack the insight needed to fully understand the generative processes which create symptoms of poverty (2000: 220). Indeed, indigenous peoples are facing extreme levels of poverty specifically because they have been conquered by invading populations who have removed their ability to sustainably carry out their life projects. While human rights can acknowledge and tackle the effects of conquest, it will take the acknowledgement of indigenous peoples' rights before the generative process of colonialism and its ongoing destruction will be acknowledged.

If 'indigenous', as an identity, continues to be used at the local and international level to fight for social equality, then it is crucial to break down this stereotype that sees the nature of the indigenous struggle as being about a struggle for the control of power. Rosengren acknowledges what he describes as 'the colonial character of the indigenous condition which requires an opposing, non-indigenous, Other in order to understand the processes' (Rosengren 2002: 25), but as McIntosh et al. note, the history of human interaction 'is far too messy to allow us to suppose that a simple dualism – indigenous/non-indigenous – can capture the true complexity of real world situations' (McIntosh et al. 2002: 24). Thus the modern struggle for indigenous peoples' rights should not be seen by governments as a struggle to reverse the roles of domination, but about self-determination largely within the boundaries and constitutions of current nation-states. With this in mind we will now discuss how indigeneity can be understood as a mediation strategy employed by indigenous peoples to seek justice through accommodation.

3 INDIGENEITY AS ACCOMMODATION

A Canadian friend, who had grown up beside a First Nation reservation, recently explained to me (Chris) his thoughts on the role of colonialism in the fate of Canada's indigenous peoples. He believed that while he could accept the role of colonialism in the exploitation of First Nation peoples in the past, he could not accept the inference that colonialism was the cause of their current problems. For this Canadian, placing blame on Euro-Canadians was simply an excuse that took the spotlight away from the real cause of First Nation peoples' contemporary problems, which, in his eyes, were the First Nations people themselves. He was very clear that while colonialism was to blame for many of the inequalities First Nations peoples experience today, the events themselves happened three hundred years ago. When asked why the wrongs of the past should not be considered in the present, he responded that the past was unavailable to the present and, besides, the First Nations can't go back to hunting and gathering – the world has moved on.

These sentiments are not simply present in local atittudes, or present only in Canada. In a 2009 interview, President Obama responded to issues of poverty in Africa with the following analysis:

> I would say that the international community has not always been as strategic as it should have been, but ultimately I'm a big believer that Africans are responsible for Africa. I think part of what's hampered advancement in Africa is that for many years we've made excuses about corruption or poor governance; that this was somehow the consequence of neo-colonialism, or the West has been oppressive, or racist. I'm not a believer in excuses. I'd say I'm probably as knowledgeable about African history as anybody who's occupied my office. And I can give you chapter and verse on why the colonial maps that were drawn helped to spur on conflict, and the terms of trade that were uneven emerging out of colonialism. And yet the fact is we're in 2009. The West and the United States has not been responsible for what's happened to Zimbabwe's economy over the last 15 or 20 years. It hasn't been responsible for some of the disastrous policies that we've seen elsewhere in Africa. I think that it's very important for African leadership to take responsibility and be held accountable. (All Africa 2009)

What both my Canadian friend and President Obama do in their statements is nothing short of a sleight of hand that removes their own participation, as representatives of dominant structures of power, in the 'problems' of 'poverty' in both Mi'kmaq or African communities. Rist makes the point more clearly:

No one seems to remember that for such 'problems' to arise two sets of actors must be involved: rich and poor, white and black, men and women. In other words the rich do not exist without the poor – to take one example. The advantage of an approach that focuses on only one party in the relationship is that it puts the blame for the 'problem' on the weaker party and removes whoever has arrogated the right to pose the question from the 'problem' altogether. By eliding social relations, this rhetorical sleight of hand brings forth a new, apparently 'objective' reality: poverty, in this particular case. (Rist 2008: 229; emphasis in original)

What both my Canadian friend and President Obama imply is that colonialism and the conquest carried out under its banner were events that have long since passed. While they both agree that the effects of colonialism are still being felt, they are clear that colonialism is not an ongoing process that continues to influence the livelihood strategies of conquered peoples. As a result, while both these commentators raise the useful point that historically marginalized groups have the ability to improve their situations, they fail to acknowledge that this ability is limited by larger structures. Crucially, they deny the reality that the limiting of power that indigenous or African people experience can be directly traced to the domination of colonial forces at home and from overseas that is ongoing today.

An example from Australia clearly highlights the point. In 2008, the newly appointed Australian prime minister, Kevin Rudd, made the landmark apology to Australian Aboriginal peoples for their historical mistreatment as a result of the policy of forced removal of mixed-parentage children. In an act that strengthened this apology, Australia signed the UN Declaration on the Rights of Indigenous Peoples (UNDRIP), after years of opposition. Despite this clear rhetoric acknowledging the existence of Australia's indigenous peoples, and the conquest they have faced, many Aborigines are questioning whether anything has changed (BBC News 2009a). Indeed, despite the hopes raised through the state's signing of the UNDRIP, the Minister for Aboriginal Affairs removed any significance from this action by suggesting, 'It's more an aspirational statement that outlines the principles and aspirations of indigenous people, and governments who express their support are committing to work alongside of their indigenous peoples to achieve the broad ambitions of the declaration' (BBC News 2009b).

In the year after the apology was made, the state introduced measures which were justified as being in the interests of Aboriginal peoples, but were regarded by Aborigines as the actions of a colonial state. The actions included the state management of benefits for Aborigines, which allowed half the welfare payments for each individual to be paid directly to shops by the state. Other measures included the complete ban on all sales, transport and consumption of alcohol and pornography within indigenous communities in an attempt to stem a reported crisis in child abuse within the communities (BBC News 2009a). As we try to understand these seemingly paradoxical actions by the Australian state we are left with the suggestion that the state, like my Canadian friend, understands the denial of autonomy and self-determination to be a historical event and is blind to the reality that its ongoing actions continue the historical processes of conquest.

In the African context this situation of ongoing conquest is further complicated because, when understood from the point of view that colonialism was carried out by European states, the 'original colonialists' were seen to leave the continent (or leave positions of power) at the time of independence. However, in reality most indigenous peoples were already suffering colonialism when the European states applied their brand of colonialism, and while independence was achieved for some sections of society in Africa it was not achieved by indigenous peoples, who were often left with their 'original colonizers'. The difficulty – as stated earlier – is that the colonial forces that restrict the freedoms of Africa's indigenous peoples today are often the very people who sought and achieved their independence from the European powers in the past.

Despite these difficulties, indigenous peoples, in clear and profound ways, continue to 'show that invasion is not a process of the past which is now finished. Rather, they go to considerable effort to explain that the process is on-going and continues to destroy people and land' (Rose 2009 [1992]: 191). At a UN meeting in New York, one participant from the Siksika Nation eloquently responded that, 'If the rights of indigenous peoples in the world were respected we wouldn't be living in deplorable conditions and we wouldn't be here lobbying so strongly for changes' (BBC News 2009b). The implication is that indigenous people continue to be controlled by dominant others who control the structures that govern their lives and modes of production. Being forced to seek validation of their rights from others is testament to their lack of autonomy. It is clear that the freedom of the Siksika people to exercise their rights is restricted by another group's unwillingness to acknowledge those rights, and that until such rights are acknowledged their conquest at the hands of others will continue.

Deborah Bird Rose's Aboriginal teacher Hobbles made the point more succinctly. In Rose's words,

> European ideologies of conquest assert that conquest is finished, and that it was the product of so many compelling and inescapable causes that it was inevitable. Ideologies throw the ball back to Aborigines, metaphorically, telling them that they cannot live in the past, and will just have to adapt to the new order. Hobbles and others disentangle the mystifying ideologies of conquest, showing that at every moment there is an act of will. They say that Europeans are living in the past, still following a law that has no future. And they ask that others make choices, exercising their will as an act of consideration for the fact that we all live, and die, together. (2009 [1992]: 196–7).

Invasion is not a process that has been contained by the past but is a process that continues in the present through the destruction of peoples and lands. What Hobbles implies is that the new world order which many dominant discourses and agents claim to be acting under, an order which relentlessly enforces its will on all it encompasses, is simply an order created and carried out by individuals. It is not an inanimate object but the creation of humanity, which can be altered, redirected and radically subverted by the very same people who claim to be under its control. Colonialism is not isolated in history but is an ongoing process in the thoughts and actions of indigenous and non-indigenous communities alike, and can be responded to through every conscious action we make.

Within this paradigm of the colonial present and of an ongoing conquest that is being continually imposed on the conquered, it could be suggested that the demand for indigenous identity to be acknowledged and valued is a naive and hopeless task. As Omura notes, 'indigenous peoples are still subordinate to Euro-American society because it is that society that defines indigenousness and controls decision making on indigenous problems' (Omura 2003: 396). If we assume that indigenous rights are inalienable then we have to accept that indigenous peoples' rights, or more specifically the freedom such rights are meant to protect, existed before the modern structures that have been designed by the state to enforce them. By demanding acknowledgement of such freedoms within modern human rights structures it could be argued that indigenous peoples are placing responsibility for redressing the crimes of the conquest with the conquerors themselves. One view of this strategy is that

> Oppressed peoples, in the vast majority of cases, have no alternative but to wage struggles for rights and redress using the language, the legal and political tools, and even the funding of their oppressors. They regularly engage in subversion, imbue the dominant with alternative meanings, find room for maneuver ... Yet these conditions also impose formidable constraints ... Audrey Lourde's ... famous dictum – 'The Master's Tools will never dismantle the Master's house' – serves as a pointed reminder of these constraints ... (Hale 2006: 111)

If this is the case then are indigenous peoples wasting their time on a system that was never designed to benefit them? And can indigenous identity and its corollary, the claim to indigenous rights, be understood only as an act of subversion?

Against this we suggest that the insistence on the recognition of indigenous identity and the rights entailed by such an identity is a much more responsive strategy to conquest than suggested by the comments above. Rose found that the Yarralin communities in Australia responded to conquest in three ways: *capitulation, resistance* or *accommodation* (2009 [1992]: 189).

Capitulation is the option offered by dominant society when it suggests that it would be better to accept the new world order and become part of it, in effect to assimilate. This response is present in the interview in Part One of this chapter, where the chairperson of the Batwa Organization, Fred, suggests that the Batwa's future lay in their ability to adapt and become like their Bahutu neighbours, to assimilate to the dominant livelihood strategies and modes of production.

The response of *resistance*, on the other hand, refuses to take the route of capitulation and aims to resist the control of the new world order (a world order that may be simply the old colonial order in a new neocolonial guise, or may be somethng different depending on our active engagement in reshaping this process). It is this response which the dominant powers in sub-Saharan Africa, and authors like Hale above, assume indigenous peoples to be taking. In Africa this is not true of indigenous peoples; the struggle for indigenous rights is far more complicated than the assumption that indigenous peoples are trying to subvert and replace the rule of authority. In addition, capitulation and resistance both fail to acknowledge key perspectives on the relationships involved in colonialism. Importantly, if indeed there is a new world order which needs to be responded to, it is important to understand that such a world order is not removed from the will of the individuals that it influences. The responsibility should not be on indigenous peoples to respond to a world order or set of events not of their making. The responsibility should instead be on both the conquerors and the conquered to take responsibility for their place in the world and their ability to effect change. Additionally, the first two responses acknowledge a situation based upon polarized identities where the only decision is whether to join or fight the colonial other.

The final response is the attempt by indigenous peoples to find *accommodation*, and this could be seen as the only choice left to indigenous peoples to regain what little they can from conquest. However, accommodation is much more reflective than that analysis would suggest. Indeed, this response acknowledges that if there is a new world order it is one characterized by the union of indigenous and settler communities, and that this reality implies an inevitable relationship that cannot be changed. Importantly it acknowledges that in an inter-related and entangled world the burden of responsibility lies with us all regardless of identity. As Rose, mentioned earlier, discusses,

Hobbles says that we all [indigenous and settlers] own Australia now. What he does not say, because for him it is so obvious, is that Europeans have already taken most of the country and ought therefore to be more equitable. They ought, in fact, to allow more opportunities for Aborigines to control land. His suggestion that Aborigines should have more land ... offers Europeans a form of accommodation. In more extensive narratives Hobbles says that the years during which people worked on cattle stations, offering their labour to pastoralists ... ought to be understood as an attempt at accommodation to which Europeans have yet to respond ...

Hobbles has offered a set of profound gifts to a non-Aboriginal audience: an acceptance of the conditions of the past as the basis from which we will build our future; some means of transforming the wrongs of the past into more equitable relationships. (Ibid.: 196–7)

With this understanding we can look at 'indigeneity' in a new light.

We suggest that the demand to have an indigenous identity acknowledged and valued by colonial states within rights-based frameworks is not a naive and hopeless task but instead a brave and courageous olive branch offered by indigenous peoples to their conquerors. It is an attempt at accommodation whereby indigenous peoples are acknowledging the joint ownership indigenous and settler communities now have of their lands while at the same time demanding from the colonial state an acknowledgement of this interdependence. Such an acknowledgement starts simply from acknowledging that indigenous peoples do exist and do have rights that are of equal value to those of other groups of people. Indigenous peoples' rights are then a vehicle of accommodation, an acknowledgement by indigenous peoples that their futures are shaped by the structures of the colonial present, but a demand on that same colonial present to acknowledge them as equal partners in a meaningful relationship. Importantly, the accommodation here demands that the previously dominant partner has to recognize the history of injustice upon which its position has in part been built and seek to find new ways to relate to others (Kenrick 2009: 22).

In the case of the Batwa in Uganda, they do not seek exclusive rights to their former forests and they do not see others as 'simply guests'. They instead demand the return of their rights to access the forests; a position which does not exclude other parties from asserting their own demands or right to the same forests. (For a similar discussion on the Baka of Cameroon, see Leonhardt 2006: 74.) Central African hunter-gatherers like the Mbuti of the Democratic Republic of Congo, the Bagyeli of Cameroon or the Hadza of Tanzania have an attitude of inclusiveness which informs their relations with everybody. Woodburn's description of Hadza inclusiveness sums up this attitude: 'Hadza society is open and there is simply no basis for exclusion. Equality is, in a sense, generalised by them to all mankind but, sadly, few of the rest of mankind, so enmeshed in property relations, would be willing to extend parity of esteem to hunter gatherers who treat property with such a lack of seriousness' (Woodburn 1982: 448).

As Asch and Samson write in the Canadian context, 'indigenous peoples have repeatedly proposed that a just resolution of outstanding issues should be based on the principle that we are *all here to stay*' (2004: 261; emphasis added; see also Asch and Samson 2006: 146; Feit 1995). For Central African hunter-gatherers, land is a metaphor for equality and for 'including in' those who wish to join them through establishing 'good relationships' based on egalitarianism (e.g. Berg and Biesbrouck 2000: 35–6; Kenrick 2005: 125; Lewis 2005: 63).

For accommodation to work it is necessary for both parties to acknowledge the need for accommodation in the light of historical injustices, to acknowledge the dependency of each party on the survival of the other, and to acknowledge that accommodation is being offered by each party. Despite accommodation being sought by many indigenous groups around the world, it seems that the response of most states is to deny the accommodation on offer and to deny their role in the ongoing conquest. And while indigenous peoples understand that '[t]he autonomy of country, species, and people is sustained by an intense interdependence' (Rose 2009 [1992]: 105), most nation-states see struggles for autonomy only as threats to stability and to the power that they presently hold.

Conclusion

'Indigeneity' proves difficult to accept for many states, particularly in Africa. This at first sight appears all the more remarkable as the authority of those actors rests on the historical deployment of the same terminology, on having demanded the same rights from previous colonial governments as indigenous peoples demand today. Governments that once understood their identity as 'indigenous' through their position as subordinate to a more powerful colonial force now understand an essentialist definition of the term 'indigenous', whereby it is defined through precedence in occupation. It is clear that African governments have failed to recognize the validity of the struggles of indigenous peoples as being their right to determine their futures and maintain their social integrity. This suggests that these governments have become the very thing they once fought against – an oppressor of less powerful groups – and that their failure may be a result of their desire to maintain their current positions of dominance. As Argyrou's earlier quote in this chapter suggests, national elites' adoption of an ideology of progress is actually a trick that allows colonialism by force to be replaced by colonialism by ideology. Indeed, Mohamed Salih suggests, 'Most post-independent African states were no less cruel towards their indigenous populations than the colonialists' (Mohamed Salih 1993: 271) and further that '[t]he neo-colonial mentality of the African neo-colonial elite is hardly distinguishable from their colonial predecessors' (ibid.: 274).

However, indigeneity is not a fact but a relationship (Kenrick and Lewis 2004a, 2004b, Saugestad 2001a). It refers to unequal relationships developed through interaction between two groups in a context in which both groups understand that one is attached to an area and that their identity is dissimilar to the other's. While this is not the only condition of indigeneity, it does help to show that the very nature of the term is relational and relies on more than just precedence in occupation of an area. For indigenous peoples and their advocates, indigeneity says more about the relationships encountered by indigenous peoples than it does about the indigenous 'condition'.

Importantly, this chapter has sought to map out three very different interpretations of indigeneity in the African context. First we framed this chapter through the interviews of two voices intimately grounded in local indigenous struggles. We then discussed some of the fears and concerns of the dominant states which argue that indigeneity is not applicable in the African context for reasons which range from ignorance of the internal migrations in African history to dominant groups' fear that they may have to relinquish some of their grip on power. Finally, we have seen that indigeneity in Africa can also be understood as an attempt by indigenous peoples to force their current nation-state colonizers to acknowledge the interconnectedness and dependency that they share with the indigenous peoples they colonize and the similarities and ideology they share with their former European colonizers. Recognizing this play of indigeneity is also a way of recognizing how the wrongs of the past continue in the present, not as a way to shame the guilty, but as a way to acknowledge the equality indigenous peoples share with their neighbours, a mutuality that is currently being denied to them.

De la Cadena and Starn suggest, 'Current indigeneity continues to challenge the Western model of civilization and progress by insisting that Euroamerican colonialism and capitalist expansion have been a misadventure of violence, destruction and the trampling of non-Western peoples' (de la Cadena and Starn 2007b: 11).

This, however, does not go far enough and obscures the reality of the destruction we all face. Indigeneity does not simply challenge Euro-American colonialism because in the African sense the current colonialism is carried out by Africans, albeit in the name of Euro-American ideals. But importantly, while the destruction and violence have been witnessed most clearly in relation to non-Western peoples, the conquest carried out by colonialism is so complete, and the world's peoples are so interdependent upon each other, that colonialism will ultimately conquer not only the indigenous world but the colonial world as well. What indigenous people are left waiting for is for the conquerors to accept the gifts being offered to them through strategies of accommodation, gifts which are fundamentally about acknowledging our interdependence, and about terminating the conquest before all the world's peoples and lands are irreversibly destroyed.

Returning once again to Rose:

> [Settler] law is a law of madness. It is based in and effected through destruction, and people cannot go on destroying for ever. Failing to understand their place in the world, and the interconnectedness of life, [colonialism's] successors continue to visit destruction on the systems that support them. From [an Aboriginal] perspective it is so obvious that this cannot continue indefinitely that offers to re-form the future are understood to be in everyone's self-interest. (Rose 2009 [1992]: 198)

We have argued that indigenous peoples' demand to reverse the ongoing histories of domination imposed on them should be seen as part of a process of liberating us all from a completely unsustainable system of property ownership and resource use, and from completely inadequate ways of responding to planetary, social and personal problems. This system is unsustainable not because it is driven by some innate human greed, ignorance, alienation or desire for power, but precisely because it is based on an understanding of ourselves and of social and ecological systems which is so completely at odds with the evidence presented to us by ecological systems and by social systems, whether mediated through the scientific literature or through our personal experience.

However unlikely the possibility may seem, might the end of the historical and ongoing dispossession and domination of indigenous peoples rest on their ability to continue to offer the gift of accommodation, and the ability of settler and dominating societies to finally receive that gift? Accommodation, as Rose describes it, is not an act born out of submission and extracted by force. Accommodation is an incredibly powerful and generous gift which is being offered because it presents the only solution to the modern constitution.

In the Collins English Dictionary the verb 'accommodate' is defined as '1. to provide with lodgings, 2. to have room for, 3. to do a favour for, and 4. to adjust or become adjusted; to adapt' (Collins 2009). As such, the act of accommodation is an attempt by one group to offer shelter and a place to live, and in the process to offer a metaphorical location for another group within their own house, their world-view and the socio-ecological places they inhabit. It is a progressive and fluid attempt to adapt to, and find mutuality in, the changing history that we are all part of. It is an attempt to recuperate from the violence that seeks to insist on the divides between nature/culture, self/other and past/present, and to insist instead on processes of continuity, accommodation and mutual belonging. The act of accommodation is inherently an equalizing process that seeks to create mutuality and the sharing of power rather than promote difference and foster exclusion.

Crucially, however, the most important component of an act of accommodation is that it cannot work on its own. It demands a response that acknowledges the gift on offer. It is an admission of mutuality and collectivity that can work only when it is responded to in the same sentiment as that in which it is offered, with an equal admission. Rather than understanding indigeneity and the indigenous rights movement as either an attempt to resist global hegemony or the last act of submission within such hegemony, it may be more useful and productive to understand indigeneity as a process of accommodation that is waiting for the right response. A response we can provide by acknowledging our mutuality and by offering the space to accept, validate and adapt to all that enables mutuality – and to resist all that fosters domination – in each other's worlds.

Comment

Editor's note: The choice of Benno Glauser from the 'New World' settler context of Paraguay as commentator for this chapter is based on making more explicit the parallels between the settler and postcolonial contexts, in the positionalities of the Ayoreo and Batwa within their respective nation-states, and the similarities in the scale of their struggles for basic survival. Benno's comments here refer beyond this chapter to discussion around the nature of indigeneity first raised in the Introduction, and then relate this to the Batwa.

Benno Glauser

I feel that the definition given on p. 2 of the Introduction ('... fighting for rights and justice for those particular groups who ...', etc.) in fact covers indigenous peoples, but not in an exclusive way: other population groups and sectors may fit the definition but would definitely not be considered indigenous. Thus I feel that there may be an additional quality missing in order to make the definition complete. And I suspect that it has to do with the following.

Rose is also quoted, suggesting that 'indigeneity is an identity that is continually in flux and is determined not by some original state of purity but by the relationship between peoples'. So far, this formulation fits the previous definition. However, from my observation and experience, I would formulate it as follows: 'indigeneity is an identity that is continually in flux and is determined not by some original state of purity but by the relationship between peoples, *on one hand, and on the other between people and nature'*.

As I said, this comes from my observation and experience. Indeed, I think that the relationship with nature (the term 'world' is often an equivalent to our 'nature', in the indigenous realm) is a distinctive quality of indigenous peoples and indigeneity, adding up to the others you highlight. I think it is essential, and similar to the relationship 'between peoples'. The relationship indigenous peoples have with nature and the world follows a paradigm very divergent from ours, placing humans among other phenomena of nature as if all of them together were a social collective, a collective held together by relations of a social nature we normally, in the modern Western world-view, reserve for inter-human relations.

In the case of the Ayoreo I work with, this is even explicit in their 'cosmovision', and in the multiple ways they describe nature and deal with what we call nature. I felt like suggesting this, as the discussion of some of the answers in the interview acquires a new weight or appears in a different light if we give importance to the relationship between humans (indigenous) and nature.

When later in the interview the answers turn around the point of the importance of the relationship with the forest, or the question of whether to go back to the forest and why and how, the fact of having highlighted the relationship with nature changes the understanding of the interview, at least for me ...

Reply

We agree that indigenous peoples tend to have a particular relationship to the land, and we are heavily influenced by the idea of relational epistemology proposed by the likes of Ingold, Bird-David, etc.

The question which needs to be asked is whether this relationship to the land is directly related to being 'indigenous' or to another attribute that is largely present among indigenous people but does not have to be present to be included as indigenous. We have written our understanding of the term indigenous based upon the international definitions that are currently available and which are largely not accepted in sub-Saharan Africa. While these definitions discuss a connection to land, they do this in terms of 'ownership and residence', and not to epistemological or ontological relationships to land.

So, while we agree that indigenous peoples tend to have distinctly different modes of production compared to most 'modern' societies, and have distinctly different relationships with their environment, we are not entirely convinced that these features are part of what makes someone indigenous. In other words, is 'indigenous identity' (as an identity born out of a colonial history) the best way to identify groups of people who have fundamentally different relationships to the land from the settlers' neighbours?

After all, indigeneity is not a real thing that someone possesses but is instead an identity/attribute that can be created and destroyed or accepted and given/taken away. This should not affect any group's right to exist and be validated as a distinct culture/society in its own right. Perhaps, then, rather than include a relationship to land within the indigenous identity, such a relationship should serve to exist in its own right separate from such a colonial history. By focusing on the way that indigenous peoples are calling on us to urgently address historical processes which are destroying their lives and which threaten to destroy us all, we are not seeking to downplay the importance of an experience of sociality that includes the non-human as much as the human, but would see that experience as fundamental to us all, and one which we recover as we disentangle ourselves from the divisive dualisms of ongoing colonialism, and instead recover relationality and an ability to accommodate difference in ways which enrich us all.

4 | Displacement and indigenous rights: the Nubian case

EMMA HUGHES

The interviews below were conducted during 2008 and are part of a number of interviews and conversations with Egyptian and Sudanese Nubians. Some, but not all, of those I spoke with would identify themselves as activists; each expressed a desire for the Nubian story to be told. Each has made a contribution to the chapter that follows and I would like to acknowledge the role they have played in shaping this account. As a non-Nubian, non-indigenous person, I have endeavoured through this chapter to let their voices speak for themselves and to document these histories of a people for whom few international channels of communication exist.

Introduction

The Nubian population was first split during British colonial rule by a border division fixed in the 1899 British–Egyptian Condominium Agreement. Nubian land was initially flooded by the 1902 construction of the old Aswan Dam, and then again after it was heightened in 1912 and 1933. More recently, the Aswan High Dam, begun in 1960 and inaugurated in 1971, flooded the whole of Egyptian Nubia and around a third of Sudanese Nubia. The new settlements to which the Nubians were relocated in Egypt and Sudan are more than six hundred kilometres distant from each other and located away from the River Nile. The effects of the resulting displacement of people and communities are still being felt throughout the Nubian diaspora more than four decades on. The construction of further dams is currently under way in Sudanese Nubia, which threatens to submerge the remainder of the land and displace its people once again. The realities for Nubians are that they have not only been affected by the separation and relocation of their peoples, but also by the differing political regimes of Egypt and Sudan and the distinct cultural environments to which they were relocated. Scholars at the time of relocation suggested this might result in the eventual assimilation and disappearance of the Nubian people.[1] In 1977 Adams wrote, no one can say whether or not the Nubians will succeed in maintaining a separate ethnic and linguistic identity under the altered circumstances of the twentieth century. Given the levelling influence of mass communication and of western technical civilization, their ultimate extinction as a separate people might seem inevitable – at least to western observers. (1977: 664)

It is now clear, however, that far from resulting in the assimilation and loss of identity that Adams and others feared or suspected at the time of displacement, it has rather resulted in remarkable efforts on the part of the Nubian community to preserve their identity: a thriving Nubian culture can be seen across the diaspora, and within Nubia itself. Some cultural elements have necessarily changed and some traditions have been lost; this has particular significance for women, who are often still regarded as the protectors of cultural integrity. It is apparent, though, that Nubians still constitute a distinct ethnic group, and what is more, there is ample evidence of politicization of this identity as the basis of reclaiming their rights from the state.

1 DIALOGUES

Interview 1 – Suad Ibrahim Ahmed, 11 April 2008, Khartoum

Suad was the organizer of the first demonstration against the High Dam in 1960 in Wadi Halfa, the heart of Sudanese Nubia. She was subsequently detained by the government and moved to Khartoum by force. She lost her job in the Department of Statistics and was not permitted to leave the country.

Under President Nimeiri she was detained again several times and put under house arrest, this time for communist activities. On one occasion she went on hunger strike for twenty-seven days in prison, demanding newspapers and a radio. She was Sudan's first female political prisoner to be detained and remains the longest-serving female political prisoner. Omdurman prison, where she was detained for over two years, became the focus for politicized non-Arab women from across the south.

I was introduced to Suad by her brother, Kamel Ibrahim Ahmed, who left Sudan for Cairo in 1996 owing to constraints on his agribusiness in Sudan, and has yet to return. Suad agreed to be part of the project and was interviewed in her home in Khartoum by Nigel Parsons on my behalf. The interview was conducted in English.

NIGEL: We want to get some women's voices into the project, there are many male activists, but it is difficult, in Cairo, to find too many women.

SUAD: You are right. But this is true of all groups ... women behind the veil – that is how I describe them, because they are constantly in the background.

N: My first question is, what are the main issues facing Nubians today?

S: It can be easily and safely said, that inundation by dams is the most important issue that has come to the forefront as a result of renewed dam activities in Nubian areas ... the ways the Nubians kept their heritage and their culture was through their language, because they lost their ability to read and write in Nubian, but they kept it orally, and it kept going from generation to generation through oral transmission, rather than through reading and writing. The area has degraded tremendously environmentally over the centuries, but it has certain resiliences that kept it going. We pride ourselves that we are different, our traditions and culture [are] different from the Arab Islamic culture and the rest of central Sudan. In our view towards the role of women in society, for example, in the way we build our houses, in the way we treat foreigners, or people who are from outside the country or the region ... we believe that for the past twenty years, the Islamist regime in Sudan has reached unprecedented levels in animosity to the Nubians. They never forgave us for the fact that, in the last democratic elections that took place just before they received power in '89, the Islamists came, in democratic elections, came out last out of six candidates. That was no problem, had not the man who succeeded in winning the election and representing the constituency, also a Nubian, been a communist, Mohamed Saleh Ibrahim. He died twelve years ago after this regime came. A great loss. He was a communist and the Islamists came last.

[Omar al-Bashir, a colonel in the Sudanese army, ousted Ismail al-Azhari's government through military coup in 1989, established the ruling National Islamic Front (later to become the National Congress Party), and installed himself as president. He instituted sharia law with the support of ideologue Hasan al-Turabi, and suspended the five regional assemblies, to replace them with twenty-six states.]

N: Which constituency?

s: Halfa, Wadi Halfa. The Nubians broke the pattern. Communists always succeeded in the capital cities, but not in the regions – the regional constituencies. It broke that pattern: he came from a regional constituency. And not only that. They never implemented the whole of the Nile Waters Agreement – not this dictatorial regime, the last one, the Abboud regime, also a military dictatorship, signed the Nile Waters Agreement with Egypt, which inundated the area with the High Dam, which allowed Egypt to build the Aswan Dam. There were certain stipulations for the people whose homes and land [were] going to be swallowed by the new dam, including transmission of power, including building of roads. All of this was not implemented in reality, so the place gradually deteriorated, because the part that was swallowed by the Nile was the heart of the whole area, was the export and import point for the whole area, for its produce and its needs, the place where continuation of education after the first elementary level used to take place. Generally speaking, even psychologically, the effect was devastating. But this was taken to unprecedented levels by this regime, actually. This regime truly is our enemy. They are the enemies of the whole of Sudan. Eighty per cent of the Sudan is against them, they are only worried about themselves, doing whatever they like, riding the wave of Islamism and doing whatever they like under its name.

So, *the* most important issue that we are facing now is *how* to stop the four dams. Already one has gone up – we can't demolish it – how to stop the three other dams and how to develop the area without inundating it by dams by providing alternative sources of power and improving education to its former levels, or even better. That is what we are trying to do now.

[The four dams Suad refers to are Merowe, which was subsequently inaugurated on 3 March 2009, Shereik on the fifth cataract, Kajbar at the second caract and Dal, just south of Wadi Halfa, 100 kilometres south of the border with Egypt. The Kajbar Dam would submerge further Nubian territory to the south of Aswan and has been the focus of recent protests. Resistance to these dams began in 1995 and the proposals were temporarily postponed; planning for the dams began again in 2007. In 2010, a contract was awarded to Chinese company SinoHydro, for construction of the Kajbar Dam (International Rivers 2011).]

N: My second question then is, what are the main issues facing Nubian women today and how have Nubian men and women been affected differently by these issues?

s: Historically, Nubian women are different from Arab women. They have more freedom and more responsibility with that. Nubian women take care not only of the house and the children, but also of the farms and the palm trees and all the social duties in the community. And because a sizeable proportion of men usually work outside the area, the role of women was actually enhanced through this action. Generally speaking, it is well known that Nubian women have a strong character and they are not shy. I think that we constitute a majority in any case; women and children constitute about 71 per cent of the Nubian population because of the absence of men.

The past twenty years has seen a huge outflow of Sudanese, who are fed up with the regime. And with decreasing opportunities for employment and the increasing operation of abuse. And this includes the Nubians as well, the numbers are increasing. It used to be just men, but now there are females as well who have made a name for themselves in reality. [For example,] Rasha, who has CDs out in Spain. This is an impossible regime. It is difficult for people to put up with it. That is why people fly away ... people fly away. But these people are incorrigible.

I think that the role of women is historically in the forefront in Nubia. Social and economic and political conditions have increased her responsibility, despite oppression, because larger and larger numbers of men leave in order to provide for the family through employment outside the country, seeking better livelihoods.

So, the economic and political situation has led to increasing numbers of people leaving the area, giving additional responsibilities to the women and children who are left there, old and young, and in addition has led to the mass emigration from the area. In Northern Province in 1993 there were 760,000 and now they have left. And that was in 1999 or 2001 with the new constitution, decentralization. They massacred the Northern Province, they mutilated it because they don't trust us. The Sudan used to have eight provinces, or nine provinces including Khartoum. Now they have been divided into twenty-six states. I should say the Northern State – that is the new name. Northern State was next to the Red Sea, but the Arabs created a corridor between us and Red Sea State in order to export terrorists and arms to Egypt: they don't trust us to do that. What they call the Nile Province.

N: Just to come back to these additional responsibilities that fall on women, would you care to illustrate?

S: We get up in the morning, we take care of the place. We go and get fodder for the goats and sheep which are part of the farm. It would have chickens, goats and sheep. She is responsible for them. She is responsible for the clean-up and maintenance of the house, she is responsible for the making of the bread, the pancakes that we make, pancakes are our bread, as it were. *Kisra* or *kabida*. The women make this *kisra*. She is the one who does it. She is the one who goes to give her condolences, or to share in weddings, and we support each other on such occasions, and generally speaking, the running of the house and the feeding of the house, and the members of the house, and guests as well, are the responsibility of the women. And mostly it is a single-parent family because a lot of the men are not available. And that is why the question of mixing of the sexes, *yani*, this unnatural divide between men and women that the regime follows in their schools, and in public meetings and so on and so forth, it is not the norm there. Women have their own independence, because of these responsibilities.

N: So they would have had these responsibilities anyway, even before the inundation?

S: Oh yes, this is the existing social pattern. That is why they are in the forefront, you will notice, of the demonstrations against the dam. For instance, in Kajbar you can see the role of women is quite prominent, the numbers of women participating in those demonstrations [are] huge, and women speakers as well, not just following men.

N: Could I put my third question to you at this point: do Nubians have a vision for the future? How can this be achieved and what are the problems?

S: It seems that oppression has created numerous visions for our future. There are people who still believe that a Nubian kingdom can be revived, independent of the hegemony of Arabs of Khartoum, that we can revive its glory. There are people who believe that we do not need to create an independent Nubia because Nubians, in their heart of hearts, believe that the whole of the Sudan is theirs, and that is why the calls for the creation of the Nubian party – which started in the thirties, it didn't start now, of the last century – did not succeed. Because the Nubians in Kordofan, or in Darfur, or in the centre or in the north, believe that the whole of the Sudan is [their] country and that [their] kingdom covers the whole of the Sudan from Chad to Ethiopa and therefore that this is [their] land, the whole place. We cannot just say that, because [Nubians] have been driven out of the centre of Sudan and have concentrated in the northern part of it, that this is Nubia. This is not Nubia, the whole of the Sudan is Nubia. So the calls for independence and so on do not seem to have taken root in society. But we still believe that the CPA, the Comprehensive Peace Agreement that was signed with the SPLM, and is now part of the constitution of the Sudan, does give the various states some degree of room to manoeuvre independently. For instance, the content of education: you can teach your language under this new constitution. In reality, the CPA is not totally ... *yani*, the ruling regime does not implement it completely. We know that Abbyei and the other regions, they are doing it piecemeal, they don't want to relinquish power, but it *is* there and it is being monitored by the international community, which for some reason the NIF, the Islamic Front, have frightened into submission, the whole of the international community [laughs]. They do not want to face them directly, they are too busy with Afghanistan and Iraq, you know, and all of that.

[The Comprehensive Peace Agreement (CPA), or Naivasha Agreement, is a set of agreements between the government of the Republic of the Sudan and the Sudan People's Liberation Movement/Sudan People's Liberation Army, which were signed in January 2005 and aimed to put an end to the civil war. The referendum provided for within the CPA was held in January 2011 and saw southern Sudan vote almost unanimously to secede from the north, with independence being declared in July 2011.]

N: So your efforts could be focused ...

S: Our efforts are, how *do* we, how do we implement a programme of comprehensive development for this area *without* inundation? This area is *very* productive, *very* productive, a natural quarantine, that can make you produce in big quantities, not like the centre of Sudan ... It is the place where ... the people who *created* how to raise water, they need help because it is too expensive to raise water and bring it to this productive land. You need big companies to come and work with the people. There are some who have already started and their work is proving extremely successful. They [other provinces] have parties when they produce eight and ten sacks of wheat and we produce *thirty* – our *minimum* is fifteen per acre. We believe there is no way out other than development. No way out other than finding alternative sources of power. People are now building huge solar power generators in Spain, South Africa, in Australia, and our sun is in one of the hottest areas – 5.6 watts per square metre – you can't get better than that. It is economical even if you produce 2.1 watts per square metre. So, we believe that with alternative sources of power, with companies, private and public cooperatives, any group that involves the local people and under a system or an agreement or a law that provides for education and health in the area and by providing alternative sources of power that does not inundate the land, clean power, and by reviving tourism – which is a major source in Egypt and has dwindled in the Sudan because of the neglect of this sector by the various governments over the years – we believe that this sector can be revived and can be a source of income for the area without inundating it. [This] will give people an opportunity to earn a decent income and stay in their beautiful large houses, not in the little dingy rooms that they live in in Khartoum. And we are good at it, *yani*. The Nubians are known for their hospitality.

N: OK, our fourth question, do indigenous organizations, local or international, play a role in this process?

S: Indigenous and international organizations have in the past and up to now played quite a significant role, a) by alerting the international community to our plight. The Nubians are known for the multiplicity of their organizations. Wherever we go there are organizations. In Khartoum we have about forty-six organizations that belong to specific villages in the area. The Nubian Club was the first club ever to be registered in 1917, because all the clubs were Armenian, Greek, British, things like that, Egyptian, but there were no Sudanese [clubs]. The Nubian club is as old as that. We now have three or four big clubs and about forty-six little village clubs all over the capital. They like to organize ... they like to organize. Whenever there are five or six Nubians in a place they create a club, anywhere, whether they are in Iceland or in Cape Town, it doesn't matter, they organize. So there are organizations. And in fact when the first idea of building a dam became known to us in June 1995, thirteen years ago, the first thing we did was alert the twenty-six Nubian studies centres that are scattered all over the world. There are various Nubian studies centres in France, in America, in Japan, in the rest of Europe. There are people who are experts in our language and our history who care about us, and we alerted them

– Help! They are going to inundate us again. That was back in 1996. And many of them wrote memos and sent protests to the regime about this. And in fact there was a solidarity day in London ... And in America there is a committee, against dams in Nubia, and we sent these protests to the international community – Amnesty International and Human Rights Watch and UNESCO and so on and so forth in the name of Nubians in Egypt and in the Sudan, particularly after the massacre of 13 June when those four people were killed and many were wounded, near the dam, about six or seven kilometres from the dam. That was on 13 June last year, 2007. That was a peaceful demonstration. The 13 June massacre.

N: In the last free and fair elections in '86, you in the north elected a communist. Do you think there was a direct relationship between the fact that you did that and the fact that they planned more dams and inundation?

S: Turabi said it in so many words, when they came to power in '89: 'This area is inimical to us', and he refused even to walk in, or to visit, the area. He just stayed on the west bank in west Dongola, but he didn't go to Halfa. They never forgave us for that. He stayed in Birka: 'This area is inimical to us' (*hadhihi al-mantiqa mu'adiyya lana*). This was after the coup, about two months after the coup, '89. And then they started hammering. They started with education, health, closing of the historical port in Wadi Halfa. They closed it down and opened another just north of Halfa. They created a customs point there, Abideer [in the Nile Province]. This is a customs point. They closed Halfa, which is the historical window to connect with Egypt. We can't sell our produce in Khartoum. For our produce it is too far from Halfa to Khartoum. It is only two hours away to Egypt. It was closed down for many years, so the trade crumbled, totally and completely. The [people] have become impoverished and poor and have left their land and home.

And of course there is another important aspect, we had a WHO project, for example. We were free of malaria and waterborne disease for *twenty-seven years* as a result of that WHO project. They [the regime] stopped that. There is an epidemic now – malaria and bil-harzia and waterborne diseases. They [the WHO] used to come twice a year from southern Aswan all the way to Dongola, along the Nile, to the swamps which are a breeding ground for these diseases. They stopped that. And they systematically ruined the education and the health system. When you have all these problems – you have health problems, you have education problems, you have livelihood problems – Nubians will not sit and wait for this. And this is why thirty-three villages are now empty. People are beginning to return now, they are beginning to be aware that it is possible to develop our area. Now people are coming back, they are trickling back. But there will be a flood when we create more projects for people, improve education and health and create means of livelihood.

They took the UNICEF programme from us. They used to have a programme. We had a very, very successful programme in one of the villages and UNICEF was so pleased with the work there they decided to extend it to twenty villages in Wadi Halfa. It included health education, support for the schools, training for the community members to be able to create income-generating activities and so on and so forth. It was a very, very successful programme, so they [the regime] were very unhappy and they stopped it. They stopped the whole of the programme in the whole of the Northern Province in order to prevent [UNICEF] expanding in Wadi Halfa. Even when you do the work with outside agencies, in order to provide some help for the people there, they stop it. They are incorrigible. I keep telling them, there is no way we can survive in marginalized areas without removing the NIF from power. And that is the next question, how can you remove a regime that is living in a citadel of law that prevents you from attacking it? With no democratic freedoms, the task becomes very difficult. It is not impossible, but it will cost even more lives than it has already ...

N: What can be done? Going forward ...

S: We need companies to invest, we need organizations to support education and health. If they start building the dams, we are gone. It has to be stopped ... Four dams in one state. Why? Why do they need to move the people? Because they are going to give the land to Islamist investors, colleagues in the NIF and investors from Saudi Arabia and Egypt.

Interview 2: Dr Ahmed Sokarno, lecturer in linguistics at South Valley University, Aswan, 1 April, Aswan

Dr Sokarno is an Egyptian Kenzi Nubian. He was born in Dahmeet, one of forty-three Nubian villages along the River Nile, and was relocated with his family as a young boy in 1963. All forty-three villages were relocated to the north of the High Dam to an administrative area known as Kom Ombo. The 50,000 Nubians from Egyptian Nubia were displaced from a 350-kilometre stretch along the Nile below the Aswan High Dam area into 25 square kilometres, 40 kilometres north of old Nubia. Kom Ombo is located in the desert, up to 10 kilometres distant from the Nile, with a sugar cane factory as the main source of employment. Nubians complained they were located far from the River Nile and their traditional sources of income, in proximity to Arab communities, and that insufficient housing was built and of poor quality. Five thousand Nubians are still waiting for their houses to be built more than forty years later. Ahmed now still lives in the relocated village of Dahmeet with his family and lectures at the university. Dr Sokarno writes and lectures on the Nubian languages and has also published on Nubian identity and their portrayal in the media. I talked to Ahmed in English, in a coffee shop in Aswan and at his home in Dahmeet.

EMMA: What do you think are the main issues facing Nubians today?

AHMED: Number one – the language, because part of the identity of Nubians lies in the language. Once you take this language away or remove the language, they would be in danger of losing their identity. This is important. Language is a defining factor and it plays an important role in the cultural integrity of the Nubians. If you deny people the opportunity to learn their language then it will be a problem, and our children now are not capable of using the language as perfectly as their fathers and grandfathers. In Nubia, the younger you are, the more likely it is that you do not speak the language.

E: Do they want to learn the language?

A: The problem is that in the past mothers were less educated. Before relocation, mothers, women in general, were not interested in education. Nowadays, women are more and more interested in education, and once women learn how to write and read they do not want their children to use Nubian; they use Arabic in conversing with their children. They believe that if their children learn Nubian they will not do well in school. This is a belief among Nubian women. They are not as enthusiastic as the old mothers in transferring the language to the next generation.

Number two, in order to appreciate the Nubian culture, we have to take into consideration the place in which they lived before they were moved to this new area. In the past, Nubians were living close to the Nile. Their whole life revolved around the Nile, you see, from birth to death. All their traditions were in one way or another associated with the River Nile. When a baby was born, certain things left by the mother were thrown into the Nile. If a man or a woman died, in the past, their clothes were thrown into the River Nile. We had a lot of traditions that were connected or associated with the River Nile. Now the Nubians live in an area which is very far from the River Nile, which necessarily changes their traditions and habits. We have Nubians who are nowadays living to the east of Kom Ombo and Nubians living to the north of Kom Ombo. Whether you live to the north or the east you are far from the Nile, no matter where you live. Therefore your traditions and habits which you have based on your proximity to the River Nile are likely to change.

E: Is there any possibility of returning to the Nile?

A: Well, nowadays we have some voices among Nubians who ask for, call for, *urge* a return to the old location, but I don't think it will be a successful endeavour, because most Nubians nowadays live in their new villages, most of them have invested their money in building or redecorating their houses, establishing the new houses and so on, so I don't think it would be possible to ask Nubians to move back to the old location. If you do so no one would follow you, because people have invested all they have.

E: So who are the voices?

A: Some Nubians who have not received their houses after relocation. Around five thousand new houses need to be built for the Nubians who have not received any houses at all since they moved from the old location. Some of these five thousand families asked for houses near the lake.

E: Where are they at the moment?

A: Some of them might be in Cairo, in Alex, in Suez, in Ismailia, in Qena, near Luxor, in Aswan ... When we were relocated to the new area to the north of Kom Ombo, 17,000 houses were prepared for the families, a little bit over. The remaining houses were promised to be built, but they haven't done this until now. These people, or some of them, need their houses to be built near the lake, Lake Nasser, but the government would not encourage them to live near the lake area.

The young men are not as enthusiastic as the older people. The older people are a little bit nostalgic, you know, about the old location. They are more enthusiastic. The Kom Ombo people have invested money in their houses. Some of them demolished their houses and rebuilt them again. They put everything, all their savings, into their houses.

How can you ask them to start afresh? How can you ask them to go and rebuild new houses?

[In the past, attempts were made to establish new communities along the shores of the lake. The re-establishment of settlements received limited support from President Sadat in the 1970s, but government support did not continue and the project lapsed. Negotiations with Mubarak's government constituted the first dialogue with the state in more than forty years. This was prompted by a wave of protest after private companies from the Delta built new villages bordering the Nile while the scattered Nubian population were still waiting for houses to be built that were promised to them in the 1960s.]

E: People in Cairo talk about the importance of maintaining a Nubian identity outside of Nubia. What do you feel is the importance of being Nubian in this area itself? Why is it important for you to identify as Nubian?

A: It is part of you, you cannot be someone else. If you are Nubian or not Nubian, Egyptian or not Egyptian, every person would like to preserve his or her identity. Part of your identity is your culture, the language you speak, the habits and the customs you have: if you lose these you will lose your identity and you will be in a very difficult situation.

E: How can it be preserved?

A: By preserving the elements of identity. In order to preserve your identity, you have to preserve the elements that constitute your identity, elements such as the language, the culture, the habits, the style of living. You preserve these, you preserve your identity. If you lose any of them, your identity is being endangered.

E: Are there organizations that help?

A: In Cairo we have the Nubian Heritage Association and the Nubian Documentation Centre. These people are responsible for translating texts on Nubia and so on.

E: And any non-Nubian or international organizations?

A: You mean UNESCO? We have the Nubian Museum. The Nubian Museum plays an important role in preserving the culture and giving people the connections they need, giving people information on Nubia and Nubians. This is considered a non-Nubian organization: UNESCO was responsible for establishing it. The government of course did not want to call it the Nubian Museum. They wanted to call it the Museum of Egyptian Civilization. UNESCO refused. They said no. It should be called the Nubian Museum, otherwise we are not going to fund your project. If you want to name it, we are going to deny you the funding. They did not want to call it the Nubian Museum. I don't know how to interpret the message [laughs].

[The Egyptian and Sudanese governments appealed for international help to rescue the historic archaeological monuments which would otherwise be flooded by the lake created by the construction of the Aswan High Dam. UNESCO in response launched a worldwide appeal which resulted in the salvage and relocation of a number of temples and the salvage of thousands of artefacts, with the participation of fifteen countries. Although many of the salvaged items are located overseas, the Nubian Museum, opened in 1997, is a key repository in Egypt for a number of the artefacts (see Hassan 2007).]

E: Are there other problems or difficulties with maintaining or preserving the culture?

A: They don't want us to preserve it, you know.

E: The government?

A: Yes, of course. There is no way to teach the Nubian language in schools, for instance. You cannot. Any language that is not taught in schools, any language that does not have a writing system, is subject to danger, to extinction.

E: Is there not much support from the government for preserving the Nubian language?

A: I don't expect any support. Nubians should support themselves in order to preserve their culture. They should not expect other people to preserve their culture for them.

E: So even Nubians within the ruling party itself might get services, schools, but nothing specifically Nubian?

A: No, they cannot. There is a line that they cannot cross. You can ask for schools, but you cannot interfere in what is taught in schools. You cannot change the syllabus, interfere in the curriculum. We can get schools built for you, but you should not tell us what to teach. I would like to teach my language. You would like to teach your language? You can look for another non-governmental place.

E: What is your vision for the future?

A: The vision is not as optimistic as it should be. The language is in danger, of course. Once the language disappears then part of the Nubian culture is gone for ever. The rest of the cultural elements of

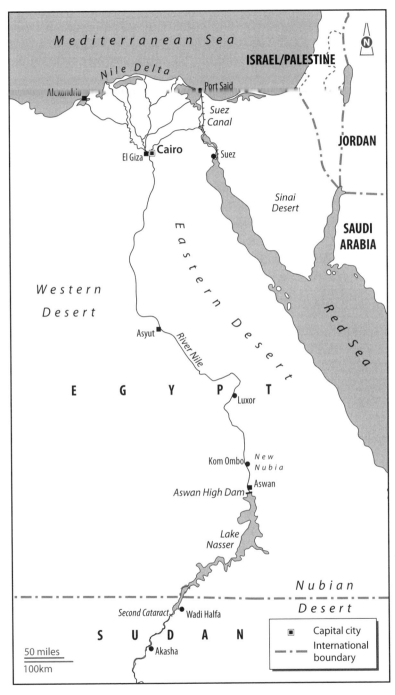

4.1 New Nubia: the location of the Aswan High Dam and the resettlement area of Kom Ombo in Egypt

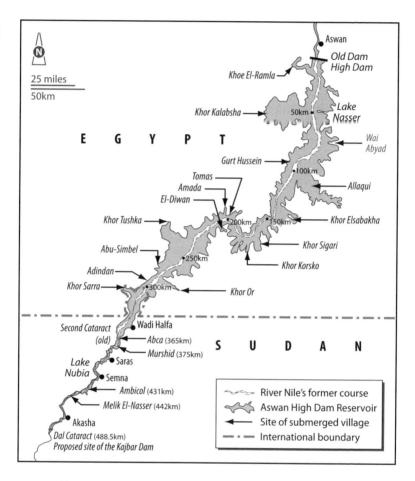

4.2 Old Nubia: the location of some of the forty-three villages submerged by the dam and the proposed site of the Kajbar Dam (at the Dal cataract) (*source*: adapted from A. F. A. Latif, 'Lake Nasser: the new man-made lake in Egypt [with reference to Lake Nubia]', reprinted from *Ecosystems of the World 23, Lakes and Reservoirs* [ed. F. B. Taub], Elsevier Publishing Co., Amsterdam/Oxford/New York/Tokyo, 1984, pp. 385–410).

Nubians are also in danger. The style or way of living is in danger. They are more influenced by what they see on TV, by what they observe near villages. Nubians are more and more assimilated, you know. One day you will have to exert a lot of effort to look for a Nubian.

E: Finally, would you say you are Egyptian Nubian or Nubian Egyptian?

A: I am Egyptian Nubian, I think, as Fernea called them, not Nubian Egyptian, and there is a difference, I think [laughs].

2 INDIGENOUS RIGHTS AND IDENTITY POLITICS

Division, relocation and gendered change

Nubians comprise three culturally and linguistically different groups, known in Egypt as the Kenuz, Fadicha and Arabs, and in Sudan as the Dongolese, Halfans and Mahas-Sukkot. But they had not been known collectively, or referred to themselves, as 'Nubians' prior to their displacement in 1963, when President Nasser of Egypt spoke of relocating 'the Nubian people'.[2] Some have proposed that the continuing process of reclamation of their rights over the intervening years has strengthened Nubian identity (Fernea et al. 1991: 184), yet this has not been the sole defining event in the dislocation of the Nubian population. It has been suggested that old Egyptian Nubia was lost much earlier: the old Aswan Dam, built in 1902 by the British, destroyed much of Nubian agricultural land and their traditional economic means of survival (Kennedy 1966: 356). Earlier still, the arbitrary border division drawn between Egypt and Sudan by the British in the Condominium Agreement of 1889 split the tribes of Nubia between the two nation-states. To this day, there is no land crossing between Egypt and Sudan, even though a distance of only 40 kilometres separates the last town on each side of the border.[3] The Nubian people were divided permanently.

Nubians also have a long history of labour migration, and this swelled as the land was flooded, again dividing families and communities. Increasing numbers of the male population migrated to cities in search of work; for long periods the sex ratio was more than two women to every man in many villages, and almost every family had at least one member working outside Nubia (Adams 1977: 654; Poeschke 1996: 46). Labour migration has continued to be a mainstay for many families, prompted by a shortage of agricultural resources in the new settlements or limitations imposed by the Islamic regime in Sudan; over the generations this has increased the numbers of Nubians in the diaspora.

At relocation, families were further divided. In Sudan, part of the Halfan population refused to be relocated and remained stoically in Wadi Halfa, where they built temporary wooden houses and moved with the lake. In Suad's family, half moved while half remained; to reach family members who relocated to the New Halfa settlement of Kashm el-Girba to the east of Khartoum then entailed a 1,500-kilometre journey by road. Communities were transferred to an area with totally different climatic and environmental conditions 600 kilometres away from their homeland. Families were relocated based on the cost of their old homes, resulting in some large families being relocated to much smaller dwellings (Fahim 1972: 9).

In Egypt, families were relocated based on family size rather than kinship structure, leaving many of the elderly, divorced and widows stranded from the rest of their families. Many families were left waiting for the construction of houses promised by the government and settled in towns and cities elsewhere as a temporary measure, which has subsequently become permanent.[4]

Communities grieved over the loss of the relative safety and security of village life. The lack of space in the new areas meant that different communities lived in close proximity; also sharing the area were non-Nubians, Egyptian Arab farmers in Kom Ombo and indigenous pastoral tribes in Kashm el-Girba, leading to a sense of insecurity among Nubians and tensions with neighbours. As a consequence, women were increasingly likely to find their movements curtailed (Sharif Saeed 1993; Poeschke 1996: 61).

Women were to a certain extent also held accountable for the weakening of cultural traditions. With the disruption to cultural continuity, women were even more likely to be held responsible for ensuring the passing on of language to the next generation and the maintenance of the many ceremonial traditions. However, their altered circumstances did not always permit this. Cultural traditions such as wedding ceremonies lasted several days in the villages, but had to be shortened in the new urban environment. Prioritizing the maintenance of indigenous languages can be at odds with what is expected of children in order to succeed in mainstream society. The reluctance of mothers to pass on their language, which Ahmed Sokarno refers to, is almost certainly linked to the fact that Nubian communities are now much less isolated from Egyptian society and children are required to meet different expectations. Since it is impossible to study the Nubian language within the Egyptian education system, in addition to the fact that the sense of Egyptian nationalism is very strong, knowledge of Nubian history, culture and language is not considered a tool for success either in education or professionally. The use of the Arabic language has thus become a greater necessity for both adults and children, leading to loss of usage of Nubian dialects. At the same time, however, the increased access to education, something historically prioritized by Nubians, saw new opportunities for women open up at social, political and economic levels. Women in the relocated areas were able to benefit from increased access to education, better provision of facilities and services and the advantages of increased communication between villages, which were closer together (Fernea et al. 1991: 126). Furthermore, owing to increasing male outmigration, women often became solely responsible for the running of the household, resulting in greater freedom and responsibility despite oppression, as conveyed by Suad. An account by Hale supports her depiction of the expanding role of women:

> Rural and village Nubian women, left alone, were among the most emancipated and autonomous in Sudan in their roles as central producers and reproducers. Over forty percent of the households were headed by women. They did everything from managing or cultivating the agricultural lands to organizing and carrying out all ritual and ceremonial activities. Women held together the economy and the culture. (Hale 1989: 54)

On a national level, great promises were made by both states regarding the bright futures the Nubian people would enjoy in the new areas,[5] and while access to some services was clearly improved, there were few who were content with the relocation; the sense of loss experienced has endured across the generations. Practical issues still remained regarding the quality and quantity of the housing and the agricultural land, plus communities were profoundly affected by the distance of the new communities from the River Nile and the restricted ability to maintain and practise cultural traditions. The combined effects of migration and relocation resulted, then, in the development of a much closer relationship with the state than was previously the case, and led to increased interaction with non-Nubians. For the communities living in relative isolation along the River Nile, this relationship had rarely been of significance. For the relocated communities, appeals were made to the state for the restitution of rights on the very basis of an indigenous identity, one that had not previously been deployed in this way. This politicization of indigeneity therefore becomes a tool in response to oppression.

Relationship with the state – the line you cannot cross

The experience of conflict with the nation-state over identity is common to both Egyptian and Sudanese Nubians; both are seen as a threat to the power and stability of the respective regimes. There have been voiced suspicions on both sides of the border that relocation was engineered in order to divide a potentially threatening population of distinct ethnicity, sever their link with the land and establish the control of the state over this geographical area. At relocation, President Nasser is said to have taken the advice of Tito, then president of Yugoslavia, who warned that the region might otherwise seek autonomy.[6] Similar allegations have been made in Sudan: opponents of dam construction in Sudan cite the lack of environmental impact assessments carried out to international standards to demonstrate the need for their construction (Giles 2006: 393; International Crisis Group 2007).

The Egyptian state appears to regard Nubians as a security issue: encouraging the existence of a separate group, potentially a separate political entity with its own language and history stretching from the fourth cataract onwards,[7] constitutes a threat to the security of the country, a position fuelled by negative media reports.[8] There is a tolerance for a certain promotion of Nubian culture, in terms of music or literature, for example, or even rights of Nubians as Egyptian citizens, but any efforts to promote the collective rights of a people have been swiftly contained. The Nubian Museum was established to promote Nubian culture, but as Ahmed Sokarno points out, the government was at pains to establish it as an *Egyptian* project.

Many activists are consequently wary of losing gains made by taking a political stance. Projects promoting Nubian language and culture, such as the Nubian Museum, are very clearly delineated as essentially *Egyptian*, and organizers are very careful to keep content non-controversial. Another example is the Centre for the Documentation of Cultural and Natural Heritage (CULTNAT), the innovative brainchild of Dr Fathi Saleh, an electrical engineer who wished to use the latest technology to showcase Egyptian heritage. It is supported by the Ministry of Communications and Information Technology and regularly hosts visiting dignitaries to Egypt as an exemplar of Egyptian culture and technology. The project began in 2000, and a Nubian heritage programme was begun in 2006. While this is a part of a mainstream Egyptian project, among sections of the Nubian community it was seen to be an extremely positive step in terms of awareness-raising. To achieve this level of prominence, however, the project leaders are in no doubt about the limits; the project is Nubian run and has the potential to create a valuable repository of Nubian culture and heritage, in addition to providing training for Nubians in documentation skills, but it absolutely must avoid political comment. Nubians may therefore appeal to the Egyptian government and the Egyptian people on the basis of human, even cultural, rights, but this is clearly circumscribed. As Ahmed points out, there is a line you cannot cross.

To illustrate further, a 2007 conference hosted by the Egyptian Centre for Housing Rights (ECHR) was the first to highlight the issues facing Nubians as an *indigenous* people. Despite invitations being issued to government representatives, only one attended – a deputy minister from the Ministry of Agriculture and Irrigation, sending the clear message that the issue is limited to a *land* problem, rather than a social, political and economic problem; that is, not a problem specific to an indigenous people.[9] Now, for the first time, a request is being filed with the UN to grant Nubians international legal status as an indigenous population.[10]

In Sudan post-dam construction, the state used various measures to compel 'the strugglers' or 'bitter-enders' of Wadi Halfa, as they came to be known, to relocate: the train service was stopped, which left them no access to food or medical supplies, and facilities and services were discontinued. They were supported by fellow Nubians, who arranged convoys of supplies, but it wasn't until after the government was toppled by a popular uprising in 1965 that the decision was made to establish a permanent settlement there.[11] Despite this decision the town was still not provided with adequate services, and to this day they have an irregular water supply. Halfans found themselves under pressure again in 1989 when Bashir's regime took power; over the intervening years their ability to trade has been curtailed and services have been ceased in order to coerce the people to move out of the area, with some success.

The current Islamist government has exerted every effort, but has been unable to gain a foothold that would enable it to establish an Islamist culture in the region. After the National Islamic Front took power in 1989, increasing pressure was brought to bear on a region unwilling to comply with the Islamist project. As they had previously held a number of influential positions in Sudan, Nubians, and Halfans in particular, were most affected by government policy to remove from public positions or imprison those disloyal to the regime (Poeschke 1996: 108). Northern State, having elected a communist in the 1989 elections, was to suffer further through subsequent state constriction of education, health programmes and trade.

As for the remaining dams, there appears to be little evidence for the benefit of the northernmost dams (Kajbar and Dal) to irrigation; the majority of benefits will undoubtedly accrue to foreign investors associated with the regime, and suspicions have been voiced that the construction of these dams is part of a further attempt by the regime to Arabize the region. The Comprehensive Peace Agreement contained provisions for the development and promotion of all indigenous languages and the shared ownership of land and natural resources: Suad vocalized guarded optimism that this could impact positively on Nubian rights. However, the secession of southern Sudan in July 2011 brought the CPA process to a close and Al-Bashir's widely reported statement of his intention to consolidate an Arab-Islamic state in the north has amplified fears of discrimination against minorities in northern Sudan (Reuters Africa 2010).

Politicization of identity

Ethnic identity is not identified by the Egyptian census, which according to Fernea et al. itself infers an 'absence of any formal boundaries between Nubians and other Egyptians (1991: 196); it is perhaps more suggestive of the desire of the Egyptian government to homogenize, assimilate and assume a single national identity, where rights are accorded only in terms of *citizenship*, resulting in the concomitant marginalization of Nubian culture and traditions. The Sudanese state in contrast is made up of more than fifty ethnic groups comprising over five hundred distinct peoples with similar linguistic diversity (Lesch 1998: 15). Nonetheless, the dominant Arab-Islamic majority has historically emphasized an ethnic nationalist model of government, and the trend towards Arabization has consequently resulted in a withdrawal of the rights of non-Arabs, Nubians included. Both Egyptian and Nubian situations then satisfy the circumstances for ethnic conflict identified by Maybury-Lewis:

> Where ... control over resources has been removed from local communities and centralized in either a national market or a state bureaucracy, access to which is unevenly available to constituent groups, the disadvantaged among the latter *will* politicize ethnicity so that resources may be accessed via the alternative route of political contest in which the state must then intervene, by either adjusting distribution, or intensifying repression, or both. (Clech Lâm 2000: 207)[12]

The politicization of ethnicity among Egyptian Nubians can be seen most clearly through the cultural revival in evidence in recent years. The revival of Nubian songs, plays, poems and literature in the diaspora has been employed to give expression to the loss of the homeland and ancestral roots; it came rapidly to the forefront of the attention of the Egyptian public through the 'Dongola' controversy in the mid-1990s. Idris Ali's novel *Dongola*, published in 1993, formed part of the growing Nubian literary movement in Egypt and was a landmark novel in that it explicitly addressed controversial issues such as a return to ancestral lands, Nubian identity and relationships with Egyptians.[13] For Nubians, identification as Nubian had always been simply to express a shared culture, customs and language which are distinct from those around them and which differentiate them from non-Nubians. Kronenberg describes this as 'Nubians are Nubians simply through the Nubian culture that they freely accept and share – a common language, social structure, oral literature and poetry, common ethics, beliefs, traditions etc – all of which create a feeling that "We are like ourselves and others are not like us"' (Kronenberg 1987: 389; Hale 1979). The significance of 'Dongola' was the marking of a shift towards a clear politicization of this identity. The momentum of the revival has continued through the use of songs, plays, poems, novels and art, among them those of novelist Haggag Oddoul and musician Hamza Edin, who have both attained international recognition. In one of the few more recent studies of Egyptian Nubian culture, Tito Eman's master's thesis catalogues numerous instances of the use of art to symbolize the Nubian case and 'meet and support their ethnic identity distinctions, ... promote their collective ethnic existence ... [and] struggle against assimilation' (Tito Eman 1997: 73–5).

The multiplicity of Nubian clubs first established as a point of contact for migrants away from their home is now a focal point for this revival of identity, and in many cases they have taken on the role of emissary to carry Nubian grievances to the government. The General Nubian Club, the umbrella organization for more than forty smaller organizations (*Gamayia*), was taken over in 2006 by Mossad Herky, a prominent businessman who has since channelled significant energy and resources into the club in addition to revitalizing clubs elsewhere in Egypt, including Alexandria, Suez and Ismailia. Although his 'softly softly' approach has not won the support of all Nubians, he has succeeded in propelling the Nubian people into the public spotlight once again and has facilitated the first direct channel of communication with the government in over forty years. There since appears to have been some movement towards accepting Nubian grievances and promises to build new villages for Nubians on the Nile and repair the crumbling houses in Kom Ombo have appeared in the Egyptian state press. However, after more than forty years of neglect, many Nubians remain suspicious. At the same time, more radical sectors of the Nubian diaspora are putting pressure on the government and advocating for a return to ancestral lands through dissident networks – namely what has become known as 'the follow-up committee', a pressure group organized almost entirely through mobile phone communication. The committee was formed in April 2007 and has claimed that its campaigns have been instrumental in the increased allocation of funds to build additional houses for Nubians, and in removing the unpopular governor of Aswan, Samir Youssef, in April 2008.

It is also the case, however, that a return to the homeland is not a simple matter; as Ahmed explains, now that many Nubians have established lives for themselves and their families, either in Kom Ombo, or elsewhere in Egypt, returning to live on the Nile would entail a significant risk and would necessitate abandoning the modern conveniences to which many have become accustomed in the urban environment.

Yet the strong desire to maintain a connection with land, culture and heritage is still evident, particularly through the activities of the Nubian societies throughout Egypt. In Alexandria, where there are twenty-four functioning *Gamayia*, a separate club known as 'the Nub' was established at the end of 2007 to facilitate the transfer of cultural knowledge, including language and traditional crafts and dress, to Nubians in the diaspora, with a particular focus on engaging women. It has been able to demonstrate increasing membership and a growing sense of cultural pride.[14]

In tandem with the cultural revival, there is evidence of increased resistance to the stereotype of the 'honest and faithful Nubian', who is traditionally portrayed as a doorman in Egyptian popular media, reinforcing the sense of otherness from non-Nubian Egyptians (Poeschke 1996: 60; Tito Eman 1997: 37). Efforts to counteract this are public, and at the same time maintain the assertion of distinctness as a people. At a 'Nubia Day' hosted by the American University in Cairo in 2008 and devoted to sharing Nubian culture with non-Nubians, Nubian students handed out flyers proclaiming that 'illiteracy among Nubians is almost 0% and there are scientists among the Nubians and there are many who work in privileged jobs'. The recent furore at the allegedly racist lyrics of a Lebanese singer again illustrates an increased willingness to oppose such long-held stereotypes and assert a collective identity in response to discrimination (Guardian 2009).

In Sudan, Nubians have traditionally enjoyed higher socio-economic status than their fellow Nubians in Egypt and in general are well respected by other Sudanese. It is of note, for example, that while in Egypt Nubians are often the subject of jokes, in Sudan jokes are often *attributed* to Nubians (Poeschke 1996: 98). While Egyptian Nubians, like Ahmed, will generally identify primarily as Egyptian and secondly as Nubian, in the much more ethnically diverse Sudan, ethnic identity is more likely to assume greater significance and be the primary identifier. In response to relocation, Sudanese Nubians maintained a strong sense of identity, and this was quickly mobilized in response to the flooding of their land (Morton 1989: 65; Poeschke 1996: 113). Although a resettlement advisory committee was formed by the government, a third of which comprised appointed Halfan members, the elected relocation site differed from the committee's choice, prompting the first public protest in 1960. Despite a government crackdown, including the dissolution of the committee and the imprisonment of a number of Nubian leaders, protests continued, both in Halfa and Khartoum. The Khartoum resistance in particular has been credited with fuelling protest more widely against the military regime, leading to the eventual resignation of President Abboud in 1964 (Poeschke 1996: 39).

Sudanese Nubians have also traditionally enjoyed a level of political power not paralleled in Egypt, including furnishing four Nubian prime ministers (Kronenberg 1987: 391). Although the political manoeuvrability of Sudanese Nubians has been increasingly restricted by the Islamic regime, they are still able to draw on their established networks, formed by Nubians and supporters resident in the diaspora, from the Gulf to the USA. There are a number of active resistance groups established to oppose the building of further dams in Nubia, including the Kajbar Resistance Committee in Sudan and the Rescue Nubia Committee formed in Washington, DC. Suad illustrates how Nubians living in Sudan were able to issue an appeal through these networks to enlist international support against government actions, alerting Nubian studies centres globally to the crisis. Demonstrations in the town of Kajbar in June 2007 resulted in the killing of four demonstrators and the wounding of many others by police forces and led to a renewed appeal for international support. The Kajbar Resistance Committee released a document in July 2007 calling on all Nubian studies centres and Nubian supporters globally to support their struggle against building the Kajbar Dam.[15] In response, the Nubian diaspora mobilized to organize demonstrations outside Sudanese and Chinese embassies in Washington, The Hague and Khartoum.[16] While the Merowe (Hamadab) Dam has now been inaugurated, it is perhaps to the credit of the organization of the Nubian diaspora that the construction of Dal and Kajbar remains pending.

This appeal to international support stands in marked contrast to the strategies of Egyptian Nubians, who told me on numerous occasions how they expected to be self-reliant and self-supporting in their advocacy and did not seek assistance from outside. When renowned author Haggag Oddoul spoke of the Egyptian government's mistreatment of Nubians at a conference in the USA, he was widely condemned, by both Egyptians and Nubians, for betraying national interests.[17]

Sudanese Nubian women are also more visible in the political arena. Although Suad describes the activities of her fellow female activists as 'behind the veil', they appear to be less affected by the prevailing Arab Islamic culture than in Egypt, and many have taken prominent and visible roles in the protests. Sondra Hale suggests that the broad reach of the Islamist regime against its detractors has resulted in a proliferation of different activist groups, liberal and leftist, religious and secular, which has had the effect of increasing the avenues open to women for political expression (Hale 2001: 83). This is also manifest in a clear politicization of ethnicity in direct confrontation with the state, with a notable prominence of women in anti-dam demonstrations.

By the end of the eighties, Fernea et al. were attesting that the contemporary situation of Egyptian Nubians 'still provide[d] a persistent set of conditions, involving shared political and economic interests which make being a Nubian important in defining this group's interests in opposition to those of others' (1991: 200). Since then a channel of expression has been opened up for these interests, through art and through direct appeal to the state for repatriation, suggesting that resistance to marginalization is likely to continue. For Sudanese Nubians, there is evidence of an escalation of resistance to a further loss of their homeland; state planning for dam construction continues.

Visions for the future

To return to the concern of researchers in the 1960s and 1970s who feared the permanent loss of a Nubian culture, and the concern of Nubians themselves, expressed today by Ahmed's fear of ever-increasing assimilation, the evidence appears to refute this. Fernea et al. surmised that Egyptian Nubians have survived as a distinct culture *owing* partly to dislocation rather than despite it:

> [T]hough many aspects of Nubian culture and social organization which existed before the building of the High Dam have changed or disappeared, the Nubians in contemporary Egypt, since their resettlement, have become, for the first time, a self-aware ethnic group. As such, we believe the Nubians are likely to play an ever more important role in the political and economic life of upper Egypt and in the national life of Egypt as a whole. (Ibid.: 184)

By the late 1990s Poeschke was also able to conclude,

> It is to be expected that in future, cultural differences and boundaries between Nubians and the rest of the national population in both Egypt and Sudan will continue to exist. However more distinctions will be drawn in Sudan, as Egyptian Nubians are in a weaker (political, economic and social/cultural) position. A total amalgamation with the Egyptian society is nevertheless unlikely, particularly in view of the recent emergence of the Nubian cultural revival movement. (Poeschke 1996: 104)

A revival of culture, heritage and language is central to the Nubians of Egypt; it remains to be seen how the development of a new post-revolution constitution in 2011 might impact on this. For Sudan, as long as the National Islamic Front, now the National Congress, remains in power and dam-building stays on the state agenda, political resistance and mobilization will continue. Sustained resistance, social, cultural and political, can be anticipated, aided to a large degree by the social commitment inherent in what Fernea et al. termed 'the Nubian polity' (1991: 141), or the social organization of communities. This has not in fact been completely lost in its translation to cities within Egypt and Sudan and elsewhere; a process beautifully illustrated to me in a conversation with the president of one of Cairo's Nubian clubs:

> If I have no food in my house, I won't ask you for help, but I will offer a small dish, of flour maybe, and you will know that this is the most I can offer. You will return a dish of food that can feed the family. This process will continue. In the city, the pride in our culture continues in the same way.[18]

Hughes

In this way Nubian resistance is built on an existing community support structure and resilient cultural values. Their ability to bring a cultural approach to bear on issues facing their people and through this devise peaceful and appropriate solutions (ibid.: 153) is evidently an enabling factor for continued cultural, social and political resistance. In the final analysis, however, there is not a single vision for the future, but many. As illustrated by Suad, oppression itself has created multiple visions, from a revival of the Nubian kingdom, to development as a tool of resistance; these are expressed, developed and enacted in respect to the environment in which Nubians find themselves, and their visions for the future will in turn be shaped by future changes of government and policy in both states.

Comment

Editor's note: The choice of commentator for this chapter is based on the awareness of the complexity of the post-colonial context across different regions of Africa, and the ways in which each region's colonial history has shaped the post-colonial aftermath. Hence the exchange here between Chris Kidd (who authors the other chapter within the Africa section) and Emma Hughes offers the opportunity to draw parallels and highlight differences beyond the bounds of the discussion contained in each individual chapter and for the contributors of this section to engage in dialogue with each other.

Christopher Kidd

One issue your chapter raises is indigenous communities' capacity to experience their contexts in different and multifaceted ways (as a denial of culture, a denial of political space and/or a denial of production). This suggests that indigeneity can be understood in different ways by different groups and more so, as your interviews show, that even within indigenous communities there can be multiple ways in which situations can be understood and responded to. A second issue raised is why do some interpretations and responses incline themselves to identify with indigenous identity while others identify themselves with a marginalized minority identity?

One response to these issues might be that the Batwa and Nubians are, in many ways, facing different sets of circumstances which elicit difference responses. Given that indigeneity is a response to a set of circumstances, we might be able to suggest that indigeneity is different for Nubians and the Batwa. In Uganda the Batwa are facing a fight for their very survival and the concept of indigeneity is useful to them as long as it is seen to be immediately productive. Central to the situation in Uganda is the belief that 'indigeneity' is valid if it can bring responsive engagement to address their situation. However, with that specific aim in mind, it could be argued that the 'marginalized minority' might have more ability to elicit the immediate response to their problems of acute poverty. The Batwa have little or no time to consider the future of their people within an 'indigenous identity' framework because they are so consumed by immediate survival strategies. However, in the Nubian case the interview with Ahmed suggests that Nubians aren't so much faced with a struggle for survival, in terms of the physical day-to-day reality the Batwa experience, but are instead faced with a struggle for cultural survival and continuity as a distinct group. As a result the interview seems to discuss how Nubians can culturally sustain themselves as a people, a concept which can only be embraced once confidence in the physical integrity of 'the people' is already assured. It could be suggested that the Batwa and the Nubians are both facing annihilation, as a result of very similar processes, but that they are at different stages of the process, and therefore forced to confront, and respond to, different aspects of annihilation.

The other interview, with Suad, offers a slightly different interpretation and does not seem to address indigenous identity explicitly. As a result these interviews fall into areas and questions we have raised in our chapter, namely is it more useful for the Batwa to identify themselves as indigenous or as a marginalized minority? For Suad it seems that the situation she describes shows affinity to a position as a marginalized minority and not an indigenous people.

Importantly, one thing which stands out in all accounts is the colonization and erasure of history that has been inflicted on the Batwa and the Nubians, specifically, we would argue, because their histories affront the national identity and sense of unity felt by the nation-state. Although they are based in different contexts, it is apparent that the biggest problem the Batwa and Nubians face is that they both are seen to threaten the state identity and are therefore repressed and/or erased from history by way of a response.

Reply

Pursuing the concept of indigeneity as 'useful as long as it is seen

TABLE 4.1 Political timeline for Nubia

Year	Government	Sudan	Nubia
	Egypt		
1899	Condominium Agreement signed		
1902			Old Aswan Dam built
1953	Independence: President Mohammed Naguib		
1954	President Gamal abd al-Nasser		
1956		Independence	
1958		President Ibrahim Abboud	
1960			Construction of Aswan High Dam begun
1963			Relocation of Nubian population in Egypt and Sudan
1964		Abboud resigns – interim government	
1965		President Ismail al-Azhari	
1969		President Gaafar Nimeiri	
1970	President Anwar Sadat		
1971			Aswan High Dam inaugurated
1981	President Hosni Mubarak		
1985		President Abdel Rahman Swar al-Dahab	
1986		President Ahmed al-Mirghani	
1989		President Omar al-Bashir	
2005		Comprehensive Peace Agreement signed	
2009			Meroe Dam inaugurated
2010		President Omar al-Bashir re-elected	Contract awarded for construction of Kajbar Dam
2011	People's revolution removes Mubarak from power	South Sudan votes for secession from North	

to be productive', one perspective which is clearly visible, both here and elsewhere in the book, is that indigeneity is frequently employed as a tool. Prior to engagement with colonizers there was no necessity to define a people or tribe in relation to the majority; it served no purpose. The significance of the first use of the term 'Nubian', by the state, to refer collectively to a group of different tribes, has parallels elsewhere: with Aotearoa/New Zealand, where 'Māori' was employed by colonizers to identify groups of *iwi*, with Thailand, where diverse highland peoples are grouped together as 'hill tribes', and with the 'indigenous peoples' of Paraguay. In the discussions of indigeneity in other parts of this book the ambivalent nature of the term is evident: on the one hand it is used by those in power to 'unite and rule', subsuming differences and naming 'the other' (see Chapter 2, p. 59); on the other it is articulated as a means of resistance. Moana Jackson and Di Grennell both highlight the utility of indigeneity as a tool to be employed strategically in the international arena, NGO participants in Thailand identify the use of a collective name 'as a tool or weapon' which can be used to create political space nationally and internationally, while for the Batwa, Fred expresses his hope that international representation as an indigenous people will lead to the end of discrimination and his people's suffering. Beatrice suggests that understanding the Batwa as an indigenous people, rather than as one of a number of marginalized minorities, may be more effective in the international arena, but also notes that it is this status which more accurately denotes the relationship with their ancestral lands. Likewise, while Sudanese Nubians are aware of their position as one of a large number of ethnically distinct groups in Sudan, their key demand is to prevent the loss of the Nubian homeland.

As acknowledged throughout this section, indigenous peoples in Asia and Africa are in a position where their status as indigenous peoples is often not recognized. Asserting the 'collective force' of indigenous identity (Singh, p. 187) and gaining international legal status and international representation as an indigenous people, then, for Nubians as for the Batwa or the Thai hill tribes, is seen as providing a means of resisting discrimination and offering a measure of protection for those rights in danger of being lost, for resources, for language, for culture and for land. This allows for a human-rights-based approach and offers the opportunity to claim rights across the continuum: for the Batwa those necessary for day-to-day survival, for (Egyptian) Nubians those which will allow cultural continuity. For Sudanese and Egyptian Nubians, and for the Batwa and highland peoples of Thailand, it is the reclamation of a connection to ancestral lands.

Acknowledgements

My gratitude goes to the many Egyptian and Sudanese Nubians from Alexandria to Khartoum who contributed to this project; their warmth, openness, generosity and hospitality made this research possible.

5 | Being indigenous in northern Thailand

KATHARINE MCKINNON

Highlanders as indigenous peoples

Unlike in nations where it is clear who were the first peoples of the land, claims to indigeneity in mainland South-East Asia are less clear. Thailand was not formally colonized and the people of the highlands were not subject to a massive influx of colonial settlers as occurred in New Zealand, Australia, North America and Latin America. The experiences of highlanders in Thailand are nevertheless similar to the experiences of indigenous peoples in colonial settler societies. The geographical peripheries of the Thai state were (and continue to be) in effect subject to the colonial authority of the Bangkok government.

The characterization of the Bangkok government as a colonial authority is not new, but it is something that can rarely be stated by those living and working under that authority. In this chapter I begin by discussing what makes highlanders indigenous. I then discuss the particular challenges faced by highland indigenous peoples under this regime. Finally I identify how indigenous groups in the country are engaging with the international indigenous rights movement in their work to obtain recognition and rights equal to those of other citizens of the Thai state.

Highlanders in Thailand have been given many different names in the decades since they first started to draw the interest and attention of state powers. The term 'highlanders' refers to the many disparate and culturally and linguistically diverse groups that have historically occupied the borderlands between northern Thailand, Burma, Laos, Vietnam and southern China. In Thailand there are nine officially recognized highland groups: Karen, Hmong, Mien, Akha, Lisu, Lahu, H'tin, Lua and Khamu. These names give only a hint of the diversity of highland peoples, and the politics of what makes up an 'Akha' or a 'Karen' identity are complex (Hinton 1983, see also Jonsson 2005; Keyes 1993; Kunstadter 1979). What brings these diverse groups together is the fact that they have historically based their communities in the mountains, away from the state powers that dominated in the lowlands, out of reach of taxation by the Tai city-states. In the mountains highlanders have led lives structured very differently to life in the lowlands. Highland economies were based on subsistence agriculture using rotational or swidden farming systems – clearing forest land in order to establish rice fields – that allowed them to eke out a livelihood on the steep slopes and poor soils. Cash crops such as opium or tea allowed some communities to make a small surplus, but never enough to allow significant wealth disparities to emerge within villages. While internal political systems were diverse, no highland group recognized a leadership beyond that of their immediate village headman or council, which means that there has never emerged a desire to establish an ethnic-based state or homeland. Instead, highland settlements were 'all mixed up', as Leach (1954) put it.

This brief description of highland cultures is written in the past tense because although many highlanders continue to live life in accordance with the practices of their ancestors, the modern era has brought many changes, and few young people are able to follow the practices their grandparents did. These days many highlanders no longer live in the highlands, and many have a way of life largely indistinguishable from that of lowland Thais. Many do continue to live in the hills and many, regardless of where they are or what they do for a living, maintain a strong connection to their home villages in the mountains and play their part in maintaining and nourishing the distinct cultural life of their 'tribal group'. But the conditions under which they do so are often tenuous. As Thailand has entered the modern era highlanders have been forced to contend with dramatic changes that affect their ability to sustain traditional leadership systems and religious and spiritual practices and maintain a livelihood based on the land.

These changes began with colonialism. Prior to the colonial era highlanders' geographic location in difficult-to-access forest and mountains placed them outside the sphere of power of lowland city-states. They occupied territories left unclaimed by any greater powers – the mountains and forests were non-state spaces forming a wide buffer zone between competing powers of lowland kings (Scott 2000, 2010; Thongchai 1994). When the British and French arrived in South-East Asia, however, the idea of a buffer zone between states was soon to be dismissed. Thailand (then Siam) was never directly colonized, but the presence of the British in Burma and the French in Indochina would lead to the introduction of fundamental changes to forms of statehood, society and culture across the region. In Siam two changes are especially significant.

One significant change was the introduction of a modern European understanding of territoriality. Replacing a previous system of power based on a complex web of political allegiances that allowed territories to exist outside of state control, the European system introduced the idea that states should maintain power over an entire contiguous territory. State control should spread out to the very edges of the cartographic line that marked on the map where one sovereign territory ended and another began. There was no longer any room in this system for a non-state space of any kind. When the borders between Siam, British Burma and French Indochina were decided in the early 1900s highland communities on the Siamese side of the line found themselves literally drawn into the state. The geographical inclusion of highland villages did not, however, equate with highlanders becoming recognized members of the Thai national community.

The second major change brought by new links with Europe was the introduction of nationalism. Coinciding with the arrival of colonial powers and the new territorial regimes they brought with them was the arrival of new ideas that the state ought to be somehow linked to a sense of national identity, based on a shared heritage, shared language and shared loyalty to one king. The Siamese leaders who set about popularizing this new idea worked, in essence, to establish a new national identity that had not been there before. Through the early twentieth-century processes of 'mass nationalism' (Wyatt 1984: 252) introduced a Thai national identity. Regional dialects were banned, and a centralized education system was introduced which taught only in the central Thai dialect and promoted a version of history that emphasized the long lineage of a unified Thai nation and its people. This new Thai national identity was founded on a set of characteristics supposedly shared by all Thai people: a Tai ethnicity, the Buddhist faith, shared language and loyalty to the monarch. Needless to say, not all those encompassed within Thailand's borders were included. Among those who were left out of this newly imagined identity were the highlanders of northern Thailand. Exactly how they fit into the Thai nation has been a point of contention ever since.

According to the brief history I have recounted, highlanders have a right to claim their status as indigenous peoples under the definitions adopted by the International Labour Organization (ILO) Convention no. 169, which states that a people are considered indigenous either because they are descendants of those who lived in the area before colonization or because they have maintained their own social, economic, cultural and political institutions since colonization and the establishment of new states. Highlanders have lived in the borderlands since before the borders were drawn, before the arrival of European colonial powers and before the mountains were divided by new state boundaries. However, because highland communities have tended to be relatively mobile, especially among groups that traditionally practised pioneer swiddening, highlanders have not been labelled as 'indigenous'. As a group of peoples who have not historically made territorial claims, and who have practised periodic migrations through the mountains, their long habitation of the borderlands has been easily dismissed. It has been much more common for scholars and policy-makers to focus on patterns of migration into Thailand across state boundaries, rather than recognizing that those boundaries themselves are only a recent imposition. In fact it has more commonly been the practice of the Thai government to assign highlanders the status of illegal immigrants based on the assertion that highlanders are only recent arrivals in Thai territory, having continued to migrate across the border from Burma and Laos over the last 100 years. From a different perspective, however, the mountains themselves could be seen as the homeland for all highland peoples, divided though they are by state borders. Highlanders can certainly claim more than others to be the peoples who belong to those mountains, and the fact that some of them have only recently entered the southern corner now claimed by Thailand is, from this perspective, irrelevant.

Unfortunately, the legal basis for such a claim is not so clear. It has been a major struggle for highland groups to claim eligibility for Thai citizenship, let alone claim their rights as indigenous peoples of the northern mountains. This is a struggle that has only recently begun, and the suggestion that highlanders should be called indigenous remains contentious, even among highlanders themselves. Because Thailand was never directly colonized, and no mass migrations in living memory swamped the first peoples of the land, it is widely accepted that Thais are themselves the indigenous peoples of Thailand. What is not recognized in this discourse is a history of Thailand in which Bangkok could be seen as the centre of a colonizing power that has, over the last century, gradually colonized the territories encapsulated by the state borders imposed in the early 1900s.

The challenges of being indigenous in northern Thailand

Like other indigenous groups around the world, highlanders in northern Thailand face numerous challenges as they struggle to survive and thrive within the confines of the modern nation-state. Political and social exclusion, prejudice and denial of basic human rights are among the challenges and difficulties that they face. Not least among these is the struggle to gain recognition as legitimate citizens of the state and as indigenous peoples of the land.

Since the earliest efforts of the Thai authorities to engage with the highland population the relationship has been based on the belief that highlanders were a problematic group. In the 1950s and 1960s, when Thai authorities first reached out to highland communities, there was widespread belief that the highlanders posed a serious threat to the security of the nation because of their cross-border mobility and because they were assumed to lack national loyalty. In addition, it was assumed that highland land use practices were a major contributor to the loss of old-growth forests in the mountains. The practice of swidden agriculture was thought to be slowly depleting the forest reserves. Finally, highlanders were thought to be a major source of opium for the manufacture of heroin in the Golden Triangle. These three issues – opium, forest destruction and national security – became known as 'the hill tribe problem'.

The legacy of that label – the 'hill tribe problem' – shapes many of the core challenges that highlanders face in contemporary Thailand. Although concerns about communist aggression have since died away, highlanders have continued to be seen as a potential threat in many respects. Even now newspapers occasionally report rumours of armed highland groups planning rebellions in order to establish new ethnic homelands – a concept which is anathema to traditional highland cultures. Opium production has diminished considerably since the mid-1980s, yet highlanders remain accused of being drug traffickers. Certainly the mountains have remained an important trafficking route for narcotics being brought over the border from Burma and Laos, but there is little evidence that highlanders are driving the trade. They have, however, suffered disproportionately from heavy-handed tactics to eliminate trafficking. In the war on drugs launched by the Thaksin government in 2003 several thousand Thais were killed by government death squads which were given the freedom to execute suspected traffickers. Anecdotal evidence from the north suggests that

McKinnon

an exceptionally high number of the victims were highlanders, many with no links whatsoever to the drug trade (multiple informants, Chiang Mai, May 2007).

Finally, the label of highlanders as forest destroyers persists despite mounting evidence that the traditional land use practices of highlanders are one of the best ways to create a livelihood from poor mountain soils, while maintaining forest cover and a healthy biodiversity (Forsyth and Walker 2008; Fox 2000; Grandstaff 1980; Hirsch 1997; Kunstadter and Chapman 1978). However, swiddening was made illegal in the 1960s, and, given also increasing pressure on land in the mountains, very few communities continue to farm in this way. Instead highland farmers are increasingly forced to keep land under continuous production, and thus are becoming reliant on chemical fertilizers, or are forced to shift to entirely different production methods, often relying on cash crops that require the regular input of chemical fertilizers and pesticides. For some communities these new practices have been the source of increased income and prosperity, enabling families to purchase luxury goods such as televisions, cars and motorbikes, afford hospital care during illness and send children to school. However, there are important downsides to these shifts. The shift away from traditional farming methods has meant that annual ceremonies and rituals that were tied to the main crop of rice have now become irrelevant, and this has contributed to a loss of traditional cultural practices. In addition, the reliance on chemical inputs has become a source of concern to environmentalists and lowland farmers, who claim that agriculture in the mountains is polluting the rivers and damaging the health of those downstream.

The accusations that highland farmers are causing new kinds of environmental damage have given fresh impetus to those who would like to see highlanders expelled from Thailand's forests. For the so-called 'deep green' conservationist groups, and many within the Thai government and the Royal Forest Department, highlanders have no right to continue to live in the mountains. Their rationale is based partly on the damage that highlanders have been assumed to do to the environment over the decades, but it is also because, according to law, the vast majority of highland villages are on lands set aside as forest reserves and are officially under the management of the Royal Forest Department. As a result highland communities do not have legal title to the land they live on, although the Community Forestry Bill passed in 2007 does give some recognition to their ability to manage forest lands under strict conditions (see Walker 2007).

The lack of land title is exacerbated by the failure of the Thai government to register eligible highlanders as Thai citizens. Thai citizenship legislation dates back to the Household Registration Act of 1956, which provided the foundation for citizenship determined by place of birth (Suppachai 1999). While most Thais were given household registration papers at that time, most highland communities were not. Without registration papers highland communities remained in an ambiguous position: 'The hill tribe people are Thai but because the officers cannot grant Household Registration and legal Thai status to them, this in effect means that in the eyes of the law their status is that of non-Thai' (Ministry of the Interior 1974, quoted in Suppachai 1999: 3; see also Wanat 1989).

Finally, in 1999, the Thai government decided to assign as aliens all highlanders without citizenship papers. In response, activists and Thai academics campaigned to 'ask the government to register hill tribe people as Thai citizens and therefore to grant nationality' (Chainarong and Suppachai 1999). Their request was granted, and over the intervening years campaigners have worked hard to ensure that as many eligible highlanders as possible apply for citizenship. The process is not simple as applicants are required to present formal documentation proving their eligibility – a feat that is not always possible for those who have only belatedly entered formal relations with the state or whose documentation has perished in the humid conditions of a mountain village. The process of registering citizens remains far from complete, and there are continued fears that the current government will follow through with a declaration of alien status even though there remain many highlanders with a legal right to citizenship who have yet been unable to obtain the correct papers.

Without the correct documentation highlanders are placed in an extremely vulnerable position. They have no legal right to travel between provinces within Thailand or beyond Thai borders. They have limited opportunities to seek education or healthcare, and those who seek work in lowland towns and cities may be subject to police harassment and in extreme cases jailed or expelled from the country.

As well as the challenges associated with dealing with the Thai authorities, highland communities face numerous challenges as a result of rapid change and the erosion of traditional cultural practices.

McKinnon

Elders across highland groups speak of the increasing loss of traditional knowledge among the young as they seek new lives in the town and cities, and enter a world where traditional knowledges seem less relevant and in many cases an unwelcome link to a vilified community they may hope to distance themselves from (Toyota 1998). Healers and shamans are finding fewer young people willing to train in their skills. A whole generation of highlanders has now been born to families living in the cities, and even though their parents may maintain links with family in mountain villages, many of these children have only a limited knowledge of their own language and culture.

As rapid change has come to highland communities, many have sought solace in one of the few readily available escapes – the narcotics that pass by highland villages on their way from production labs across the borders to mass markets in Thai cities and beyond. Because many highland communities are on trafficking routes, drugs are readily available, and furthermore are relatively cheap. As rates of opium production dwindled in the mountains, rates of opium and heroin addiction have soared, especially among young men. Now a much more commonly available drug is methamphetamine, called *yaa baa* or 'crazy medicine' in Thai. As with many indigenous communities worldwide addiction is an increasing problem and a sign of the desperation of peoples who are coping with the restrictions and oppressions of life on the margins of the nation-state and the shock of rapid cultural change.

This raft of contemporary challenges is being met by a committed group of highland activists and NGO workers who are using all means available through political processes, development strategies, activism, media engagement and community outreach and education to engage with these challenges and address them on their own terms. With allies in the Thai media, Thai academics and highland activists have been working successfully to counter many of the negative stereotypes that prevail and to work to change government policy. The citizenship campaign is one example of the successes of this movement, but alongside this work there has been a range of initiatives to introduce after-school programmes in traditional culture for young people in village schools, to record traditional land management practices and translate this knowledge to contemporary circumstances, to record ceremonies and oral histories that are in danger of being lost, and to alter public perceptions of highlanders as dangerous and damaging – instead highlighting how highland communities have helped to care for the precious forests of the north. Most recently efforts have focused on developing links with the international indigenous rights movement to help support these efforts and help create awareness among highlanders and Thais alike of the status of highlanders as indigenous peoples.

Working to claim indigeneity

One issue that remains a challenge for the rights movement is finding ways to continue to work together to maintain the struggle for highlanders' rights in the state. Maintaining a united sense of purpose across disparate cultural and ethnic groups, and continuing to find ways to have their interests and concerns taken into account, requires ongoing work. One possible path forward is to seek official recognition of their status as indigenous peoples. What this new designation would mean, whether it is a name highlanders in general wish to adopt, what Thai language term would be used, and what the implication of such a decision might be are all issues that highland activists and NGOs are beginning to address.

For many years, highland leaders and NGO workers have quietly been forging links with the international indigenous rights movement – attending international meetings, forming cooperative relationships with organizations like the International Work Group for Indigenous Affairs (IWGIA). Until very recently, however, few efforts had been made to enrol the support of the wider community of highlanders and to push for the recognition of highlanders as indigenous people among the Thai public and state authorities. In early 2007 a group of twenty-five highland village leaders and highland NGO workers gathered in Chiang Mai to discuss first of all whether it was appropriate to pursue recognition of highlanders' indigenous status and how this might be done in context of the second Indigenous Peoples' Decade. This discussion is recorded in the transcript of the Indigenous Futures Workshop that accompanies this chapter.

The workshop came about as a collaborative effort between me and three prominent indigenous NGO workers based in Chiang Mai, Thailand. I wanted to organize a small round table discussion to contribute to this book, and my collaborators happened to also be looking for an opportunity to initiate a conversation about indigeneity with their compatriots. The small round table I had initially envisioned thus grew into a much larger event as my collaborators insisted that the conversation should include village leaders, representatives of each tribal group, men and women, as well as some non-highlander activists and academics who had long been engaged in the fight for highlanders' rights.

The meeting began with short presentations to outline some of the issues around the term 'indigenous' and why we believed it to be an appropriate term to describe highland people.[1] The gathering then divided into two: one group made up of NGOs and activists and the other made up of village leaders and representatives. Both groups spent the rest of the day discussing these questions: 1) What does it mean to be indigenous in the contemporary Thai context? (is the term 'indigenous' useful/appropriate?); 2) What are the key issues and concerns for indigenous people in Thailand at this time? How can local IPOs best respond?; 3) How can local IPOs benefit from interactions with international indigenous peoples' movements? What are the challenges that need to be overcome?; 4) How can local IPOs engage with the second Indigenous Peoples' Decade?

As the discussion below shows, the NGO workers present fully accepted the relevance and importance of adopting the label of indigenous peoples. The timing of the workshop came at the beginning of the second IP Decade, and after the ousting of the Thaksin government in a military coup in 2006. With the flux in Thai leadership that came after the coup activists and NGO groups saw a chance to again place the needs and concerns of highlanders on the government agenda, and hoped that this could be a chance to attempt to displace prejudiced policies of old with a new era of engagement that could be based on recognition and respect for highlanders as indigenous peoples.

The village representatives, on the other hand, were not so sure. The term indigenous was new and controversial and not all were convinced that it was necessary or appropriate to adopt this new designation. Thus before any action could be taken very lengthy discussion was necessary around the questions of what it really means to be 'indigenous' in northern Thailand, whether the term was relevant or appropriate, and – hardest of all – how these terms would best be translated into Thai.

DIALOGUE

NGO/activist views

In the discussion of the first item on the agenda, what it means to be indigenous, the issue of naming came up often. It is a topic that has long been part of debate around highlanders. The official names used by the Thai state and early anthropologists in the region were not necessarily the names that groups gave themselves. Akha, for example, were called Ikaw, a term which can also mean slave. The term Karen is also problematic as the many subgroups included under that name do not necessarily regard themselves as belonging to an overarching 'Karen' grouping. Efforts to have autochthonous names given official recognition have had some success over the last two decades, and the experience of this success was discussed in relation to debate around whether a further struggle should be launched – to replace the common term 'chaokhao' with a Thai-language term for indigenous peoples.

NIRAN:[2] I think that if we really want to push [for recognition] it is not too difficult. During the first Indigenous Peoples' Decade, we, especially in Chiang Mai, have submitted our declaration to the government regarding what we want to call ourselves; there have been several changes [positive]. We have made some progress and such negotiation works. If we want we should make a declaration. If we want to confirm the term and definition of ourselves, we should make [a] 'loud and clear' declaration.

[...]

There has been acceptance of using our original names. For example, Karen call themselves *Pgakeryaw* and this term is widely accepted now (although even among Karen people themselves there is some confusion [about the term]).

BUNMA: The issues are [on] two levels. First is the issue of self-identification – *Pgakeryaw*, *Hmong*, *Lahu* – what names we call ourselves. Another issue is about a more generalized naming, meaning what others call us: *chaokhao* [hill tribe] or *chonphao* [tribal people]. [*Chaokhao*] has condescending implications, but *chonphao* has been widely accepted and used. The academics try to avoid the use of *chaokhao* and use *chattipan* [national ethnic peoples] instead.

[The term *chattipan* is used to label ethnic or cultural groups that are widely seen to be part of the nation, unlike the term *chaokhao* or even *chonphao*, both of which are used to describe highlanders who are both citizens and non-citizens, recent migrants and those living in neighbouring countries.]

For *chon klumnoi* [ethnic minority group], it's different, it doesn't mean

McKinnon

155

chonphao. Even within the administration division when they refer to it, they mean the Vietnamese immigrants, Lao immigrants, Pakistani immigrants, Malay immigrants, Indian immigrants, they don't mean the *chonphao*. So I think there is a clear distinction between ethnic minority and *chonphao* or ethnic peoples.

SOM: There are different dimensions to the issues and how they are looked at depends on who you are ...

Looking at it from [the] globalization period perspective, if we are too rigid in the definition, it will be to our disadvantage. If we make it broad, those we try to protect will get the benefit too. We would be better off. I would recommend that we should use the term that has broad meaning ...

[Selecting a term with a broad meaning was seen by many participating in the discussion to have the advantage of being wide enough to include other marginalized ethnic groups within Thailand. This would allow solidarity with indigenous groups in the south and east who have also had difficulties in their negotiations with the Thai state. The complication is, however, that such a term might exclude highlanders who have recently crossed the Thai border, and who are currently classed as recent or illegal immigrants.]

Now even using the term '*chonphao chattipan*' [mountain minorities of the nation] we are judged by those friends who work with migrants' issues that we are narrow minded, not trying to help others.

SUCHIN: We need reform of the term we use so that it is useful, but ... whatever innovations we make also need to be about self-identity first, rather than political goals ...

I am mocked by my colleagues that I am narrow minded in my use of terms which do not consider or help our *tangdao* brothers and sisters ...

[The group of NGO staff were clearly aware that there could be several implications to introducing a new project to seek recognition of their indigenous status. On one hand there were other groups in Thailand who could be included under this new title and who could benefit from it; thus there was discussion about how this group of activists have a responsibility to extend that project to others within Thailand who were eligible. On the other hand, some participants also expressed a sense of solidarity with other groups which could not so easily be called indigenous people of Thailand. Their responsibility to these groups as advocates and activists could potentially be compromised if they campaigned for an indigenous identity that was based on an understanding of indigenous as original inhabitant and people of the land.]

AWUT: We may not have been colonized, but we were there before the modern state. Many groups already resided earlier. This meaning can apply to our situation, it's not in relation to colonization. ... The indigenous peoples' movement is progressive in many countries ... but in the South-East Asian region we must admit that the movement is rather weak. Ours is also weak, right? Which means that it is necessary that we hang on to [the existing strength of the indigenous peoples' movement] so that we can benefit from it also? Therefore, when we hang on to the process, we need to define ourselves. The issue is what word or term we want to set for ourselves and which term can be mutually agreed and accepted that it has meaning equivalent to indigenous peoples ... The term carries with it both the promotion and the protection of the rights in the context of being in a country. We depend on the process so that we can get protection. It has become necessary, so what term do we want to use? We need a term that is equivalent to 'indigenous peoples' [as it is used] in an international context.

[The NGO discussants recognized that by using the term indigenous they would be able to access international support and become part of an international network that was not open to them if they simply accepted their designation as 'chaokhao' or ethnic minorities. For this group there was general agreement that they could and should seek to be recognized as indigenous peoples.]

AROON: It has always been problematic to define ethnic and indigenous peoples within the nation-state ... Even though there is acceptance of our rights as being 'chao thai phukao' [Thai highlanders], it is still not the same as being recognized as a real insider [of the country]. How to find a term that does not relegate us to the margins? ... If we can get a term that is good for us ... if it makes justice for us in the new society ... if we use the term that is inclusive, and encourage the networking of ethnic groups in the region, it would be good. We need the term in Thai, which is close to indigenous peoples, and a term that makes them [us] protected.

[There was an acknowledged need to have a word in the Thai language which would be recognized and would protect those that it named. The question of how best to translate the term 'indigenous peoples' was, however, very difficult for both the NGOs and village representatives.]

ARAN: ... the term indigenous peoples has been recorded and is useful for us ... Is the problem how to get small groups linked to it and have acceptance or recognition at the national level? It is that, we are not denying the use of the term '*chon pheunmuang*' (indigenous group) in the context of Asia, we are a group of indigenous peoples in Asia. Even though there is no space for the term in Thailand, but we are indigenous peoples here, and we are the indigenous peoples that do not have opportunity, and are disadvantaged, something like that, this is the issue we need to work [on] together. But the issue that is problematic is that the Thai state do not accept the term '*chon pheunmuang*' and still use '*chaokhao*' [hill tribe] with us, or *chao thai phukao* [Thai montagnards].

[...]

CHANARONG: I want to suggest that the use of [the] term '*chon pheuntin*' [indigenous, people of the land], it includes everyone, ethnic peoples and mountain peoples, etc. But *chonphao* [mountain people] would include only ethnic highlanders.

[...]

AWUT: From my analysis, the other ethnic groups in other regions [within Thailand] are not strong yet. Only us in the north, we are together and strong. We should then think for them too for the moment. At the moment, we are like the frontliners in this struggle. I want to give [as] example the Suay people, they are shy to identify themselves only as 'Suay'. In the term[s] of identity, they are not strong enough.

KLAHAN: Referring to what Niran said ... The term includes all [within and beyond Thai borders] ... i.e.: for the Hmong, they would not divide Hmong Thai or Hmong Lao, they are '*chonphao pheunmuang*' [mountain indigenous people]. I am concerned: if we use a term and the government does not accept the term, [then] they might take measures against us ... [They may perceive] that we are taking the space of the '*khonmuang*' [people of the northern province] ...

[Klahan is here referring to the term *khonmuang*, which is used to describe the people of the northern region who were historically linked with the ancient Lanna kingdom. In the modern era of Thai statehood Lanna was incorporated into the state under the rule of the Siam kings in Bangkok. But *khonmuang* is a term used to differentiate northern people from central and southern Thais – a people with their own dialect, script and cultural practices. The key distinction, however, is that the northern province also encompasses people who did not come under the rule of the Lanna kings. These were the highlanders, the people of the forests and the mountains. The term *khon pheunmuang* used by Awut below refers to a movement to describe 'native' northerners, and the concern is that by claiming indigenous status the state may perceive that highlanders are trying to usurp *khonmuang* native or indigenous status.]

AWUT: We have to refer to the definition; the *khon pheunmuang* are the disadvantaged group; the indigenous peoples are not the mainstream, but the *khonmuang* are the mainstream, thus they fall out of the indigenous peoples' definition.

MONGKUT: [We have to] educate the public.

[...]

[It was very difficult for the group of NGOs to come to some agreement about what term it would be best to use, whom it ought to include, and whether the northern highlanders should just act for themselves or seek to include other minority groups elsewhere in Thailand. In the end, most seemed to agree that it was most practical to use a term already in circulation that would involve a recognition of indigenous status, but whether that term should include reference to mountains/mountain people could not be resolved.

At this point the NGO group took a break before coming together again to discuss the next item on the agenda: 2) What are the key issues and concerns for indigenous people in Thailand at this time? How can local IPOs best respond?

In this part of the discussion, debate arose around the need to get a space within Thailand for highlanders: a space to discuss policy issues, a space to practise their own culture and pass it on to their children, a space to be free to be acknowledged and live as equal citizens. The current use of the term '*chonphao*' and the possibility of being renamed as 'indigenous' (or *chon pheunmuang*) started to be discussed here as things which were limiting and enabling in different ways.]

ARAN: We haven't got a channel to national policy formulation. And our organizations have not been upgraded to national level where we can participate in decision-making or policy formulation.

McKinnon

AWUT: If we analyse [the situation], there are the conditions for a push ahead ... International participation is good because there is space [for IP], but at national level it is not good, because there is no space.

CHAIYA: We should expand or open new space in the state's political structure so there is social space

[As part of this discussion, participants started to speak freely about the colonization of indigenous education systems and languages by Bangkok, and to speak about a need to find room alongside this for themselves to ensure that their children did not forget their highland roots.]

SUCHIN: In our period, there is this much loss. I think in ten or twenty years I don't think there is *chonphao* any more. We might change the name but we cannot solve this, I don't think it works. For example, even we NGO workers, many of our children cannot speak our language.

If being *chonphao* has a condescending meaning, who will want to be *chonphao*?

CHAIYA: The space in the classroom is the space that is confiscated by the Bangkok Thai – how do we open a space in the educational institutions?

KASEM: Even learning our language is seen as an issue of national security; but in fact even Thai language is not really Thai, it's Khmer and Bali Sanskrit.

[Language is an issue of national security owing to government fears about the implications of highlanders' cross-border connections. The concerns date from the Cold War when the Thai government highlighted the dangers of highlanders' 'lack of national loyalty' and the possibility that they could assist or be recruited by communist rebels. Only recently has legislation on citizenship been altered to allow people to become citizens even if they are not fluent in central Thai – the language in which all education and public life is conducted.

The final discussion among the NGOs group was a discussion of the Second IP Decade. The group was concerned to think about how to get involved in the Second IP Decade in a way that would maximize the possibility of achieving a positive response from government and the Thai public.]

AWUT: The first Indigenous Peoples' Decade has passed by and the Thai government did not respond or do anything about it ... We are now in the second Indigenous Peoples' Decade. We could say that IPOs [in Thailand] were not strong during the first decade. But now, it is more tangible, we have IPOs in place, we have IPOs network, we have joint forums in which to meet and discuss. Now as IPOs, using our capacity, can we push for any change? Can we get the government to respond to the decade? What should we do by ourselves to respond to the Indigenous Peoples' Decade?

BUNMA: What is interesting is that the Thai government has ratified the Convention on Biological Diversity which contains Article 8j [which deals with traditional knowledge and recognizes indigenous knowledge, and the importance of the participation of indigenous and local communities]. In practice, how can we push for incorporating it into policy or using [the Convention] to influence a change in government policy to support this?

NIRAN: We can open the issue up to the public as much as possible, at national, regional level, forums, even on TV and other media. If we each could contribute some money the TV programme can happen. If we need to rent space, we should do it. It's important.

CHAIYA: The TV media people themselves have a certain level of interest, if we could connect with them.

NIRAN: We should use the public space continuously and consistently.

KASEM: We could present the picture of 'chonphao'. The audience are the city people; they are those who do not understand us.

We could use cultural performances as an entry point. This reminds me of my trip to China. They asked each ethnic group to perform. I was very impressed. I do not know about the background, but it looks like the government supports them, and each ethnic group has a cultural preservation of songs, dances, etc. I think that it is valuable, it creates visibility and awareness of the existence [of ethnic peoples]. The good image will come out. Then we could insert human rights issues, bit by bit. If we directly focus on the human rights issues, they would not welcome it. So we use the cultural aspect as an entry point.

But for Pgakeryaw people, we do not have cultural performance: dances, what do we do, we only have our way of life; outstanding cultural performances, we do not have, like that of Akha, Lahu; well, that's OK, but for the groups that have cultural performance they could use the space to create awareness.

AROON: In Thailand, there is no *chonphao* commission or *chonphao* council or direct IP mechanism yet, but the National Human Rights Commission [NHRC] is the closest we can get. If we can push for having a mechanism within the NHRC to help in monitoring the human rights situation that the government will conduct, or the impacts on *chonphao* in this decade, ... or support *chonphao* in solving the problem relating to human rights and link the process with that of the NHRC. ... If we want to start pushing to have such a mechanism then starting from there to protect human rights is an interesting option ... It would be more interesting than pushing the other sectors of governments [to do it for us]. But now, I can't think of it yet, after pushing it, whether it would help in solving our problems realistically.

Village views

The discussion in the group of village representatives contrasted with the NGO group in many important respects. They spent their discussion time focusing only on the first item on the agenda, which was what it means to be indigenous in the contemporary Thai context and whether the term 'indigenous' is useful or appropriate. In general they were not as convinced as the NGO group was that a new term was necessary – opinion was divided. Yet the fact that their debate went on so long indicates to me that they did recognize that the issue of what they are named has important implications. In the summary of their discussions below I have chosen quotes that highlight some of the important distinguishing features of their discussion. From the opening of the debate the Pgakeryaw (Karen) elder, Virote, made the important point that the name should first of all recognize the humanity of highlanders.

BUNMA: The two main terms are: *chon pheunmuang* [indigenous group] and *chon klumnoi* [ethnic minority group]. The question is what terms we want to use so it covers other indigenous groups in Thailand, not just us who are called hill tribes.

VIROTE: We have fought for hundreds of years. If we look at it from Pgakeryaw's perspective, Pgakeryaw means we are people, not animals. I suggest we use '*khon*', which means people, not *chao* this or *chao* that ... Let's use '*khon pheunmuang*', not '*chon pheunmuang*'.

[...]

BUNMA: In the past, they defined us, but this time, what do we want to define ourselves?

162

KHAMKHAENG: I have participated in several forums. Thai people are used to the term '*chaokhao*' [hill tribe]. Our *chonphao* brothers [and] sisters are usually happy to flow with what they define and call us.

What we do, we inform others, UN or Thai people, that we are indigenous peoples. For me, I would suggest we use '*chonphao*' or '*chattipan*'. I used to be invited on TV, that time we used '*chonphao*'. If we keep changing it's confusing.

In Lisu, we have terms '*wikala*', which means those who are not us, who do not understand our life [the others], but the term '*Lisu liwa*' means 'us'. I think it is acceptable to use '*chonphao*'; we are not inferior to others. We are what we are.

[After more discussion and a break the group reconvened to continue discussing the question of definition. Khun Kamol began by summing up the morning's discussion.]

KAMOL: This morning, there were several terms we proposed together with the reasons and values for each proposed term ... We have not yet agreed on the term to be chosen but we have summarized the meaning, definition of each term. However, whatever term, we should be keeping in mind what and how we want to present ourselves to the public, or to the society. We have some criteria for the self-definition: 1) It must have its universality [be internationally recognized/known]; 2) It must reflect our identity; 3) Being native to the area.

We talk about having rights. We talk about having social space. Bunma clarified that the terms we proposed are appropriate to be used at different levels, at regional level within Thailand [north], at national level within Thailand [Thailand], and at regional level [Asia] and at international level. OK, I would like Bunma to continue to give us more details. After we are clear about 'self-definition' we will move to the next topic.

[From this point the group of village representatives engaged in a long discussion about the pros and cons of each potential translation for 'indigenous peoples' and its component parts. The nuances of using a term that means 'native' as opposed to a term that means 'from the region'; a term that would include all highlanders including brothers and sisters from beyond the Thai borders or a term that would refer only to Thai highlanders; a term that would recognize a special relationship with the land or a term that would not. Alongside much of

McKinnon

163

this discussion was a concern that the terms being suggested had not previously been used in the way proposed, that they were unfamiliar and could be problematic because they were not already known and used. However, there were also voices saying that the unfamiliarity of these terms was a positive thing which would allow highlanders to give it the meaning they desired.]

WANAT: For me, I am not just used to the term. I am and we are much more used to terms like *chonphao* and *chattipan* or *chao thai phukao* or Thai highlanders. I think that words like *chonphao* and *chattipan* are already known and used.

WAEN: A word would not have meaning until we use it.

BUNMA: That's right. We are discussing that in the past we are defined and called by different terms by others, right? But now, we will not be stuck with the terms defined and called by others, but we will define ourselves, and choose the term to call ourselves. Therefore it is possible to erase those terms [the terms used by others to call/define us]. And we can create a new term.

SOMSRI: Creating a new term, would it be difficult?

TASANEE: I don't like the term *chaokhao*, or *chonphao*, or *chattipan*. They are the terms they call us, because we are a group of people. I want it to be like we are Thai with different nationality or ethnicity. We could not choose who to be born to. I want it like ... we were born here with this or that ethnicity, not this tribe, that tribe, etc. ... I think we can make the term ourselves and [although] the new term might not be accepted, we should not be afraid, we should define ourselves. I advocate for the term '*chon pheunmuang*', which does not mean the *muang* people but the native people who have lived in Thailand, wherever in Thailand. We are this nationality, that nationality. We can also include other groups of people.

Hearing '*pao*' [mountain] I don't like it. [It means] highland people but not all of us are in the highlands, not any more.

So do not worry about using the new term. For example, before they used '*maew*', we don't like it, now not many people use this any more.

[The term *maew* was one of the Thai words used to describe Mien in the past. But the term also means 'cat' and was derogatory. Efforts by activists to establish the authochthonous term 'Hmong' have been largely successful.

In these lengthy discussions about the intricacies of what name to choose and what it would mean there seemed to be a clear recognition among the village representatives of how important it was to choose the name they wanted. Unlike the NGO groups, who articulated concerns around how to link up with international IPOs, etc., what this group spoke about was the importance of taking possession of their identity as one way of strengthening their communities and battling public prejudices.]

KHAMKHAENG: I think it is like a tool or weapon. The process of mobilization is important. The important question is whether all of us have a common understanding. I think that the change of the term does not matter much or make you stronger ... I don't think changing the name matters much, it is more important we are firm in ourselves.

WILA: We discuss so that we come up with an agreed term. Let's choose, one that is acceptable by most people. Whatever term we use, there will be problems. Like Siam was replaced by Thailand was possible, as it was done by the government, but for us it might be more difficult, because we are small people, but it is possible I think.

WANAT: If we only follow the international norms, do we erase everything we have? We already have our identity. In Thailand, if we change our name, we should use the term that still has the sense of being 'chonphao'. For me, chonphao implies our identity; changing names cannot delete the bad images in the mainstream view and inscripted in the education curriculum. Today the curriculum still projects the image of us as bad forest destroyers. If we want to change, we need to change the whole system. We cannot change the curriculum in school, we should think about this.

WILA: Time is almost up, let's choose one term.

VIROTE: I want to maintain khonpao, I mean 'khon' [people] as the prefix, not 'chon' [group]. [Khon] stresses being human beings. Use the word 'khon', which is our original language.

WILA: If we insist to use chonphao, that we are chonphao, is it possible to also have the same protection as the term indigenous peoples?

KHAMKHAENG: Only one word can make a big deal.

[Although the group had still not discussed the second two points – the contemporary challenges for indigenous organizations and the role of IPOs in the second IP Decade – they had run out of time. Their whole day of discussion had been spent thinking through the question of what to call themselves and how this could impact upon the pressing

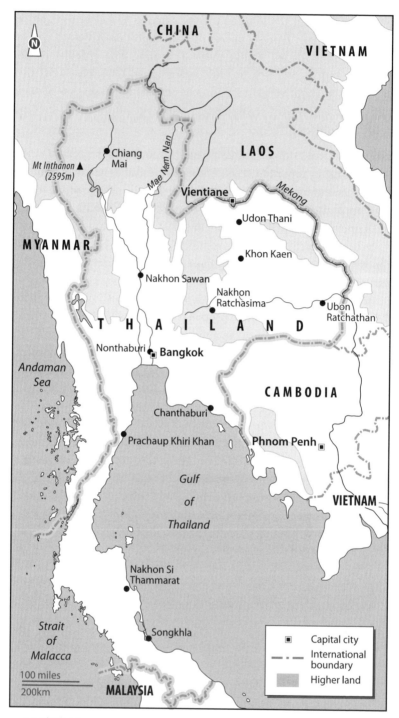

5.1 Thailand

issues that face their communities: citizenship, natural resource management and the waning interest of young people in learning about
their cultural roots.]

Analysis

There was no decisive conclusion reached by the end of the day's
discussions but the debate touched on a number of important issues
which I would like to highlight here. The first thing that was striking
about the day's discussion was the energy and passion that all participants brought to the debate. To my surprise the village group spent
the entire day debating the first point on the agenda: What does it
mean to be indigenous and is the term 'indigenous' useful/appropriate?
In this group there was strong recognition of the importance of a
name, and much of their discussion focused on how to define themselves and how best to present themselves to the public. The debate
among the village leaders seemed to go in circles around the merits
of various possible terms: should they simply stick with the terms
that were already familiar, such as *chaokhao* (hill tribes) or *chonphao*
(tribal people)? Should they continue to push for newer names that
emphasized a more positive identity and had been in use for some time,
such as *chao thai phukao* (Thai montagnards)? Should they support the
suggestion of choosing an entirely new name which would designate
them as indigenous?

The merits of different terms were extensively debated and although
no one term was agreed upon by either the NGO group or the village representatives there was shared recognition that the label they
chose could be extremely powerful. As one participant stated: 'We
are discussing that in the past we are defined and called by different terms by others, right? But now, we will not be stuck with the
terms defined and called by others, but we will define ourselves, and
choose the term to call ourselves. Therefore it is possible to erase
those terms [the terms used by others to call/define us]. And we can
create a new term.'

Regardless of whether the term used meant indigenous or not it was
important to claim a name that they had chosen for themselves as a
way of rejecting the labels given by others and the negative connotations
that came with those labels. To me it became clear that there was an
understanding among both groups that we live in a world where group
identity is important and labels we use place people and give them

McKinnon

167

meaning, assign them rights, and ascribe certain kinds of power in different social and political contexts. With the wrong name you are easily marginalized and disempowered.

There was also broad recognition among the NGOs and village representatives that the power of a name could spread beyond their identity as highlanders. By including other marginalized indigenous groups in Thailand, such as the 'sea gypsies' of the south, many felt that they could help to support the struggles of these 'brothers and sisters', building on progress already made by groups in the north. What was particularly evident in the discussions of the NGO groups was that by adopting the wider term 'indigenous' all of Thailand's indigenous peoples could benefit from the stronger links that could thus be established with a global movement towards human rights. The 'indigenous' label has become, thanks to the hard work of many, a name that can now grant valuable political recognition. The United Nations Declaration of the Rights of Indigenous Peoples is an important outcome of this, and potentially an important source of guidance as indigenous peoples seek redress for years of injustice. Thailand voted in favour of the Declaration, and if they also decide to recognize the indigenous status of highlanders and others, this could provide the foundation for a much more positive future.

For the majority of NGO staff participating, the value of adopting the 'indigenous' label was clear. It was clear that the use of the term indigenous was not only appropriate, but would assist in their struggle for equal rights and recognition in the eyes of the Thai state. As one NGO representative stated in the workshop: 'The indigenous peoples' movement is progressive in many countries, but in the South-East Asian region we must admit that it's rather weak. ... [So] it is necessary that we hang on to the strong indigenous movement so that we can benefit from it also ...'

By identifying as indigenous, highlanders could access the support available internationally through organizations such as the ILO or IWGIA.

NGO participants also discussed how the term could provide an impetus for mobilization of indigenous groups within Thailand and help to create a new political space in which to claim rights and recognition by the state and the Thai public.

The definition [of 'indigenous'] is for creating political space, not just in our country but also at an international level. In deciding the term we choose to define ourselves we should think of the pros and cons. Let's think how it would be reflected at all four levels – regionally within Thailand, at the national level in Thailand, at the regional level in Asia and internationally. Whatever term we choose we need to fight for its acceptance.

The fight to have highlanders accepted as indigenous peoples has already begun and has won allies in the Thai mainstream. International Indigenous Day was marked for the first time in Thailand on 9 August 2007. Coinciding with this celebration, indigenous groups in the northern city of Chiang Mai organized a six-day festival of Thailand's indigenous peoples 'to highlight the diversity of Thai society and to deepen the understanding about the culture and traditions of Indigenous peoples in Thailand' (UNDF 2008). The festival was given support at the local government level with the vice provincial governor of Chiang Mai chairing its opening session.

The fact that the festival took place with such support is a hopeful sign that the effort to create new political and social possibilities through identification as indigenous peoples is working. By taking on the new label of 'indigenous', highlanders are seeking recognition of rightful claims to remain in the lands they occupy, of their rich cultural heritage, and of their great knowledge and skill in appropriately managing their communities and their forests. With this they are also able to claim a new position in relation to an international community and begin to draw on the support available internationally through the indigenous rights movement. But most importantly for the daily lives of highland peoples, being accepted as indigenous will allow highlanders to claim a new position in relation to the Thai state – a position of greater legitimacy. By making their indigeneity visible to the Thai public, highland activists are creating new avenues to secure community rights to land and support in efforts to sustain highland language and culture. How the new Thai government will respond to these efforts and what strategies indigenous groups will need to employ in the coming years is yet to be seen. Perhaps at long last the state will make some room for highland people as valued and respected members of the Thai nation and relinquish an unjust and inflexible vision of Thai nationality that has excluded highlanders for so long.

McKinnon

Comment

As in the Africa section, the commentator for this section is someone who is familiar with another region within Asia, namely India. There are strong cultural links between Thailand and India and much traffic between these two nation-states. Sita Venkateswar's comments further our understanding of the politics of indigeneity and the shifts and nuances across the varied polities of colonial and post-colonial Asia.

Sita Venkateswar

What's in a name?

The discussion above on naming practices and their implications resonates with the situation prevalent across India. In the Indian context, the term *adivasi* or 'original inhabitant' is a Hindi word used by the general population, often as a pejorative, when describing aboriginal groups. It is meant to be synonymous with their 'primitive' condition and marginal status. But those referred to as *adivasi* are also included within the list of Scheduled Tribes, which in turn confers certain rights and is part of the affirmative action apparatus written into the Indian constitution. However, each group has its own name derived from their own language with which families refer to themselves. *Onge, Munda, Nayaka* are some of the names of groups scattered across India and the Andaman Islands, each referent encompassing very specific linguistic, cultural and geographic attributes. Within the current political climate in India, the 'original' connotation of the *adivasi* is ignored or contested, since all Hindu Indians also assert their 'originary' status based on the scriptures.

The term *indigenous* has currency within the international sphere, and those groups from mainland India who have been connected with the mobilization of indigenous activism internationally have embraced that term and its associated discourse of rights to assert claims within the national context of India. There are some politically astute individuals, whose personal biographies would be interesting to explore, who skilfully navigate and play the politics of the domains signalled by each of the appellations mentioned above. Such parallels are likely to extend across much of South and South-East Asia or Africa and are markers for the ways in which colonial and post-colonial histories intersect with and are embedded within the social landscapes of these regions.

Additional aspects of the post-colonial political context of India are provided in the chapter from the volume published by Berg entitled

Indigenous Experience Today, in which Amita Baviskar (2007) offers an insightful glimpse of the ways in which 'originary'/'indigenous' claims have co-opted some *adivasis* to become complicit with the anti-Muslim, fundamentalist, Hindu supremacist agendas within the contemporary Indian political landscape.

Reply

As Sita Venkateswar identifies, the complex politics of naming are similar for many different indigenous peoples. Having the right kind of name is a conduit to a whole set of political possibilities within the nation-state – some positive, some less so. It is a sad reality that those struggling for rights and recognition within the state cannot simply be known by the names they call themselves but are forced to engage in a naming 'game'. For those with the appropriate know-how this game can be played to great effect to counter racism and institutionalized discrimination.

Glossary

Chao khao	Hill tribes
Chao thai phukao	Thai montagnards
Chatti pan	Ethnic/ethnicity
Chon klum noi	Ethnic minority group
Chon pao chattipan	Tribal and ethnic groups
Chonphao	Tribal people
Chon pheunmuang	Indigenous group
Chon pheuntin	Indigenous, people of the land
IPO	Indigenous peoples' organizations
Khon muang	People of the province (*muang*) as opposed to people outside provincial authority, i.e. forest people
Pgakeryaw	Tribal group, known also as Karen
Pheun muang	Indigenous, original people
Tangdao	Illegal immigrants

Acknowledgements

I would like to acknowledge the contributions of my indigenous collaborators in the north, who made the Indigenous Futures Workshop possible and so generously allowed me to be a part of the discussions on the day. I hope that this volume creates new opportunities for the kinds of networks and connections that are needed to help support and foster their good work in Thailand.

McKinnon

171

6 | Chupon's dilemma: a dialogue

SIMRON JIT SINGH

Prologue

If one can single out an event that turbulently shook the Nicobarese society and culture from its very roots, it was the tsunami of December 2004 and its immediate aftermath. To the Nicobarese, the catastrophe represents an incisive cut in human memory, an event that clearly separates the then from the now. It delineates the most passionate point of reference for the Nicobarese, and rightly so, as their life now rarely resembles the past. The Nicobarese, numbering 26,565 according to the 2001 census, inhabit most of the Nicobar archipelago located some 1,200 kilometres off the Indian coast in the Bay of Bengal. Having migrated from the Malay–Burma coast over two thousand years ago and having lived in relative isolation, the Nicobarese provide answers to some significant and interesting questions surrounding South-East Asian cultures.

By virtue of their location on an important sea route to the Spice Islands, the Nicobar Islands were often visited by trading vessels either for the replenishment of food and supplies during their long and arduous journeys, or for refuge in times of unfavourable weather. As a consequence, a certain amount of barter trade took place between the inhabitants and the traders, which was of little economic significance to the latter. The islands were lightly colonized by the Danes (1756–1869) and then by the British (1869–1947), who were the first to set up an administrative system on the Nicobars under a nation, until they became part of independent India in 1947. Since 1956 the government of India has afforded protection to the Nicobarese through special legislation, the Andaman and Nicobar Protection of Aboriginal Tribes Regulation, which regulates entry to these islands. During the past couple of decades, the Indian government has introduced a variety of welfare programmes for the Nicobarese, covering education, health services, transport infrastructure and a few subsidies, including the sale of cheap fossil fuels used to run outboard-motored boats (Singh 2003).

Nicobarese villages are located along the coast, sheltered by mangroves or natural bays, with their dwellings perched on stilts facing the sea. Outrigger canoes provide for easy access to villages located either along their own coastline or on another island. By and large, the Nicobarese are rather shy, and live in their (metaphorically) secluded world with few needs and a preference for leisure, festivities and rituals. Largely subsistent, the Nicobarese exhibit an economic portfolio that combines hunting and gathering, fishing, pig and chicken rearing and bartering copra (dehydrated coconuts) in exchange for rice, sugar, cloth, kerosene and other necessities in the nearby market located on Kamorta Island, where the administrative headquarters of the Indian government are also established. Money rarely exchanges hands and capital accumulation is absent. Some families maintain food gardens, where they grow an assortment of crops such as bananas, pineapples, yams, sugar cane, oranges, lemons, papaya and jackfruit. Besides these, the Nicobarese select from a large widely available range of edible leaves, tubers and fruits, as well as seafood from the surrounding mangroves (Singh 2003, 2006). With their 'limited wants and unlimited means' (including the generous subsidies), it takes only a little more than an hour of an adult's time per day to fulfil all economic activities combined (Fischer-Kowalski et al. 2011).

Owing to their proximity to the epicentre, the Nicobar Islands were devastated by the tsunami of 2004, which took away thousands of lives as well as destroying their villages, material culture and economy. Following the catastrophe came another wave in the form of national and international humanitarian aid. Driven by its own logic, the Nicobarese were very soon overwhelmed by huge amounts of money and material goods, thus increasing consumption levels and causing changes in lifestyle among the population within a very short time. At the same time crucial parts of the pre-tsunami means of production or supply were made dysfunctional while increasing dependency on aid. The new profile brings in a high potential for social conflicts in terms of access to resources, land, leadership, social coherence, family structure and an interest in continued aid flows.[1] Why, according to the logic of the (non-capitalistic) Nicobarese, should one work when one needs no food. As long as there is money in the banks, and a free flow of food provisions, the willingness to work is low.

However, as is often the case, a few (politically influential and articulate) soon overcame this cultural constraint and were able to take advantage of the immense opportunities that were presented to them. With wealth and power combined, the select few create a middle ground that is now hard to cross for any meaningful intervention, a

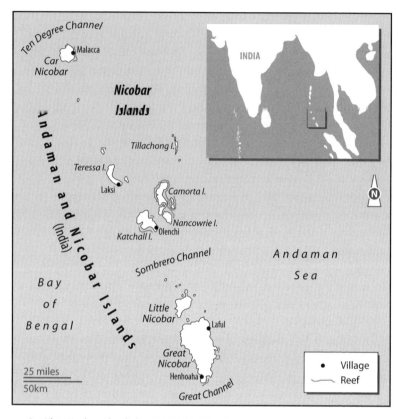

6.1 The Nicobar Islands (*source*: Ulrich Schueler)

wall between the outside and the inside. Sufficient aid and (politically) filtered programmes on the part of the local elite have undermined any effort on the part of the Indian government and NGOs to revive the economy and enhance self-reliance. Below is a dialogue that took place (in November 2009) between the author and Chupon, an eminent leader, who oscillates between despair and hope in the search for a better future for the Nicobarese.[2]

Chupon's dilemma

Chupon was waiting for me in a modestly furnished office. It was a simple setting with no overtones. Pictures of rural life, awareness-raising posters, a few books and files clearly conveyed a sense of dedication, as a matter of fact, to making a difference in people's lives. It was the field office of the Tata Institute for Social Science in Port Blair, the Andaman Islands, in the Bay of Bengal.

Chupon greeted me warmly, taking my hand. I had known him for more than ten years; striking a positive chord from the very first moment we met in my quest to understand the Nicobarese indigenous culture and way of life. Chupon lived on top of a hill in the village of Champin on Nancowrie Island (in the Nicobar group of islands). His cottage, made of concrete, was mainly used for receiving guests and for spiritual meetings. He himself lived in a sort of tree house behind, where the hill rolls down. 'It is much cooler here, surrounded by palms and fruit trees,' he had explained proudly. The floor too was made of split bamboo so the breeze could pass freely in all directions.

I do not remember how many times I had trudged atop this hill where he lived, and the innumerable hours I had spent talking to Chupon about the Nicobarese culture and the challenges they face, accompanied by a ritualized sipping of lemonade from freshly harvested lemons from his orchard. He stimulated me with his insights, revealed his memory on the age-old customs and traditions that shaped his culture, shared his dilemmas, agonized over the ongoing changes, and organized several storytelling sessions with his peers. Chupon was in truth my mentor and guide, who showed me the way into the Nicobarese culture and inspired me to search deeper and document all there was to document. He was then fifty-eight.

We sat down. His smile expressed the usual warmth. However, the look on his face conveyed a sense of urgency. I did not know what to expect. 'I had been waiting for you,' he muttered. I tried to read between the lines. 'I missed you,' he added emotionally.

'You have always been on my mind, Chupon, and I am really happy to see you again,' I answered. I realized this was not going to be one of those thrilling conversations of the past, about the affluent culture and traditions of the Nicobarese. It was now about rescuing the little that was left in the aftermath of the tsunami of 2004.

'Is there any hope for our islands?' Chupon took me by surprise. I started to feel uneasy. I was not prepared to answer that. In fact, it had always been the other way round. The questions had always been mine, and Chupon would answer. It was as easy as that. He always reflected before answering and I respected his views and opinions. Was I now under investigation, the expert on the Nicobarese, to reciprocate his hospitality, generosity and guidance, a sort of '*guru-dakshina*'[3] after all these years? I suddenly felt very insecure.

'What do you mean?' I asked innocently.

'You know, people are fighting with each other, there is hatred, the families are divided and also the people. There is no leadership that binds us. Why, even the government does not invite our tribal councils as often as they did before. They don't consult us and take us seriously,' he retorted in one breath.

'Why do you think it is like that?' I asked, in an attempt to gradually shift the responsibility for that question he had thrust at me.

'Probably the tribal council has lost its credibility and confidence with the administration,' he said sadly. 'There are a few people who control the power and the resources and have become rich after the tsunami. They favour their own family and friends to benefit from aid and the new opportunities. These are also the present leaders. Several of the older known leaders have either died or are ineffective. We are truly divided,' he added.

I nodded. I knew what he was talking about, but I wanted him to continue.

'There was too much compensation money after the tsunami, too many resources to be distributed. It depended a lot on the leaders to ensure a fair distribution. Sadly, only a handful of responsible older leaders have survived, and so the younger ones took over. The younger ones also had the advantage of Hindi so they could better communicate with the government and NGOs. They became the middlemen, the "tsunami captains" as we call them,' Chupon explained.

'But that can be good as well. To have younger dynamic leaders is also an advantage in this time of crisis,' I chipped in.

'Yes, but if you have no experience and get so much responsibility to decide for a lot of money, the situation can get worse. Many became greedy and corrupt, took to alcohol as they became richer and richer, controlling most of the aid resources for themselves or for a few favourites. So now there are those who have plenty and others who have little or nothing. This has created jealousy and conflict in the community,' added Chupon.

Chai was served. I was glad about it. I needed time to think, to wet my lips and to occupy my tense hands.

'I am aware of this, Chupon,' I admitted. 'I have been thinking a lot about this as well. It is definitely not an easy situation. What about elections? Can't you change the situation by electing new leaders?' I asked.

Chupon looked at me as if I had asked a very naive question. 'The common Nicobarese have lost their voice and power. Elections are not fair and meaningful,' he answered in his patient style.

'Hmmm,' I murmured, trying to regain my credibility. 'So what can we do?'

Chupon looked at me, fidgeted a little in his chair. I knew he had been thinking a lot about this. I was beginning to get the feeling that he was looking for someone to share it with who could make it happen. We both took a sip of tea.

For a few years Chupon had become quite inactive in the society. He had completely withdrawn from social issues and politics, and gave much of his time to spiritual meetings and prayers. In part, it had pained me to see such loss at a time when dedicated experienced leaders were needed. Chupon was related to, and had worked closely with, the late Rani Lachmi, the formidable leader of Nancowrie. And he had been one of the senior executives of the colossal MML (Manula Mathai Limited) cooperative society, which had slowly collapsed after the rani's death. Among other things, Chupon's greatest strength lay in self-reflection and articulation, a quality everyone acknowledged. In fact, he was one of those rare figures in the archipelago who was clear headed, experienced and adhered to a set of societal principles. Indeed, the loss of such a person was not easy for me to accept. However, I was glad that he continued to mentor me and share his views and concerns, which served as a stimulus for me to act.

'I am very concerned too, Chupon, but I am still not sure how to deal with this complex situation,' I encouraged him, seeking to provoke further discussion.

'We must revive the cooperative system, our economy.' Chupon let his plan out in one breath. He waited for my reaction.

'And what will you sell?' I asked.

'Vegetables. We have many successful examples among us who have learnt to grow vegetables: pumpkin, beans, gourd, okra, eggplant, bitter gourd, etc. At present we have to import them from Hud Bay, and by the time they reach here they are withered and expensive. They are not even organic. The growers use a lot of fertilizers and pesticides. There will be a lot of demand for fresh organic vegetables,' Chupon answered.

'And where will you sell the vegetables?' I asked.

'Here, on Kamorta. We can also export them to other islands where they do not grow.'

'Vegetables are a good idea. But to initiate a cooperative movement

Singh

we need an entire transportation and marketing infrastructure. And in order to sustain this, we need enough vegetable production. As far as I can see, there are only about a handful of people who are enterprising enough to grow them,' I said.

'Yes, but we can show the others how to do this. How to procure seeds, how to nurture the plants, irrigate the soil, etc. And once they learn this, they know they can earn enough money for a living,' he answered.

'I have seen that the agriculture department made a lot of effort to introduce agriculture to the people. They brought in seeds, know-how, organic fertilizers, tillers and other equipment. But most could not adopt this new way of life,' I replied, not ready to accept.

'Yes, I know. Anything new takes time and the right way to introduce it. Unfortunately, a lot was imposed on the Nicobarese from above: the choice of land, choice of vegetables, use of technology, and fertilizers. It also involved a lot of labour they were not used to, and the harvest was rarely good. Many were shy to come forward and ask a second time if the little they did failed,' he explained.

'What about the power tillers? Wasn't that useful to save labour?' I asked.

Chupon let out a stifled laugh. 'The tillers were lying around with one person in the village, the Captain. Once something went wrong, they were never repaired. Nobody knows how to fix them. They lie rotting in some dump yard in the village. On Katchal they use the tiller for transportation,' he explained.

'I am not sure if agriculture will work so easily in the Nicobars,' I said, bringing in my scientific observations. 'Agriculture is very different from the coconut economy you had. The trees once planted fruit for decades without any maintenance. Copra is made only when the food at home is running out, at best a week in advance. The Nicobarese are not used to working with seasons, long hours under the sun, toiling away in the fields and planning for a harvest months in advance. How will this transition work?'

Chupon thought for a while. It was indeed a challenge I had put in front of him. My anthropological insights were based on years of observation. I was sure he would have no answer to that.

'I am not sure about that.' He took me by surprise. 'The Nicobarese also plant the *yom*, the horticultural gardens, where we grow an assortment of tubers, fruits and some vegetables. For this you need to prepare ahead, right from organizing labour and clearing the forest to fencing, planting, grafting and weeding, and it is a work of several months. If not done on a regular basis, establishing horticultural gardens is an integral part of festival work that requires planning, sometimes a year in advance.'

I felt my transition theory crashing to the ground. How could I have overlooked that? I knew about it of course, but then why had it not occurred to me? It's true that the Nicobarese are able to plan a great deal ahead if you consider the festival cycle and the work required to establish the *yom*. I had been part of several of those planning meetings and the various stages of the festival following one another, guided by elders and *menluanas* (Nicobarese for shaman or witch doctor). I had of course separated the subsistence system from the cultural system when considering the concept of time in Nicobarese society.

'You have a point.' I slightly humbled myself, though not ready to give in altogether. 'But I am not sure how many of the Nicobarese actually maintain a *yom* on a regular basis. It has usually been optional, or linked to festivals. Moreover, I still do not see how this links to large-scale agriculture. We need plenty of produce for the market to be able to run a cooperative society.'

'At least twenty-five per cent of the families maintain a *yom*, I would say. All we need is to find ways to introduce agriculture based on the *yom* system. The Nicobarese know very well which land to choose for planting a *yom*, when to plant, nurture, harvest, etc. Why can't we build on what they know? We can introduce some cash crops in the *yom*, vegetables that are easy to grow and care for, and don't wither so easily but also fetch a decent price. This way the *yom* system can gradually evolve to serve both subsistence and market needs.'

What Chupon was saying was really exciting. I could really see his point now. The agriculture intervention had not taken into account the local system and built on it, instead trying to superimpose an entirely new idea of which the Nicobarese had no previous understanding and over which they had no control. Taking the *yom* as a point of departure made sense indeed, and was worth the effort. Vegetables would be a good livelihood option under these conditions, if only the idea found acceptability among the Nicobarese. Still, vegetables alone were not enough when thinking of reviving an entire economy.

'Chupon, you really have a point. However, I am still concerned about the success of a cooperative society that supposedly needs more turnover for it to be sustainable. We would need to have additional products to be marketed by the cooperative society so it could meet overhead costs, distribute risks and earn profits. What about copra, something you have been making for half a century? Do you think it has a future?' I asked.

'Those who did not lose all their coconut trees in the tsunami are already making copra. The new coconut palms are slowly coming up again. In a few years they will begin fruiting. The Nicobarese will not give up their coconut economy. It is their lifeline. But I have a good feeling that we should begin producing virgin coconut oil for the market. As you know, we make this at home by grating the coconut and squeezing the juice with our hands. I know it is a laborious process. But we can find out if there are mechanized ways of squeezing the coconut and making oil.' Chupon was now on a completely new track.

I shrugged. 'Are you suggesting that each household should now start producing virgin coconut oil instead of copra? It took you sixty years to make a transition from selling coconuts to selling copra. How many years do you think this transition would take?' I asked cynically.

Chupon ignored my sarcasm. 'The Nicobarese would only have to transport the coconuts to the oil mill for processing. The by-products can be used here on the islands. A great benefit is that the coconut flesh after it has been squeezed will remain on the islands and then can be fed to the pigs. With copra this was not the case. It was all exported,' Chupon continued excitedly.

'We would save so much firewood that we now use for making copra. It would be good for our forests. Also, if we can find a market, we can make coir from the husk and the shells can be used for producing energy for the mill.' Chupon's thoughts trailed off.

I was now beginning to get annoyed. 'So what you are suggesting is that from now on the Nicobarese should supply some sleazy fat capitalist with cheap raw material who could then reap enormous profits from oil extraction just for himself. Probably even sell the by-products to the Nicobarese at exorbitant prices,' I retorted.

'I never said this.' Chupon paused, suddenly realizing the tense situation. 'The cooperatives will process the oil. The people's cooperative. All profits will be divided among member households who sell their produce to the cooperatives. It will also generate employment for many.'

I stared at Chupon. He had indeed been thinking a lot, putting the pieces together for an economic revival.

'Do you think the Nicobarese would be willing to make this shift?' I asked softly, slowly giving in, and prepared to take the lessons.

'It is a backward shift. The Nicobarese have much less work. They only have to harvest the coconuts and bring them to the nearest mill. The cooperatives can employ technically minded Nicobarese to do the rest, while the profits are for all,' Chupon answered calmly.

'Why do you think there is a demand for virgin coconut oil?' I enquired curiously.

'This oil is of very good quality, absolutely clear, and no smell, which a refined coconut oil made from copra has. I am sure there is a demand for it. This way we can get a better value for our coconuts,' he answered.

'We have to find out, Chupon. Someone would have to explore its potential for the market, and the necessary infrastructure needed to transport it across. We would need to compare the number of coconuts required to make a unit of copra, and a unit of oil, and the gains from it in terms of labour time and income.' I muttered some of my jargon in an attempt to rescue some of my scientific dignity.

But why was Chupon talking to me about all this? Was he returning to the people again, thinking about their problems and possible solutions? Was he willing to take up his original role as leader? Or was he just mentoring me as usual, expecting I would carry out his ideas to help the people? It had been now more than five years since he had left active social and political life. I had missed him very much in that role, so powerful and effective. It would neatly turn the tables if he returned. I did not dare ask him directly and make him self-conscious, but pretended to go on casually and let him come out with all that he was thinking about the new economy.

'What else do you see as part of the cooperative movement?' I asked.

'Nicobarese are very fond of fishing, not only for their consumption, but also for leisure and sport. There is a great demand for fish in the local market. The non-indigenous settlers, the administration and defence are all consumers. Unfortunately, there is not enough fish catch to meet the local demand. If the Nicobarese began fishing for the market, they could make an income. Fish can fetch sixty to seventy rupees per kilogram,' he replied.

'Are you sure the Nicobarese will be willing to sell fish? I often heard that the Nicobarese don't like the idea of selling fish. It is against their culture. Excess catch is distributed to family and neighbours,' I challenged him again.

'Yes, there are a few who still find it offensive, but times are changing. There are some enterprising youths who are already doing this. For example, there is a person in Payuha who sells fish in the neighbouring village of Munack. Some youths from Tapong, Champin and the Inakas are already selling their catch in the market in Kamorta,' Chupon answered.

'Wouldn't there then be a risk of overfishing once the product enters the market?' I asked carefully.

'As long as the catching methods are not commercialized and the Nicobarese continue to respect the seasonal cycle of species regeneration, as we have done for centuries, this would be no problem. There should be strict rules at the cooperative society on the fish species that can be sold in a particular season and the methods used for catching them. There is plenty of fish in our sea around us to give us some additional income without harming the productivity,' Chupon answered confidently.

'Hmmm.' I acknowledged what Chupon had just said, although not quite convinced. Perhaps this was my scientific apprehensions over the free market and culturally inappropriate practices. But who was I to romanticize their life as cultural entities and ecological sustainable people, deny them the material standard of living they were now used to and their right to self-reliance from the resources they owned? What could be worse than to be dependent on aid for years, to have an addiction to it, which then continues to transform the entire social and cultural fabric, allowing people to lose all there is to lose?

'We can use the same infrastructure as for the vegetables since both need cool storage facilities, handling and transportation. The village cooperative office should be the storage point before bringing them to the Kamorta market every second day.' Chupon was deep in his plans.

He paused for a minute, and continued again. 'One day we can process the fish into a variety of pickles and chutneys and sell it as organic, ecologically sustainable and marketed by people's cooperatives. This way we can add value to our fish without increasing the catch,' he retorted in one breath.

I listened, and smiled. There was a level of determination in Chupon's voice. I had not heard him speak like that in a long time. I looked at him gently, still not sure how this transformation had taken place. But it seemed it had. It was overwhelming.

'Is there hope for the islands, Chupon?' It was my turn to pose this question now.

6.2 Chupon and Simron Singh

'Yes, yes,' Chupon replied eagerly. 'There is so much we can do. We just have to do it. Organize the people. We need some support, though, some education. Only a little bit; invisible intervention.' Chupon laughed at his own creative expression.

'Yes, *invisible intervention* is a nice term. I hope you are not asking me to organize that, Chupon,' I replied, highly amused.

'Well ...' He laughed again.

'Chupon, I still do not get the connection between the economy and the political situation you started off with. How will that change?' I asked.

'Once the people are well off and are not dependent on aid, the situation will change. At present aid is organized by the leaders who then dictate what should happen in the village. The people do not have the courage to go against them. Once the basic necessities are met with a sound economy, the people will have no fear of changing their leaders,' Chupon replied confidently.

Chupon had indeed made a convincing point. I could see the connection now. It was as simple as that, yet it needed a clear mind to get that straightened out.

'Life will become even better than before the tsunami. And we can continue with our lemonade and analyse all that has happened sitting in my tree house,' Chupon added dreamingly.

'What is your commitment to this invisible intervention, Chupon?' I

Singh

183

was not willing to let him off the hook so easily. He was almost there, and it was time to nail his responsibilities down.

Chupon paused. He began thinking. Was this a trap he had got himself into? I thought. No, there was no regret on his face at all. He looked rather calm. I waited anxiously. He then looked at me and smiled earnestly.

'I will give honest advice to my people, set an example, help them when they ask for it, share my experiences and knowledge with the people, with the captains. I will guide them the best I can.' Chupon's answer was straight and clear, conveying the toughness I had known in my early days.

I stood up and held his hand. I looked into his eyes. They were sincere. We hugged, a long, yearning embrace pending for years.

Epilogue

This conversation with Chupon had a deep impact on the author's understanding and future engagement with the Nicobar Islands. This was precisely what was needed at that time. In the years after the tsunami, the situation looked rather grim, despite good intentions and the support of quite a number of well-meaning actors. As a researcher untrained in community mobilization and rehabilitation efforts in a post-disaster situation, I felt challenged to provide (it seemed a moral duty) some relief and a sense of a possible future to my research subjects. But the odds were stacked high given the cascading effects of inappropriate aid. Chupon has instilled new hope for the islands, pointing to the fact that collective action inspired by culturally appropriate ways is the only way forward. He laid bare some of my scientific insights and humbled me by his forceful arguments, building on a sense of community and indigenous identity. The issue for him was not only their livelihood, but a sense of being in the world, inextricably linked to what it means to be a Nicobarese. He has effectively portrayed the complex interrelations between their biophysical and cultural existence – an understanding that must precede any form of intervention or aid from outside. In effect, he has implicitly pointed to the root of all the problems the Nicobarese faced – the inability of the outside world to appreciate the fabric of a long-evolved community, reflected in their intricate relation to nature, in their myths and stories, as in their spirituality, subsistence and leadership. Chupon was ready, and so was the community, to take the future into his own hands.[4]

Comment

Editor's note: Benno Glauser and Simron Jit Singh have been brought together again here to extend their earlier discussion in Section One and to offer further insights that make connections or highlight contrasts between disparate parts of the indigenous world.

Benno Glauser

Listening to Simron's dialogue with Chupon, among the different voices or messages I distinguish, I can hear 'there is only one way: forward, and becoming active' ... 'it is important to rely on one's own culture, on one's own known ways, ways of being and ways of doing' ... 'let's be hopeful' ... 'there is room for intelligent, well-thought innovation' ... 'it is important to provide an example to others with one's own actions' ... 'the leadership needed here is a natural one, it is not important to be leader in the formal sense' ... And: 'change *must* be oriented in one's own collective cultural characteristics' ... 'they are at stake, they must be preserved'.

The cited messages are Chupon's, but Simron, being the host of this conversation, listens attentively and, as he goes along, comments about his feelings to us. He does not seem to disagree with Chupon, but he is cautious and even sceptical, while Chupon maybe cannot afford to be sceptical – his life is at stake! Instead, in his case a doubt seems to come through, with an implicit quest for external approval. It implies the acknowledgement that the Nicobarese, who are not alone in their own world any more, have become inevitably interdependent with others, whose favourable attitude they need to be able to count on for their own future. Simron in turn is careful and wise enough not to dispense any external approval lightly. Simron's underlying question, which he puts to Chupon – if I understood rightly – is: Is there hope? And maybe Simron is not asking this question with only the Nicobarese in mind.

In this way, the dialogue to my eyes reflects the main issues and challenges indigenous peoples face, and, although this is not perceived by the global mainstream of our time, those that humanity faces. Could we say that both Simron and I interview indigenous leaders because we are worried about ourselves? Or because we would like to make sure that at least their worlds and realms are safe, and have opportunities for a survival we are uncertain to still have for ourselves?

A dilemma obliges you to take a decision. Simron seems really sceptical and doubtful, surely on the basis of having seen and lived through many

185

similar situations elsewhere. Chupon, however, to Simron's surprise, has made up his mind. We cannot do other than applaud and express our support for Chupon's good spirits and determination. Chupon is not only a former leader, he is an elder. He does not need leadership any more. Yet the seriousness of the situation of his people, the present-day Nicobarese, can be grasped if we realize that this elder, instead of spending his days in prayer, a little work and ritual celebrations, has gone into himself, has shed some light on a possible way out or way forward, and, most importantly, has decided to come back, this time as an elder, not as a leader. Doing this, he is putting his life, his integrity, his peace at stake. I think he cannot do less, because he has no future if the Nicobarese do not have a future all together. However, the fact that he takes this decision just shows how deadly serious the situation is.

With regard to my dialogue with the two Ayoreo leaders, the two conversations at first sight do not really seem to compare. The Ayoreo leaders in the interview are not dealing actively with the question of 'what to do'. But there are – among others – two important coincidences. Both peoples have been affected by a man-made or man-induced major disaster: in the case of the Ayoreo, the forced contact and subsequent deportation from the forest habitat to a meaningless realm, and for the Nicobarese, the 'complex disaster' brought upon them, not by the tsunami, but by the outside world's helplessly unhelpful ways of wanting to give a hand, which ends up imposing, invading and taking the energy out of the natural forces and ways of the Nicobarese.

The second coincidence is the message – more explicit in Simron's text, more implicit in what the Ayoreo say – that there is force in the collective way of being, in every people's culture, as something natural, as something which comes by itself, something which does not need the enormous effort demanded by change, improvement, innovation. There is benefit in the natural force of remaining one's own self, or of recovering it if it is lost. For the time being, this is a total anti-message or anti-value in the present day's globalized world, but it is possibly a crucial message for our future: not to change but to get back to being ourselves. This is the challenge Chupon puts to his people, a challenge shared with the Ayoreo leaders and elders, Mateo and Aquino.

Reply

Upon reading Benno's commentary, what seems to emerge more strongly is a contrast between the indigenous worlds driven by a sense of 'community', as opposed to our own loosely bundled 'society'. The two worlds are separated by their own logics: the first based on obligations and responsibilities, and the other on the notion of individual rights. The worries of the indigenous leaders are more for their people than themselves, as they ruminate over what has befallen them. They are not ignorant of those who threaten their existence, are aware of their motivations and interests, but are still able to face them with dignity and honour. They do not represent themselves as victims for want of pity, but what we see is the wisdom of accepting the way the world goes, of understanding it, while still being determined to find one's own place in it, even under changed conditions. Despite varying geographical contexts, the indigenous identity does indeed come out as a collective force in both cases, with a strong sense of responsibility and integrity.

Acknowledgements

The author is extremely grateful to the Nicobarese community, who shared the intimate details of their lives and taught me the concepts of indigeneity during the course of my decade-long research; and to colleagues, in particular Marina Fischer-Kowalski and Willi Haas who accompanied me through the difficult process of the aftermath both on a scientific and personal level.

I would also like to thank the Indian Andaman & Nicobar Administration for their logistic support in the field. The post-tsunami research and writing were made possible by financial support from the Austrian Science Fund (Project RECOVER – L 275-G05) and the fellowship in Urgent Anthropology from the Royal Anthropological Institute attached to Kent University, UK.

Singh

THREE | **International**

7 | Indigeneity and international indigenous rights organizations and forums

SITA VENKATESWAR

I want to preface the discussions that follow below by explaining the basis for my connections with Survival International (SI) and the International Work Group for Indigenous Affairs (IWGIA), the two leading international indigenous rights organizations that feature in this section. My engagement with these organizations and their interventions originated with my involvement with the Andaman Islands, first as a PhD student conducting fieldwork with the indigenous groups of the island; later as an activist working in tandem with local organizations in the Andaman Islands, to take the Andaman administration to court over their policies regarding the indigenous groups and their encroachment into the territories allocated to them.

It should be reiterated here that all the activism referred to above occurred on *behalf* of the islanders. None was initiated, led or participated in by individuals from among any of the indigenous Andaman groups. It is for this reason that there is no discussion convened with them within this book, but their situation informs my interlocutions and is illustrative of the vast majority of indigenous peoples in many parts of the world.

My first contact with SI occurred just before I started my fieldwork in the islands in 1989, when I wrote to them, primarily, to enquire whether they were involved in any research in the islands or could fund the research that I intended to undertake there. Their friendly though regretful response was filed away in my Andaman folder. Many years later, when I was based at Massey University, New Zealand, as a lecturer in social anthropology, I received an urgent message from Sophie Grig, who was in charge of the Asia desk at SI, to serve as an 'expert witness' and submit a testimony to be used in the civil action suit brought against the Andaman administration, who sought to resettle the Jarawa, one of the semi-nomadic indigenous groups of the island. The Jarawa were in the throes of a severe crisis at the time, unwittingly re-enacting a scenario familiar from colonial times as they struggled to survive assorted epidemics of measles, pneumonia and influenza, and thereby also underscoring the ongoing colonial context of their quotidian existence in the islands.

The correspondence with SI at this point also led to my contact with Diana Vinding at IWGIA, who invited me to write a piece on the Jarawa for the IWGIA publication *Indigenous News*. This was high honour indeed! I had extensively consulted IWGIA's monograph series during my thesis-writing period, obtaining the framework for 'ethnocide' which became central to my own research, from the literature they made available in print. To be accorded recognition within their publications was an unanticipated privilege for me at the time. Subsequently, it also led to IWGIA publishing my monograph on the Andaman Islands in 2005, just as the 26 December tsunami unleashed its fury on the inhabitants.

Later events, which altered the substance of my interactions with these organizations, are alluded to farther down in this section, in my response to the series of dialogues and interlocutions that follow.

Beyond my own relationship with SI and IWGIA over the years, there are other more representational reasons for their selection and inclusion within this book, i.e. for the *kinds* of organization they are and their specific *forms* of engagement with indigenous issues. These distinctions will become clearer during the discussions with the organizations and the ways in which they can be positioned within the range of international NGOs (INGOs) and their transnational strategies for addressing the situation of indigenous peoples across the world.

I also include a brief discussion with Ida Nicolaison, who was a nominee of the Danish government to the UN Permanent Forum on Indigenous Issues (UNPFII), a body that worked in conjunction with the Working Group on Indigenous Populations in the drafting of the Declaration on the Rights of Indigenous Peoples. During the same research-related travel in 2007 that resulted in the interviews with SI and IWGIA, I also tried to convene interviews with Professor Rudolfo Stavenhagen, who was UN Special Rapporteur for indigenous issues at the time, as well as with Vicky Tauli-Corpuz, the chair of the UN Permanent Forum. However, their very busy schedules and numerous travel commitments made it impossible for our travel paths to coincide. Hence, I thought it was quite a scoop to be able to meet and talk with Ida Nicolaison while I was in Copenhagen to interview IWGIA, and thereby insert a UN perspective into this section.

Unlike most of the transcripts in the rest of this book, the ones that follow below have been edited minimally and allowed to speak for themselves. The interlocutors involved in the discussions are media savvy and used to presenting their views at a multiplicity of forums nationally and internationally. Moreover, the discussions were held in English, and so did not require any translation to render them into a form that is accessible to the general public. When there are annotations these are mainly used to clarify my own role as an interviewer over the shifts and turns in the dialogue, or to address some of the issues that emerge from the interviewees' responses to the questions that I posed.

DIALOGUES

Interview 1: Stephen Corry, Survival International, 4 December 2007

The transcript that follows is a discussion with Stephen Corry at the Survival International Office in London. It was a grey, winter afternoon and our discussion was punctuated by the sound of a loud drill from ongoing construction work elsewhere in the building (which rendered the later transcription work really difficult and time-consuming). Stephen Corry was an extremely articulate person but quite unlike the person I imagined as the fiery front for that organization because of his demeanour, which was so reminiscent of that of an efficient civil servant.

SITA VENKATESWAR: I want to start by asking you the first of the questions on my list, which are:

- What in the view of Survival International constitutes indigeneity?
- Who are indigenous people?
- How do you identify them?

STEPHEN CORRY: The first thing I would say is that Survival would make a distinction between more broadly indigenous peoples and tribal peoples – they are not necessarily the same thing, indeed they don't necessarily define themselves as the same thing. Indigenous peoples are obviously the descendants of those peoples who were in a country or part of a country before it was colonized by other peoples. So long as they retain a sense of their own identification (however that might be expressed). I think tribal peoples are obviously a sector of indigenous peoples, though not all tribal peoples are necessarily indigenous to the area. But then they weren't necessarily there for very long. Looking just at tribal peoples we would say they are peoples who are clearly self-identified as being different from the mainstream. Generally the markers are old-fashioned anthropological markers,

193

language, kinship, material, culture, belief systems. So they recognize themselves as being different and to retain the notions of tribal peoples it is necessary to them to live in some way more or less self-sufficiently. If they are completely integrated into the market economy of the nation or of the mainstream (however you like to define that), then it becomes harder to assert that they are identifiable tribal peoples. So basically what it means is they are getting most of what they need to live, not necessarily all of it, but most of it from their local environments.

[Here, Stephen seems to have missed the main focus of my question, but it could also have been the result of the flurry of questions that I directed at him; despite opening the discussion stating that I would start with one question, in effect I bombarded him with several quite distinct ones, each one leading in a somewhat different direction.]

sv: OK, so when you distinguish the two, sometimes you're talking about one and the same groups of people, indigenous people are also tribal people ...

sc: Yes.

sv: in terms of their social organization. But often indigenous people have to be distinguished from other tribal people who may be living in that area as well or have come to that area as a result of other ...

[I attempt to disentangle the various components at stake in my original question and Stephen's somewhat fuzzy response.]

sc: Well, although the indigenous peoples' movement, which has grown up over the last thirty years or so, thirty-five years, looks at it as kind of one spectrum, in reality of course, to all purposes, there is no connection whatsoever between the problems faced by a Pequod in New England who might be a millionaire as a result of having a casino on his land but who self-identifies as indigenous, and derives that self-identification through technically one-sixteenth ancestry. There is no connection whatsoever between the problems faced by that person and in the Andaman Islands a Jarawa. They are completely different issues. So I think the concept of indigenous peoples as one issue is itself highly questionable because what has happened in the last thirty-five years is that the organized, articulate, effectively more mainstreamed indigenous peoples have tended to dominate this cause, whereas actually the most significant problems are faced by the more remote, numerically smaller peoples who one categorizes as tribes.

[Stephen may not have intended to, but seems to suggest some ambivalence regarding the self-identification prescription, which is an important article of the Declaration, and a decisive move away from the more quantitative basis for ascribing indigenous identity in North America and elsewhere. On the other hand, he draws attention to the situation of more vulnerable groups who remain remote from the transactions and advances made in international domains.]

SV: So would you say that the people whose interests Survival International represents are the ones who are most isolated, groups who may be not much in contact or just recently in contact or not a part ...

SC: Yes.

SV: ... of or are not politically articulate, have not learned to work the system.

SC: Yes, as a priority, not exclusively, but as a priority – unquestionably.

SV: What are the some of the political tensions around the ways in which you, Survival International, operate? What are the things that the organization has to balance out as it goes ahead?

SC: Well, the organization is an advocacy organization standing up for these peoples' rights. In that context, it is not our role to compromise on those rights. We are in the position of an advocate in a court, say; our obligation is to give the best possible argument for our clients, if you like. So, in terms of tribal peoples' land rights, we say, well, the international law says tribal peoples have various legal rights to the lands they use and occupy, that is the legal position, that is our position. Now, if those peoples wish to negotiate to give away some of their land rights that is their concern but it is not up to us to be party to compromising their rights. So, the problems we face are of course governments are, and always will be, opposed to the idea of peoples within their boundaries who are not part of the mainstream for psychological reasons, financial reasons and so on and so forth, so the idea that governments are going to acknowledge and accept these peoples' rights willingly without pressure is fallacious, is not going to happen. So Survival's role is basically, it is an *adversarial organization* which is set up to challenge the status quo [*my emphasis*]. *So the point of it is, we don't accept the status quo* [*my emphasis*], which is that tribal peoples' lands are taken from them – literally.

SV: It is interesting you say that, that you take an adversarial role. Do

Venkateswar

you find that often that might make your task harder in the sense that it might be easier to be more conciliatory?

sc: It depends on what your objective is. If your objective is to work out some agreement which will apparently facilitate good relations for the next five or six years, then yes. If your objective, as ours is, is to change the world's view of these peoples, radically, that might sound like an ambitious goal. In fact it is already happening in a lot of places, it's a goal no more ambitious than opposing slavery some two hundred years ago. And actually we think there are quite a lot of parallels. The proponents of slavery argued that it was for the benefit of the slaves, they argued that it was vital to economic expediency, was vital to government interests that there should be slavery. If you are going to take that mindset, deeply ingrained, and change it in a permanent way, you have to challenge the view of tribal peoples prevailing in many governments, development organizations and in many universities, among many academics. You have to say, look, these peoples have the right to live as they wish to live, it's got absolutely nothing to do with being backward, or forward, or modern, or less modern. It's got to do with peoples' rights to a way of life which they have chosen. Everybody's way of life is changing and adapting all the time, always has, always will, it's got nothing to do with keeping people in isolation or anything like that. It's to do with acknowledging their right to, generally speaking, lands that in most cases they've lived on longer than the Englishmen in England.

sv: How do you decide, whose rights to advocate for?

sc: We are looking primarily at the most vulnerable, and so that means ...

sv: And vulnerability is identified as ...?

sc: ... the peoples who stand to lose most. So if you have a numerically small group of people of a few hundred, living on their land in relative isolation, history shows us that they stand to lose everything, including themselves as a viable group of people, they face being wiped out, which is what is still happening in parts of Amazonia and elsewhere, so obviously they are the most vulnerable. And so that is where we would seek to make our focus whereby there will be parts of the world where there are such peoples about which we know nothing at all and there's no information ... we are unable to get information to them, and there's no point in trying to do anything. So there are pragmatic concerns such as information, continuity of information ... and there are other concerns such as, it will be clearly inappropriate for us to be focusing on a particular area if fifteen miles over there, there was a tribal people facing a worse situation. And basically, obviously the most vulnerable people would be peoples that are getting physically killed, shocked and so forth, and then it basically boils down to land. As long as people are not actually getting killed, massacred and their land invaded by people with guns, although that is still going on in some places, so long as that is not happening, then the question fundamentally boils down to land. So if people have, at the moment, retained their land and are using it, but are faced with having it taken away from them, or most of it taken away from them, they're more vulnerable clearly than the people who, even one could argue who had it taken away from them a hundred years ago. So there are both pragmatic concerns and concerns deriving from what is the ultimate purpose of the organization, and it is basically two strands, one is to take individual cases and attempt to effect change on the ground, tangible, visible change, and the other, running in parallel with this, is to change attitudes, to be part of the process ... I am not claiming we are the only ones, but to be part of the process by which enlightened world opinion on these issues is changed permanently.

[Here Stephen seems to be using the terms 'indigenous' and 'tribal people' interchangeably, although he tried to distinguish between the use of those nomenclatures earlier in the discussion.]

sv: Now, the second strand that you identified, whose mindset are you looking to change? Who are you reaching?

sc: Everybody – if some two hundred years, two hundred and fifty years ago, slavery was accepted as part of Europe and some other places ... but [the] European way of thinking. Everybody ...

sv: Survival supporters exist all over the world, but it seems to me the majority of people who support your efforts are based in the Western world. Am I right in that?

sc: Well, the majority of people who pay to support our efforts are based in the Western world – obviously.

sv: But through your efforts are you able to change the mindset of the mainstream in the various other parts of the world, where the tribal groups exist?

sc: Of course, of course.

sv: How do you do that? How do you reach the people there?

sc: Well, basically you reach them exactly the same way you reach them here, which is through the media and, nowadays, the new media, through radio, through the press, through pamphlets, publications. Effectively those ways of changing, of confronting these kinds of issues haven't changed for centuries and it's time to do up those pamphlets, for mileage, pamphlets which might be printed in the newspaper. A generation ago in many parts of South America and in the sixties, there was a case in Colombia where a colonist who had shot and killed Indians who were called Quiva, for which they were to go on trial, they said that they did not know it was wrong to kill Indians, therefore they were acquitted. That would no longer be the case, there's now an acknowledgement by government, by the media, generally among people that you can't treat people that way because they happen to be tribal peoples. The changes in Botswana over the last five or six years, if you follow the media, obviously we do very closely, are absolutely clear on this, there is now far more sympathy from the media in Botswana to Bushman issues than there was five years ago.

sv: This particular year is quite an important year with the declaration being passed in the UN. How do you see that declaration impacting on the movement for indigenous rights?

sc: Well, I think it is important to take a long vision on this. This problem is not going to be solved in the next five years or ten years.

sv: No.

sc: But we think that it is going to be solved in the next fifty or sixty or seventy years. That's not to say there's not going to be incidents of the abuse of peoples' rights, of course there are! But by and large the climate would have shifted massively in favour of these peoples, but any of these single initiatives including the UN declaration, court cases, the Botswana court cases, the Mabo case in Australia, challenges that come up in North America, the creation of the Nunavut in Canada and so on and so forth. They're all part and parcel of a progress. None of them by themselves I think are any necessarily more or less significant than anything else. I mean, the fact that the UN now recognizes indigenous peoples in the way it has done with the Declaration is a great step forward. The ILO 169 was a great step forward, the ILO 107 actually, in spite of its shortcomings, considering it's fifty years old, was a great step forward.

sv: Despite the Declaration, what are the problems that you antici-pate in the future towards realizing those aspirations that are voiced in that declaration?

sc: As thinking moves with this movement that Survival is part of, there of course will be a backlash, there is a backlash in parts of South America, there's increasing hostility among some sectors of populations in some places like Australia and Canada, the States, that is inevitable. It's not helped by the anthropologists who deny the existence of indigenous peoples, although that is nothing new. If, I mean, if I was to respond to what you were saying in the beginning, you said we're all moving forward towards the same goal! I don't think there is any evidence of that at all actually. I think that anthropology, just like missionaries, just like anybody else, covers a huge spectrum. This movement has been promulgated and pushed by some anthropologists and deeply opposed by some others and always has been. I mean, Survival had a lot of hostility from anthropologists in the seventies, for instance, when we started supporting the Yanomami in the efforts to get land rights. We actually had a letter from Sir Edmund Leach who was the grand old man of British anthropology and he was saying that these are the most homicidal people on earth and should not be, they should not continue into the future basically. So there's nothing new in the ideas that people like Kuper and Suzman, he now works for DeBeers full time. These people saying there's no such thing as indigenous peoples in Africa. None of that is new; there's always been a sector of anthropology which basically doesn't like the notion of indigenous peoples having definable rights.

sv: Yes, I think it's also important to put those peoples or those views, the people who are articulating those views, into the context that they exist in. It is not incidental that they are all coming out of South Africa, which has its own history of rights.

sc: Well, you say them all, I think we count three, there are three of them, Morwen, who is now a full-time employee of DeBeers, it is not normally viewed as an institution for the pursuit of anthropological advancement, and then there's Kuper, who based most of his stuff on DeBeers on Suzman and what he said, he hadn't been in CKGR [Central Kalahari Game Reserve] for thirty years and then whatever his name is in the States, you know who I mean. Anyway, there's a lot of noise from very few people, in fact, and it reaches the anthropological community who therefore think there's some controversy about this. Of course, there are NGOs in Botswana who are deeply hostile to Survival – always have been, as they are deeply hostile to the notion of the people who are living in the CKGR. So none of those is unexpected, none of those particularly new. But I think it is fundamentally a mistake to think that everybody involved in indigenous peoples' issues from whatever side is necessarily heading towards the same goal, and they're not at all.

[Stephen is referring here to the series of heated exchanges that occurred between some social and cultural anthropologists within the pages of *Current Anthropology*, a debate that I refer to in the introduction. Prior to the interview, there were some increasingly acrimonious exchanges regarding the situation in Botswana and SI's interventions there that were published in *Anthropology Today*.]

SV: No, which is the other thing which I probably was not that clear [about] in my statement at the beginning, that in looking at indigenous futures, there are going to be many differences in how people are thinking about those futures and ...

SC: Yes, of course.

SV: ... and so to ask this question of an academic, and to ask a question of an NGO, and to ask a question of an indigenous activist is going to raise different kinds of replies.

SC: Well, as you know, there is no standard anthropologist, NGO or indigenous activist.

SV: But what I am really interested in is trying to see what is the path towards this realization that has been marked out by all of these groups of people, whether it is an academic ... What kind of steps do they see themselves taking if they're working with indigenous groups? What are the steps of indigenous rights groups at Survival International, how do they see themselves going forward with the declaration, which supposedly ... another path being opened out with the recognition at such a high level that these are the aspirations of a group of people that must be recognized and acknowledged?

SC: Fundamentally we have to turn it into public awareness. UN may be a high level but it's what people think on the streets that matters. The democratic governments respond to what they think the constituency wants, so the only way to effect any lasting change is to change people's minds on the street. That does not necessarily come from universities, it does not come from governments, does not come from the UN. It largely comes from the media and that brings along everybody else with it. There are people's views that these kind of issues will be changed if they continually – if they often see these stories appear in some depth, reported accurately so that they can then see that there is an injustice, there's a violation, they think these are crimes that are going on. We shouldn't sit back and say, well, that's how things work in Brazil or Botswana, of course that's how things work, but that's the problem – they are also crimes – therefore they must be denounced as crimes, exposed as crimes, and it doesn't matter who's perpetrating them at what level, whether it is government or big companies, big industries. They must be shown up to be what they are, and if that happens sufficiently, ordinary people, and [it] doesn't have to be the entire population, but sufficient grounds for public opinion is created, which is what's happening and has been happening.

sv: But it doesn't change governments. It is not incidental that the four nations, Canada, US, NZ and Australia ...

sc: Of course it changes governments, but of course it changes governments, of course it does – I mean in the twenties there were still people riding out and shooting Aboriginals in Australia – that is changed. In the sixties there were people dropping sticks of dynamite out of aeroplanes in Brazil – that has changed. There are still massacres but there're small, they're hidden, but when they are brought to justice they are often dealt with severely by the courts in Brazil now. I am not saying everything is solved by the government; we have, as I said, if you take a broad movement, if you look at the last thirty, forty, fifty years, things are immeasurably better for most tribal people around the world. The notion that the Jarawa should be forcibly integrated is now largely absent from a lot of thinking in India. Well, it wasn't even five or six years ago. The problem about lobbying people in government is they change all the time. Whereas if you're trying to get your issues known on the street, that's where government derives its ideas from. *So, I see Survival, it's a popular movement, it is deliberately not talking to academics, or even to governments, it's talking to the person on the street – and because that is the way we think that in the long term, change – permanent change – can be effected* [*my emphasis*].

sv: When you look at rights, do you look at those rights in isolation of some of the larger social injustices that might exist, for instance within indigenous groups, there are other kinds of problems and iniquities that might need to be addressed. Do you include those, like for instance – issues of violence, issues of gender?

sc: Yes, I would say Survival has no specific policy on this; my view is that all peoples are barbaric, have the most barbaric customs. The way we treat our old people in England is, to many people, utterly barbaric.

It is not, however, our role – Survival is a very narrowly focused organization. What we are pushing for is tribal peoples' rights faced with their effective annihilation by outsiders. In that context, what they do in their own society is not up to us to sit, pass judgement or attempt to change. We wouldn't oppose people who are trying to change it; we don't oppose people who are trying to stop female circumcision, it's a heinous custom. However, it is also true that a lot of those are actually dying out quite quickly and there are movements within the bigger ... numerically bigger groups opposing those things, and those are kind of [a] natural process of attrition by which they are dying out. The infanticide of twins which was not uncommon in Amazonia, for instance, is and had been rapidly dying out in the last fifty years. So we're not here saying everything they do is fine; it's a very specific target. We are saying if we want these peoples to have a place in the world in the next three or four hundred years as peoples; and why shouldn't they. They can't, they won't, unless they have basically their land rights.

sv: So are there any success stories? Are there groups whose rights Survival has advocated for a period of time and then decided that, OK, we've done as much as we can, they're on their own, they're on the path now to be able to ...

sc: Well, they are in the hundreds, I mean the whole movement is a success story, as I say, if you go back forty years and look at the attitude – in a way the biggest success story will probably be in South America. If you go back forty years and you look at the government attitudes in South America, missionary attitudes, colonist attitudes, you find very prevalent was the idea that the future can only be in integration. There's no other future, these people have to get integrated or die out. That is completely changed. In its changing, a lot of Amazon Indians now have acknowledged land rights. In particular countries like Peru, most of the Amazon Indian communities have land rights. In Brazil, most of them have some measure of land rights, might not be title but it's a measure of land rights. They might not be always adhered to by local colonists or by the state but nevertheless it's there. It doesn't mean that it's there for ever, there will always have to be some kind of vigilance, there will always have to be people taking some kind of vigilant role for the inarticulate, very poor, the dispossessed in any context. Of course they will – we are not going to have a world really in which everybody can stand up, articulate their own defence on a level playing field – that's not going to happen. And if you've got a multibillion-dollar industry stacked up against you, they are going to play dirty, governments play dirty. So of course there is going to be a need for the non-governmental sector to be speaking and acting in their defence. Of course, one of the problems is that nowadays the NGO sector is increasingly a government-controlled centre. So actually NGOs are increasingly less genuinely non-governmental or now have been taken over by government, and a lot of the organizations set up [at] more or less the same time as Survival, including IWGIA, Cultural Survival, are now actually acting really just as arms of the government, which is tragic in our view, but don't get me on that, we'll be here all afternoon.

sv: How do you see Survival working in tandem with other international rights organizations?

sc: The key partners that Survival is seeking to work with are the people on the ground, and that doesn't even necessarily mean the NGO on the ground, it might mean the communities on the ground, NGOs can be good or not so good and they can change. So, if there is a local NGO, which genuinely articulates the wishes of the people in the communities, that is the NGO we want to work with – that's the absolute primary goal.

[I am aware of the extent of efforts made by SI to work closely with an organization like SANE in the Andaman Islands in their efforts to draw attention to the plight of the indigenous groups in the islands. I am also aware of how wary Samir Acharya, the director of SANE, was of the perception of alliances between the two organizations by the government or the media. Samir trod a careful, independent path to avoid any accusations of being a mouthpiece or a front for 'foreign' interests.]

sv: But in any group there's always bound to be multiple interests and divisions.

sc: Of course.

sv: But by aligning yourself to any of those groups do you see that as engendering more tensions or problems?

sc: No, it might engender more tension, but that might be necessary. If there is a group of people, as there are all over, whereby principally the young men are taken out – this is the common Protestant missionary way of acting, take out the young men, train them as leaders and put them back in wanting what you, the mission, wants, the

Venkateswar

governments do it, the United States did it with their tribal councils. So of course in any group of people there are going to be people who are working against the interests of the majority! And they are often going to be better resourced, who are articulate, with back-up from industry, government, whoever it is. That's always been the case. Does that mean where everybody has got to have a equal say, if a group of people who everybody knows is going to be destroyed, if they give their land away or sell it for not much money, that will effectively destroy the people. There'll be some of those people who'll be actively pushing for it. Do you give them equal say in what happens? No, you take a stance which says people's rights cannot be bought and sold even by the people whose rights they are – you cannot sell your own rights. So it is not up to individuals to give away the rights of their children, great-grandchildren or their people – it's not in that sense their choice. Either we take the view that people have rights, and those rights are inalienable – cannot be given away. No society wants to self-destruct, so if you see a real concrete threat and the people themselves don't see it, you try to fill them in. If you can't show them because they're Sentinelese and nobody else speaks their language and you can't get close to them or anything and you say OK, we will attempt to stop that threat, and by doing so, of course, we're acting for and on behalf of the Sentinelese. And of course they don't know who we are and they didn't ask us to do it. And if that's going to stop us, then the Sentinelese haven't got a hope in hell of lasting another twenty years. So, there's always been peoples who do not have the ability, they don't have the resources, the language, they don't have the literacy to be able to guard their wicket, so other people will have to do it if they care about them. There's nothing new in any of this. I entirely reject all the criticism which Survival has had over the Botswana affair, not one part of which I accept.

sv: What do those criticisms amount to? What are they saying about Survival?

sc: Well, actually there isn't anything they're saying which is true. They say things like – well, we came in without knowing what we were doing; in fact Survival has been involved in the issues before most of the NGOs and individuals were even created, that's what we were talking about, CKGR, in the early eighties, to the government of Botswana. So if you strip away all the things that aren't true, you're not really left with anything. What it really boils down to is that the local NGOs don't want foreign criticism; they want foreign money because that's what

supports them, but they don't want foreign criticism. They're not separate from government, so they are close to government, that's why they
don't want foreign criticism. There are other reasons, they want the
money, and they want to be seen as the people doing the action. We'll
be the first people to bow out if they are actually doing the action. We
would never have got involved; we're not picking the most problematic
areas we can pick. We're looking for the most vulnerable peoples in
any given area. But if there's a local organization doing everything that
needs to be done, fine, we've got plenty of other things to do, nothing
we'd like more. So there's xenophobia, there's kind of, well, we want to
be the one seen to be doing the thing because we get our funds from
doing that. There is: we mustn't upset the apple cart, mustn't upset the
status quo too much, which is an advantage of being distant because
you don't care about the status quo. It is vital that an organization
in Survival's position doesn't care about the status quo. It is here to
challenge the status quo – that's why it's here. So if you say – wow, we
must go very carefully. I mean, the anti-slavery movement didn't say
we must go very carefully, the anti-apartheid movement didn't say
let's go very carefully. You're not going to change significant human
rights abuses by treading carefully. We cannot find in any historical
relevant context where that has ever happened. So why on earth is
something going to happen in the case of indigenous people? So, but
that's why they don't want [the] status quo upset, they don't want to
lose their funding, they want to stay close to government because ...
you can understand that point of view, they live in the country, they
live with government, the government dominates everything, controls
everything. They don't want to sour that relationship – I think also one
has to raise a question, I mean if you look at [the] CKGR issue, the NGO
KURU is essentially a mission-derived NGO. It doesn't really believe
that these peoples should be in the CKGR, it wants peoples in centres,
where there's the school, the mission and the church, and if you apply
a South American context to that, it will be extremely clear that what
we are talking about is basically a missionary organization that's
looking for schooling and all those traditional missionary things, it's
not looking for rights, and therefore mention of rights is dangerous.
Again, it's not news, it's not surprising, it's not going to end – it's OK.
We shouldn't get too worried about it.

[There is a veritable thicket of quite contentious issues in Stephen's concluding paragraph. Some of his assertions may be valid in the Botswana context, but to extend that to other NGOs across the world is likely to be overstating his point. SI too needs to be perceived as 'taking action' by their supporters and their funding hinges on such a perception. SI's unmitigated adversarial stance seems to place them in difficult relationships with local NGOs which often need to work with governments and local administrations to reach the same goals that SI has set out to achieve in that context, but also need to walk a somewhat different path towards that realization, which seems to be hampered if they ally themselves too closely with SI's efforts. As I have noted in the Andaman context, there were marked shifts according to the situation on the ground; whether or not there was unreserved support for SI's actions or attempts to maintain a distance from SI's sometimes strident publicity drive.}

SV: Thank you very much, you've been very eloquent.

Interview 2: discussion between Sita Venkateswar and IWGIA members Lola García-Alix and Jens Dahl, Copenhagen, Denmark, 12 December 2007

Lola is the current director of International Work Group for Indigenous Affairs (IWGIA), while Jens was her predecessor. Jens continues to be actively involved in IWGIA's various initiatives. Both have considerable experience and expertise through their involvement in various international forums.

SV: I'll start with my first question – what distinguishes IWGIA?

LG: I think what distinguishes IWGIA, in the context of the work of the international arena, perhaps, is that we have tried to link it with the local processes, and at the same time also link it with documentation and publication.

SV: OK.

LG: So I think one of IWGIA's priorities is to support indigenous peoples to follow and participate, as full actors, in all the discussions of the UN.

I think IWGIA was one of the first organizations that, together with a few other NGOs, the whole idea was to secure indigenous participation, to secure that. They were able to come and present their cases to the UN, particularly from those parts of the world where they were suffering abuses of human rights. But not only that, how do we link that with our work supporting indigenous organizations in the region, in the countries, and also how do we somehow document their situation in the country, that could also be used in the international arena. And I think [that], for me, still today, is one of the distinctions of IWGIA, in that work. It's not only that we are supporting people to be there, not so many other NGOs were involved in the international processes dealing with indigenous peoples' rights. Unfortunately we are very few in that context; of course, IWGIA is one of the big ones. But that is because there are very few organizations. In general, human rights NGOs, they haven't been involved at all in the discussions of indigenous peoples' rights and those NGOs who have been involved, they have been for some European NGOs, very small NGOs. During the last ten years, they have come up with some other NGOs, from Canada mostly. But we are very few. But, perhaps, the main difference, that I can see (Jens may be able to say more about it, and perhaps he may have another idea), is there is not an international profile just alone. But really how can the work of IWGIA, the support of IWGIA for [the] indigenous in the region, in the countries, and our documentation work, fit together into the whole promotion of indigenous peoples' rights, at the international arena.

JD: I agree completely, IWGIA talks about its holistic approach – which means combining different things, combining human rights with documentation and project support and lobbying activities, and I think this is usually what an NGO would do, one or two things, but not very often you will find an organization that will do or have the capacity, or want to do, these four different kinds of things and I think that is a main characteristic of IWGIA.

Another you could say linking characteristic of IWGIA is that IWGIA only works with indigenous peoples, that you could say, in some respects, is a strength, and of course is a weakness in other respects. I think the strength is very obvious, that from 1984, when the first discussion started about a draft declaration, you only find one organization that has followed the process for twenty-three years, and that's IWGIA. This means that we have accumulated a lot of knowledge, we have accumulated a lot of credibility and we have created a huge network among indigenous people. We know them and they know IWGIA, which, I think, is creating trust and it is also creating a situation where indigenous people know the limitations of IWGIA. I think that's important.

We often talk about who will be there as the support organization next year – oh, maybe only IWGIA. It is not a critique of any organizations, it's just a [de] facto factor, that if you take minority rights groups, they do a lot of good work there, but they have only been with indigenous peoples for some years, take Amnesty International, a section of AI are doing a lot of good work with indigenous peoples, but it's also only two years and they're not there any more. You have few, like you have a Dutch organization, which has been there for many, many years, and indirectly you have Anti-Slavery International, but you don't have a lot.

LG: I think that's a weakness. I've always seen it as a weakness that there are not more human rights NGOs, who were interested, really, or were engaging themselves in the discussions of indigenous peoples' rights. I think there are many reasons. Part, I think it's indigenous peoples themselves, also the ways in how indigenous peoples ... and, I think, it's not only fair but I think IWGIA has also been in the forefront to say, OK, that indigenous peoples are the main actors in this. It is not our fora, as such, we can support, facilitate, lobby – we have many channels. But when we come to the UN, they are the ones who have their right to speak, the ones who are the main actors. I think that issue has been very difficult to understand, for many of the big NGOs, in the sense that they have to respond to their constituencies, as such. So when they, you can see it very clearly, in the issue of the speaking time, in organizations that have this ECOSOC [UN Economic and Social Council] purpose, so they normally don't give speaking time to any other organization, even indigenous people, they present their own statement. They, of course, propel themselves and their constituencies, and the objectives, by themselves. I think IWGIA has a completely different approach in the indigenous context, and it's we'll facilitate the participation, and we help them with whatever financial means – even procedural means, that includes giving them our speaking time to present their statements.

SV: OK, that's important.

[This is an important area of distinction between IWGIA and Survival International, which also highlights the very different kinds of populations the two organizations work with and try to support. Stephen Corry would say their efforts are to ensure the survival of very precarious indigenous groups which have no voice at either national or international forums, while IWGIA's work supports other indigenous groups which have the ability or are empowered to represent themselves in the international arena.]

LG: I think that's very important. That has also created credibility, in the sense that we have never tried to promote ourselves, in that sense, in that context. But mostly, to bring indigenous people to this platform, so they can somehow promote their own issues or defend their own. It is not only us now but I think there are very, very few NGOs who are ready to give speaking time, even give accreditation, to indigenous peoples because they have their own models of procedure and all this, and I think it's just something that shows how we understand our role in the international arena.

[Lola is drawing attention to a very important issue here: having speaking time at the UN is something that is jealously guarded because it is so difficult to be accorded that privilege, and to step aside and hand it over is very unusual indeed, and sets IWGIA apart from other organizations operating in that domain.]

We are there to write our reports, to document through our publications, to help also to facilitate a dialogue with specific governments to see the possibilities or the niches where they can, somehow, bring their issues. *But we don't see that much as a place where IWGIA can publicly present our own strategies or our own visions but more really to support indigenous visions and demands, of abuse, comes in front* [my emphasis].

SV: It leads me to the next question. You're not well known. You *are* well known but you're also *not* well known. You're well known in a certain domain but people, even domestically, in Denmark, don't really know much about you. And certainly internationally IWGIA doesn't ring a bell, unlike, say, the most obvious organization by contrast is Survival International, where the ordinary lay public seems to know more about them, and my question is, you've already said something that you are more effective by locating yourself, somewhat, behind the scenes, so that you are facilitating indigenous presence and indigenous capacity-building, but you don't want to beat the drum about yourselves very much, publicly?

LG: Not in that context.

JD: No, no, but I think you are wrong in a way. I don't think we are more effective but you asked what is peculiar about IWGIA and I think we explained what, in our understanding, differentiates IWGIA from the others. I don't think we're more effective, we're effective in the ways we've explained.

SV: Yes ... yes, so do you find in the ways in which you operate, do you have reason to find yourself at cross-purposes with other international organizations working on the same issue? Does that ever occur? Do you all, kind of, work in a way that – do you need to be consulting with each other, do you find yourself in a region where you're often not working along the same platform, or you're working at cross-purposes, is the word that comes to mind?

LG: I don't know if I can answer that now. Before you mentioned that IWGIA is not known, we are not that public.

SV: Yes.

LG: And if you put that ... Survival International, I think they somehow, they profile themselves more to get support from the public, and I think IWGIA has never done that. And I think it is not our objective, in that sense. I think IWGIA is known, within the people, organizations, academics and activists related to indigenous people. And I think because we have discovered sometimes, even with the Danish government, have felt that they need to sometimes bring the issue of the need to show the public encroachment, and we have always said, I mean in Denmark, we do not work towards the Danish public. We feel that, more, our constituency is more indigenous peoples – an indigenous peoples' organization. We want to be known by indigenous peoples' organizations, by activists, by academics that are working on indigenous peoples and work together with them. And this links to your second question, I think in general, my perception, is a good cooperation between organizations, NGOs, as I said, the few who are active on indigenous issues. We have a good cooperation, for instance, in the context of Europe, we have tried to establish a kind of informal network on how to really promote indigenous rights, and indigenous issues within the European Union, together with other European organizations. With Survival I haven't had much experience, perhaps you know more about that. But, I think, we don't have the same, not the areas of work, but I've never been in issues where Survival is also – except in Asia, Botswana, but except for that, Survival has never ever, somehow, directly been involved in international processes. I've never met them in Geneva, very few times, as in one or two, but they haven't been associated with regularly following the process of anything.

sv: OK.

LG: And the issue of promoting indigenous peoples within the European Commission, for instance, what would have worked from the indigenous organizations in Europe at the council, and other NGOs, like Forest People's Programme in England or in Germany, in Holland, and my sense is that we try to cooperate as much, I don't feel that there is any kind of competition, in that sense. Perhaps what I said the weakness with IWGIA is that we are not big enough sometimes in those frameworks to, perhaps, make a big difference. For us, it is really very important that the kinds of networks in Europe, in the European context, are strengthened. I think NGOs in Denmark, while working in some way with indigenous peoples, have known about IWGIA, and if they consult us or ways that we work out and/or we contact them, so I don't know what cooperation you have in mind but ...

sv: It depends on particular issues, say, for instance, what's been happening in Botswana – that's very special, and it's very politically charged and extremely polarized, and I wondered, because I was aware of the fact that IWGIA also had a presence over there, in some capacity, and because of the controversy publicly, so many anthropologists have taken public positions on the issue and Survival has taken public positions on the issue and I don't know to what an extent that has actually augmented or exacerbated the problem, and I wondered how IWGIA was operating in that context. Did you find your efforts were being undermined by some of the ways in which the whole area/region has become so politically charged?

LG: I think Jens should speak here. You have been much more involved in the work.

JD: In that work I don't think we should discuss Botswana.

[Jens was showing political acumen here in not being drawn into discussing the situation in Botswana.]

sv: No.

JD: I don't think we should specify projects.

sv: No, you shouldn't, but this is just an example to suggest the kinds of tensions that might occur in particular parts of the world because so many ...

JD: I would say Botswana is the only case I know of where there really have been, as you say, kind of conflicts between organizations, between all organizations, indigenous and non-indigenous, it's a really conflicting case. I think it doesn't promote the case of the Bushmen to discuss that.

There are always conflicts and I think it's more important to work and cooperate instead, and I want to say that I'm not surprised that people don't know IWGIA but it says a lot about the public in general. It's not interested in, first, indigenous issues, secondly, they are not interested in international issues, and if you take the country around here, I know how many other times we have tried to get the press interested and the case is always, how many killed persons do you have? They might be interested in the tsunami but go out and look in the media because how much is there about the Andaman Islanders and the Nicobar Islanders or Ache – it says a lot about ... and it's not because IWGIA hasn't provided, I mean your book was widely distributed to the press here, how much were they interested, nothing at all. Have they been interested in the Picnas in Rwanda, no. They are interested in the monkeys, or what are they called – so that's one issue. The issue is not interesting and it's not a sexy issue, the sexy issue of the Tasaday in the Philippines, and these kinds of things. This is one reason; the second reason is that also international issues are not really interesting to people, UN issues, not for the press.

What sometimes bothers me and makes me a little bit irritated, I have to admit, is when I see a PhD written in the United States about indigenous peoples in international ... and they don't refer to IWGIA anywhere and my question is, is it my fault also, or is it bad research? I don't know, I don't have an answer to that, but I'm not trying to say it's not a problem because it is a problem. It is also a problem for IWGIA that it could be much better known, no doubt about that.

LG: That's true, but on the other hand, you said these were the Danish press in all this and to do that – it demands a lot of resources. It is an issue to say, OK, what is our main objective? Of course, we try as much as we can to bring the issue to the Danish media whatever the issue is. It is very, very difficult and because of that, if you really want to do something about media in Denmark, to reach their public and all this, you also need the resource to do that.

SV: For publicity ...

LG: For publicity, it needs a lot of effort to do that. In that sense it's much more than IWGIA can try and devote ... we try as much but first of all we are into a handicap is that all our documentation is in English and Spanish and even if everybody speaks English in Denmark ...

SV: How about in French too?

LG: A bit in French, yeah, and Hindi ...

JD: And Thai.

LG: But I think one of the issues that we have been discussing quite a lot during the last month is we have been trying to develop our publication and information strategy. How do we raise visibility about, not IWGIA, but the issue and about the documentation that we have? How do we reach the people that would be interested in the documentation and information that we have, and in the work that we do? For instance, how do we link our work in the regions, also to promote the visibility of the documentation using much more, for instance, this launch, relating some of our publications to some of the political processes in the country and related to some of their national processes? That, I think, we haven't invested much on that – this issue of raising visibility. And I wouldn't say only about IWGIA but about the issues and about the documentation that is available and it is an issue that we want to put much more resources on that, but I see that differently than just the public, I see, for me, it's more identifying which are the target groups we want to know about IWGIA's work, and this normally, in many cases, they're out in the countries where indigenous people live. And that is where we have to put our efforts, and I think we have had a lot of dialogue with the Danish Ministry of Foreign Affairs on that because we have to put efforts in place, I mean our priority is to put efforts there and not so much into the Danish public.

[These preceding paragraphs are extremely useful in enabling a clear sense of who IWGIA are, how they identify themselves and how they operate, i.e. primarily to ensure that indigenous peoples' voices are heard where they matter and stepping aside to make that happen rather than speaking for them. Then, playing an educational role with their documentation to create awareness and lobbying on behalf of indigenous peoples. IWGIA also has a clear sense of how to be effective in the tasks they undertake through the kinds of networks they build among governments and international organizations. These attributes offer us an understanding of the differences between the main international NGOs and the ways in which they can be distinguished. In terms of comparing the preceding discussion with Stephen Corry of Survival International with the current discussion under way with IWGIA, there are marked differences in how they choose to engage with the wider public, outside the indigenous realm.]

sv: I also note, and I may be wrong in this and you can tell me so, that one of the other characteristics of your approach internationally is to take a kind of softly, softly, gently, gently approach with government rather than a directly adversarial or more confrontational mode to engage with them, and that has its pros and cons, but that also, I think, distinguishes IWGIA, in some way,

[In addressing this issue I attempt to obtain a better understanding of the kinds of strategies IWGIA apply to their endeavour.]

JD: Yes, in some ways, not all. In the sense that I don't think we would criticize the government without being in touch with the indigenous organizations in that country. It doesn't make any sense to go farther than the indigenous if there isn't correspondence with indigenous peoples there. So, if we take the case of Bangladesh, for example, I think we have criticized the Bangladesh government, I have had the great honour of being called a terrorist by the Bangladesh government in Geneva. On the other hand we don't do it unless what we are saying and doing fits into the relevant strategies of the indigenous peoples. So that might be because indigenous peoples often have to be more soft and then ... but there are differences, of course, because in some cases they have been quite critical. In the case of the African governments, we have been very cautious and I think that we have reached, IWGIA has reached, what it has reached in Africa, because of the cautious approach. I mean, you can bang all the African governments on the heads for violating human rights and they don't listen any more and that has been, you could say, a soft approach. Obviously it hasn't in America, I don't think we have taken a soft approach.

[Here too we should note a point of contrast with what we can infer of strategy as enunciated earlier by Stephen Corry for SI. Of course, it should be noted that SI more often than not operates in areas where the indigenous population are not in a position to speak and act on their own behalf.]

LG: I wouldn't call it a soft approach. It's more, I think, and you have mentioned it, Jens, dialoguing with the indigenous peoples in the country, and also how the political situation and how we could promote best their interests with regard to political dialogue and in many cases and most of indigenous peoples, what they promote is really establishing a political dialogue and not a more confrontational approach, but in many cases we have been also supporting [a] more confrontational approach. We have been very much criticized by Indonesia, as we were in West Papua, East Timor ...

JD: East Timor, for years and years!

LG: Jens mentioned the issue of Africa. I don't know about this *soft, soft* idea, but if I can take one example, the issue of the whole discussion on the Declaration and the position of the African governments, when the African government, unexpectedly, suddenly stopped everything, postponed the final decision. So there were two possibilities, take a very confrontational position and denounce the African government, or take a more soft approach, and say can we establish a dialogue with the African government, can we really convince them that there's some framework of all these rights in Africa and that Africa has its own understanding and its own practice on implementation of these rights and which, not IWGIA, but together with indigenous peoples from Africa, their networks, and other NGOs. That approach, and I think it was an approach that really helped, at the very end, to get the African government on board. Of course, there are many other issues that play also – but I think with a very confrontational approach, debunking African governments and complaining about their human rights positions, I don't think we could have moved, and I think it was positive that the African governments took the position to postpone it because, I think, they were forced to reflect on the Declaration. Perhaps, if they had been positive and just accepted without anything ... I think [it] gives us another possibility, not only IWGIA, but indigenous peoples' networks in Africa. Really, to establish a dialogue – which kind of rights, which kinds of people are we talking about. And somehow create a better base of understanding of this declaration and the rights included in that declaration. So I see soft approach and soft approach, what do you want to achieve, and that's the issue, I think, for us is that *can we move things forward* [*my emphasis*].

JD: And I think too, international relations are about creating neutral understanding. If you want to do that, if you want to achieve any kind of compromise or any progress, you need somehow to have a soft approach. At least a non-confrontational approach, otherwise you don't really, I mean, when you asked about international relations, I see why do you go into divided nations if you are not interested in creating some kind of understanding. And if you start criticizing me, then of course I'm not so happy with you, so it's a bit difficult to create any understanding and get any results.

[This is another aspect of strategy that distinguishes IWGIA from other international NGOs.]

LG: And I think you mentioned, when you presented how the idea of this book came about. I think even in the UN, it's one of the things that was very clear from the very beginning, [the] working group on indigenous populations, the importance of this networking among indigenous peoples and listening to each other's situations and establishing these kinds of linkages among themselves. But also, with governments, in the sense that many of the indigenous representatives who participate in the session normally, perhaps, they don't have points of entry to their governmental institutions and normally, when they are participating in this international process, this is the very first time that they have an entry point to their governments, governmental delegations, and I think this is really something that they can see having pivotal value, because in many cases, most of the cases, I think they are listened to. And they can have an impact there that they cannot have at home. They feel much stronger there and they have much more power, in many ways, there. Even their views, I think, they are taken much more into consideration by these governmental delegates and, I think, it has helped in many, many ways to develop further dialogues at home that, perhaps, would have never been possible if people had not brought those issues and had been at the international arena.

SV: Yes, except with moving forward with the African government, it was not possible with the other four nations that stood apart. They, the four ...

LG: Canada, Australia and New Zealand ...

SV: And the US. Even internationally, with your success, and how diplomatically you are able to work in that forum, with those four countries, you couldn't make any headway, I suppose, towards getting them on side?

JD: No.

LG: You should count also, frankly, these four countries, they have very, very strong indigenous movement[s] so it's much more, I think it's more related to national political processes than, I think, in the case of the African governments, I don't know if IWGIA is so clear on that, but I think their concerns, they will frame in their own countries, but they were not related to specific national issues, in many ways. Of course, there was the way they interpreted their rights there, but while Canada, New Zealand and Australia, I think they are very much related to national politics and national interest, and their own dialogue of their own confrontations with indigenous peoples in those countries. I don't know if you agree [*aside to Jens*]?

JD: Maybe the issues are more political in those four countries than in the African, political in the sense, party political things. I don't think it's party political in Africa. I think it's a nationalist thing, so the question is different. Just in Australia now, they've turned a hundred and eighty degrees and they want to recognize the Declaration, with the new government.

LG: It's going to happen in Canada.

JD: In Canada now, they have a conservative government, you saw it with the Carter administration, in [the] US, and as soon as Ronald Reagan took over they took a completely different position on indigenous issues in the UN and the Organization of American States. I don't think you see these kinds of things, not to the same extent, in Africa, because more or less they agree all of them, that they hate the issue if you put it up in a confrontational manner. So, no, you couldn't move these four countries.[1]

I was part of the dialogue with many of the African governments and I would say, of course you could say, they could have participated in the process much before, but, I think, some of their concerns are related, I mean they were really issues but it was related, for instance, of course they are from young countries. The issue of borders in Africa is seen as a big issue. There were those concerns we were raising, which, I think, were fair in many senses, but I think they were also open to understand, in the very end. They were not very, very worried and there were very few and that was also a reason it was a success. I think it was, in fact, only two or three African governments who really had problems, who at the beginning they really were able to kidnap the African group. But at the very end, of course, because they were so few, and I think it was Botswana, it was Nigeria and perhaps Kenya, a bit also in that group. But the others, they couldn't see so many problems, and they were not so concerned about it.

SV: I was quite puzzled by New Zealand because it seemed it was quite contrary to the way in which the government presents its efforts with Māori in the country, where there does seem to be a consensus –

we're going to make every effort to construct this as a bicultural nation; that there is a treaty process under way that addresses past wrongs and makes reparations and yet, internationally, it seems when there is an opportunity to take a stand ... To say this is where we stand, and New Zealand has taken a contrary stand internationally on so many matters, where it could have toed the line set by the US, whether it's on nuclear policy, whether it's on Iraq and Afghanistan, they've taken a completely different stance, and yet, on this matter, I could not understand why they just became part of the crowd, and not a distinctive New Zealand position, so I was surprised.

JD: The same with Canada. Canada has a much more progressive policy at home than they have internationally, in relation to indigenous issues.

LG: I think my interpretation of that, I think it is very much related to how that declaration can be used in a legal system ... and this is what worries them. The legal system gives the possibility to make jurisprudence.

JD: I think in the case of Canada, it's about mining companies. Big Canadian mining companies not operating in Canada but operating in other countries and they are afraid because a lot of these Canadian mining companies are operating on indigenous claimed land. That is what worries them really.

LG: I think in all four countries, the US is a bit different, but in general, I think, that they have the issue of land – a natural resource. It was not self-determination, they have a long argumentation on those issues, but at the very end it was the issue of legal advice, many of those countries they have long legal cases on the issue. Of course, the Declaration is a dangerous instrument in their legal context, and how those indigenous peoples could use the Declaration in that context, so this also is a reason why they have been very, very clear in their statements explaining how they moved – that this is not applicable in their countries and how to protect themselves from using those instruments that are based for future jurisprudence.

SV: So, where to after the Declaration?

[I attempt to steer the discussion forward at this stage towards considerations of the future.]

LG: I see, very clear, three periods in the whole discussion of indigenous peoples in the UN. You have the first ten years, I would call it from

1985 to 1995, in which a lot of these indigenous peoples were coming
to the UN, bringing their cases, bringing indigenous peoples into all
these UN issues. From 1995 to 2005/06, say, it's the standard setting
of their whole process, the discussion of the Declaration, the issue of
recognizing these facts that it was moved from all this information
that came to the UN, to a more standard setting discussion, a bigger
frame or UN legal frame to put all those claims on. And, of course, now,
it's how do we use that. Where, how, do we put this in practice which
we are starting now, and it's not only in regard to the Declaration, I
think the issue of implementation, it's also with regard to all of the
international mechanisms now that exist with regard to indigenous,
the special rapporteur, or even the Permanent Forum. The Permanent
Forum has been meeting six years and I think it's the same tendency.
I think the first six years has been a lot of coming, with a lot of recommendations, a lot of statements, and I think now, everything has
been set and recommended. How do you secure that, so that this goes
farther and is implemented and has an impact, on the indigenous
peoples? The same, with the special rapporteur, he has come with a lot
of recommendations, but how can we go farther? And now the Declaration, which can be the legal frame also for all these mechanisms, which
kind of monitoring can be done which will really protect and promote
indigenous people? I think there are many, many possibilities and, of
course, there are many levels we can see from an international arena,
in the UN, what can we do? Regarding the UN, for instance, now when
I think one of their following or implementing issues, is the establishment of a new mechanism, under the Human Rights Council, to
monitor and advise the Council on how to better promote implementation of those rights. With regards to the special rapporteur, exactly the
same, how do we secure now, with the Declaration, with a legal frame
some of the recommendations from the special rapporteur? The Council can be more proactive to assist governments to really move forward
in the regional arena. You have regional policies of the African Commissioner. In taking the first good step forward to communicate with
the African Commissioner you should recognize the validity of the Declaration within the frame of the commission's work. I think those are
the first steps of implementation, and there is the Intra-American Commission, exactly the same now, there are indigenous peoples from Latin
America filing many, many cases every year, in [the] Intra-American
Commission. I think the Declaration needs to be used there. I think the

issue is how many references do you have to the Declaration? As many references, as much as can be used in the international indigenous frameworks. At the national level, I see the Declaration as a dialogue tool, a political tool, for most of indigenous peoples. *For most of the indigenous peoples in the world the Declaration is not a legal document, it is a political document [my emphasis].* And the political document also means it is to be used for open dialogue spaces and in various specific issues, and the issue of consultation, with regard to development projects, in those countries, now they will give indigenous a foot to really, to demand their rights with the endorsement of the international community. I don't think it will be the governments who bring them the Declaration. What is needed now is to identify entry points in the different countries, how do you contextualize the Declaration? I think it is very important. I think it is an issue I think we learned also from the process with the African government. I think it is very, very important that the Declaration is contextualized in the different countries, in the different settings, because I think it will open many, many doors for indigenous peoples. But perhaps it is a positive approach.

[It is necessary to put this extended response into context. IWGIA are evidently thinking about the future in terms of the forums within which they operate and the kinds of processes that characterize such domains. And hence their response is abstract and legislative rather than specifically directed to particular indigenous groups and how the Declaration can impact on them.]

sv: Maybe we should talk about the obstacles.

jd: The obstacles! We all know about the obstacles.

lg: Many obstacles. Not easy, and I think it's important to see step by step some of them ... to communicate from the African Commission, what does it mean? But on the other hand it opened a lot of possibilities of going farther.

jd: Denmark has a nice policy but do they implement it? No.

In some respects they have a toolkit, in some respects it is very detailed and concrete, do they do anything? No. So, how do you get them to do something? The first step is, OK, you have a nice policy, but often you have this nice policy, you could say, against government's will because it is, somehow, forced to do it by parliament in the case of Denmark, maybe by public opinion, but in other countries, I don't know. So, what do we do to get this done and the same with the

Declaration? The Declaration, in my opinion, should have an impact on the World Bank. The World Bank has something they call free, prior and informed consultation, and now you have a declaration that talks about consent. So how can you get the World Bank to change their policy? Well, they will not just change it but, let's say that the World Bank, and the other agencies, they might have nice policies and they might even, like the African Commission, adopt the Declaration. But will they do anything? No. These government institutions, they don't do something under pressure because the issue is, none of these issues are popular. You don't become elected on your policy on indigenous things. Go down the street and ask a member of parliament, what is your opinion about indigenous ... you become elected on local politics, not on these kinds of issues. So, there needs to be someone like IWGIA, or indigenous peoples' own organizations, that tell government, 'no, you have to do it'. But also telling them what to do, I think. So, and that's a challenge. It's on the country level and it's on the more international level.

[This is a useful illustration of the strategies that an organization like IWGIA could bring to bear within a national context.]

LG: And the good thing now, with the Declaration, is that you have other mechanisms in place also, that have been there before the Declaration. And now you have other mechanisms in place that I can see have much more meaning on the work of the Permanent Forum. For instance, now with the Declaration, because, as you mentioned, with regard to UN agencies, I think now the Permanent Forum has a very important role to follow. To really make an impact in the agencies, which have part of their work, on really reviewing their policies and their programmes according to the Declaration, and in there I see an enormous value of the Permanent Forum, for instance. And I think there are some things that can be moved at that level. At the level of national government, I think, there are a lot of obstacles. But indigenous peoples, I think, during the whole process of the Declaration, also really tried to show government what is the value of the Declaration. The Declaration has some values that are both for indigenous peoples and government. That by recognizing those rights, governments or states are not losing power in that sense. That there are some benefits for the whole community, and I think this message in the whole Declaration work, on the whole implementation, I think it's very, very

Venkateswar

important to try and admit because I think it's better to see the benefit, to see the Declaration as a base for a new dialogue based on international human rights standards, that we benefit both parts, rather than seeing only benefit for indigenous peoples.

JD: As Lola said, it's a critical document. And the political situation varies a lot from country to country. And one thing is that where, in Botswana, where indigenous peoples make up a tiny minority. Another thing is in India, where, of course, the dialogue is completely different. And if the Naga people start to go, oh no, we have the right of becoming, creating our own state, then you have lost the first round of the discussion with New Delhi. It's also a learning process for indigenous peoples, how can they use it? Or how can they misuse it? Or lose the discussion, and the number of examples of indigenous peoples who have lost the discussion simply because they don't have the right understanding of their own situation.

LG: I think with regard to implementation, now we talk about the Declaration, but you have, in fact, many countries, in all parts of the world, but somehow they have not very proper laws about indigenous peoples or they are not implemented.

SV: I know if they were, then you wouldn't need ...

LG: You have the Philippines, you have Latin America, even I'm thinking about Australia, as a different case. But yeah, OK now, they have adopted, at a national level, the Declaration, but how are we going to implement it? Even in many countries in Latin America, you have it in Ecuador, you have many of the components of the Declaration, even in constitution, but, for instance, they have not developed further laws, or there are other laws that come on top of that, mining laws, or whatever, they're not ... the issue of implementation. This is what I mean, they can put it, frame it now, into the Declaration but I think really the challenge for all of us who are involved in indigenous organizations is, really, now you have the frameworks in place, you have the international framework, first of all, but in many places you have also national frameworks and the gap is implementation and, I think, that is a challenge for the indigenous movement in the years to come, and of course for IWGIA. I think it's very important to have the context in place and I think they have different entry points but perhaps from our side it is more to identify entry points in some countries because we work all over the world and really try to identify what can we do from here.

SV: Right at the beginning, you said that it was a weakness but then you focused on indigenous peoples and you talked, it was interesting, I was listening to you identify IWGIA as a human rights organization, but issues of human rights and social justice spill over, beyond indigenous groups to other people living in close proximity to them, and you see that particularly around the Amazon area, and the landless movements over there, and indigenous peoples against logging and soya farming and all that. How do you see that context, in terms of advancing the rights of ...?

LG: Marginalized?

SV: Yes, because what I've come to recognize in the Andaman Islands is in all these years of focusing just on the indigenous groups and rightfully so, that especially after the tsunami, there's important issues of social justice that apply to the settler communities who are also dispossessed and marginalized, in so many ways, and some of them are also as much cast out by the mainstream political structure, in terms of obtaining some of those basic human rights. And my conundrum, my dilemma, in this context, is how do I go on to address these issues, I can't address them one in exclusion of the other. Does IWGIA have a position on this? And I am sure you see it yourselves, that you are addressing something in one region and you know of something else happening but that's not your area of focus, how do you deal with this?

LG: I think it is a difficult question, I think because we, from our side of things, we have also been raising this issue.

SV: Jens mentioned that IWGIA's working with non-indigenous groups and I thought that was very interesting. And it is probably quite new that you're doing ... but it's important.

LG: Yes, it is.

JD: In a way, you could compare it, a little bit, with a discussion on women's rights and gender rights, I mean you have poor and rich women while promoting something only for women, when you have poor men.

SV: Yes.

JD: But still, sometimes you have to focus your efforts and see that where there are people who are discriminated against, or in less favoured positions, and that other people who are also in less favourable positions are not the focus, but you need to focus on something, people with a certain kind of sickness or indigenous peoples and so on. So I think in that way it is fairly simple. I mean, you can't focus on

Venkateswar

everything, but the other thing is, of course, that you need to take a specific position in a specific situation, and I know I've come to ask in Argentina, where this has been an issue, that you have settlers there who have stayed there, I don't know for how long, and you can't really deal with indigenous rights without also considering the situation and the effects on the other people. And I think … follow the situation in northern Norway with the Saami people there. Where they have really fought for the Saami rights but the day when it comes to discussing practical issues, of course, I need to know that my neighbour is doing exactly the same for me, s/he is Norwegian. So that you have rights that do not limit the rights of the other person. On the other hand, in ninety-nine per cent of all cases, it is indigenous peoples who don't have the rights to see as other poor peoples. Because indigenous peoples are maybe nomads or they may be hunters and gatherers, but in the very concrete situation, you need to take in too that there are other people who are as poor as you are, for example.

LG: I think it is a very conflictual situation. I know Alejandro [another IWGIA staff member working in South America] has worked with the Afro-American community in Colombia, in some cases, in the same situation as indigenous peoples, and the way that we have worked has tried to promote a dialogue and understanding among the Afro-community, of course, they have the same rights and, of course, not to compete in that sense and see the benefit of recognizing their rights to land, exactly the same as indigenous peoples' land. I mean, the complication, I think, in general, is there's a big discussion, I have friends there discussing the issue with many of our partners. It is our experience that we are with the losers, indigenous peoples in many cases, are in an even weaker situation.

JD: I think the situation in Chittagong Hill Tracts is a typical case, it may be extreme but is still typical. I just saw in some emails, in Chittagong yesterday, that there now some of the Chakmas have been pushed off their land and they have certainly been settled in Bengal. And, I think, it is a more typical case than the case of indigenous peoples, to get rights that the others don't have. *As a matter of fact, it is also a matter of not letting five per cent of the cases determine a hundred per cent situation [my emphasis].*

LG: And I would say that because we defend indigenous peoples' rights it does not mean that we are opposed to the others' rights. That should be very, very clear, because that's not the approach. But perhaps, from our perspective, from our work, that we support the promotion of indigenous peoples' rights. And in the cases where there are conflicts in the specific cases, we try to see the ways of establishing some dialogue and understanding between the parts, because [when] you support one you are not against the other.

sv: How do you decide who to support and who to work with?

lg: I would start the way that IWGIA ... and then perhaps, you'll have more historical background, from our network entrants. So, if somebody from IWGIA went to their country, to the areas and so identify first of all who are the organizations, the situation, the political situation of the country, and then the problems of the indigenous peoples there, which kind of organization, where they are meeting with different people and to make an assessment on what the situation is, and what were the indigenous problems in that context, and see and talk to them and identify what could IWGIA do for supporting that context. In some issues, we couldn't do anything, but in some issues we could support, whether it's more support within institutional building of the organization or if it was, of course, abuses of human rights, how do we link it with our international work documenting the situation in our publications. So, first of all, I think, our basic point of departure was really contextualized on an assessment of the different countries and the actors in the country. I think, during the last many years, we have also started some long-term relationships with different indigenous organizations, which means we believe that it is not just ad hoc support but we commit to some kind of support so we can have some time perspective also. That they are able to, and of course we cannot support everybody, so we take the point of departure where we start with small kind of support and we see if we can develop and see together if this can be developed into something more. In some cases, the organizations, the indigenous organizations, the non-indigenous are static, so the organizations that we are working very close to, but they have come into crisis. We have more or less withdrawn or we can try to support through the crisis. But in some cases, our support has not developed into more long-term relationships and [on] the other hand, in other cases we have had now for many years with different organizations in the different regions a very long-term support. What we have tried also, we have discussed and we have different seminars about which kind of partnership IWGIA has with these indigenous organizations, with those [with] whom we had a long-term commitment, what is IWGIA's role?

What are the expectations? What is our expectation of them? Because, in that sense, we don't feel that we are – we don't want to be considered simply donors but are part of a relationship that we can play a role and can play another role. So, I don't know, how can I say, that we choose this specific one against another. No, I think, the same as with rights, because we only support those, perhaps is more limited to our possibilities and the ideas of, perhaps of developing long-term, expanding our support to one organization so they can develop some work, instead of, perhaps, just disseminating small support everywhere. So, can you add something [turning to Jens]?

JD: You can't make, well, we've had the discussion with DANIDA [the Danish government development organization that funds a range of interventions across the world]. And they also want us to put up some logical, I mean, they want us to put it into a logical frame, how do you choose? And you can't do that. You have to take into consideration your own organization's history, well, what you have by tradition, what is your network? What are you good at doing? What is your capacity? Where are your priorities? And then a little bit but it's by accident, and you say someone walks through the door, oh, that one seems very nice and it's a very relevant thing, and it may be, also it's, it's a group of persons, or theme that no other one takes, there are a lot of mainstream projects among indigenous peoples, where IWGIA would rather say, but why don't you try to approach that and that donor agency, or something like that, if it's a question of money, instead of IWGIA going in, and in other cases, I think, we have been explorative. I want to mention the networking thing. In some cases we have seen, oh, this is something we should do, I mean, let's try and investigate what we can do there for my own instance. I recall how we got into Russia, for example, and I think there we did an investigation thing, and IWGIA was the first organization really working closely with the indigenous organizations and that was a way to develop in Russia. In other cases, like the Cordillera Peoples Alliance, in the Philippines, we published a book that the leader of that organization read and she got in touch with IWGIA and it was nothing to do with Asia, it was nothing to do with missions. So, it's not always logical but I'm sure there's a pattern in it.

LG: I think you can use a lot of objective criteria in many ways that, at the very end, also the subjective criteria, are very important.

JD: Exactly, that's what it is about.

LG: And that is what it is about. You can, of course, say what is the objective criteria and put them all there, but at the very end also they assess, what you make of the leaders. There are all these more subjective criteria, of course, play a role and then their way to build capacity, and build trust between IWGIA and the organization we are working with, and all those things, the subjective criteria, of course, play a role.

sv: Do people approach you out of the blue?

LG: In some cases, yes.

sv: And you follow the same process by sending somebody to look at the context, explore it and ...

LG: Not now, everywhere. I mean, now we have much more defined programmes and I'm saying that because, of course, IWGIA has developed quite a lot in the last fifteen years, and also approach, support our programmes, and we are now much more developed into some kind of strategies with defined original priorities, the thematic priorities. We are not supporting ...

sv: Any and everyone.

LG: Any and everyone and, for instance, normally we do not support specific projects related to how, on issues like this, and it's not because it's not important, because we think IWGIA, perhaps there are many others who do much better work than us in this kind of support. So, we have, of course, our priorities of land rights, the issue of capacity-building or the institutional building of indigenous organizations, political dialogue, so we have those priorities.

JD: But sometimes, what we have seen, OK, this is becoming interesting, like urbanization in indigenous people's living in urban areas, so we take, you could say, become proactive on it by publishing, maybe approaching indigenous youth organizations, or something, then we have to come to give priority and look at our priorities, and give priority, because we think this is an important issue in the future. So this kind of thing, you could say, they are straight initiated by IWGIA.

LG: What is given, I think the difference between fifteen years ago and now and perhaps our work now with many of our partners, I think, our side, we try to identify, are there some trends? What are some, for instance, issues that result with respect to poverty and indigenous people, and we were one of the first who brought the issue of the poverty concept and indigenous peoples, of tourism and indigenous peoples, of urbanization or the whole issue of communication, you know, promoting, somehow, this creation of communication networks on indigenous peoples and, of course, through the work that we are

Venkateswar

doing with the regional partners, identifying some areas [where] we can see a trend on an important issue. And [where] indigenous peoples in the countries also somehow see this as a big issue, an important issue, in these contexts.

JD: And there is, of course, a personal thing that there are some people we like and some people we like less and there are some people that we have become acquainted with. This morning I wrote a letter to a person in Greenland. We were students together and he, later on, became president of Inuit Peoples Circumpolar conference and of course we have known each other for thirty, forty years. Of course that makes him easy, we have cooperated since that conversation was started in 1977, thirty years ago. So, of course, you don't just ... in a way you know each other. Maybe you disagree sometimes, maybe you agree, but at least it is a continuous relationship. And we have some of these long-term relationships with some organizations, the Russians, the Saami, the Inuit, there are some of the Peruvians here, and the Philippines and so on. It's also that we communicate very good. We understand each other. I think that's important, I mean personal things we shouldn't underestimate.

LG & SV: Agree.

JD: There are people that we don't trust and there are people that we trust to the end.

SV: You work with the Danish government? I would imagine that, given your presence in the UN, does that require ...

LG: Depends what you think working closely with the Danish government means. I mean, we receive most of our money from the Danish government.

SV: Does that mean you have to toe a certain Danish political line, or ...?

LG: Not at all. I would say the contrary. I think for us, in connection with the Danish government and with DANIDA, the relevant agency, much more give us an entry point to make a difference, make an impact on them, much more than they can do on us. I'm not talking only about the Danish government, I would say the Nordic government, we receive money also from Norway. We have never received any kinds of conditions. On the contrary, the first I have heard that, they got money from Australia for something. So, it was to ... we wrote a book about it.

JD: It was about Hitchcock, land rights. That was funded partly by the Australian government, the other part was IWGIA. They never fund IWGIA any more.

SV: No certain Danish political lines?

LG: No.

JD: Not directly but, of course, they have their agenda. Like, you should support indigenous women. So we have a discussion every year, why we are not so active with indigenous women. They sometimes, you could say, express happiness or they support that we work a lot with indigenous peoples in Africa because now this is government policy. On the other hand, there is a lot of action in Latin America which the Danish government did not really appreciate but they have accepted it and in the end, I think, that was part of their change in policy on some of the Latin American countries, in Nicaragua, Bolivia, which a lot of other governments support. So I don't think, for some years we have a discussion once a year with a Danish minister ... or with [an] indigenous minister of foreign affairs, it always ended that we agreed to disagree on basically everything.

LG: The impact is more on our side on the contrary, they know that, of course, somehow they support us. I think it is, somehow, recognition of our work. So, we have some doors open and many people in the ministry and they are open to listen to us. So, I think, it's more that way than the other way around. It is not because they demand support [for] the Danish policies on this and that. On the contrary, I see more our work in many ways we have those possibilities to play a role of a little bit of a watchdog.

SV: Does your work, did IWGIA's work, influence the government's timber certification policy and all that?

LG: No, OK, we have been to talk to Sille [another IWGIA staff member] about it, Sille has been the one who has been involved in that. We were part of our working group, established by the Environmental Ministry, on the issue. Last year, I think, the whole of last year, BBF and WWF brought people to discuss the issue and to develop some kind of a guideline of certification, and one of the issues we were there to promote was indigenous peoples' rights on ILO 169 and all this. That it was at least their guidelines. So, in that sense, I don't know where it is now but I think it impacts the policies. But I think we have different entry points. But, of course, in many cases, I mean, we are kind of working on all the issues and we haven't been directly involved on that issue. But we saw we were invited to follow that working group, the kind of entry point or some possibility at that time.

SV: Thank you very much.

[The repeated use of the phrase 'entry point' is indicative of IWGIA strategy, always alert to the possibilities of augmenting or building on their interventions with indigenous groups or seeking to promote them even if only through indirect means. Or their willingness to both dialogue with governments/states as well as support or build capacity at the grass roots.

This wide-ranging interview with Lola Garcia-Alix and Jens Dahl offered a comprehensive understanding of the various ways in which IWGIA positions itself with respect to indigenous peoples, as well as the strategies that the organization uses to address their situation in a variety of contexts. The presence of two people jointly responding to the questions that I posed worked to enhance the quality of the ensuing discussion, providing a means for each to confirm or extend the other's reply, thereby resulting in a much more satisfying discussion.]

Interview 3: discussion with Ida Nicolaison, Nordic Institute, Copenhagen, 13 December 2007

The UN Permanent Forum on Indigenous Issues (UNPFII) came into existence when the UN General Assembly voted for its establishment in July 2000. It was to function as an advisory body to the UN Economic and Social Council and conceived as a subsidiary organ to it. Hence it was situated at one of the highest levels of the UN hierarchy.

Ida Nicolaison was a member of the UNPFII and was nominated by the Danish government to that position. She served two terms within the forum after it was first convened in 2002. She has long experience of working within the UN system and with a variety of indigenous groups in Africa and South-East Asia. She is also a Senior Research Fellow at the Nordic Institute of Asian Studies, where I met her when I visited Copenhagen in December 2007. This interview with her provided a means to look more closely at processes within the United Nations.

SV: Ida, I want to ask you about the Declaration, which has just been passed. Where do you go to from here? What happens in terms of the UN processes once that document has been passed?

IN: It's evident that the passing of the Declaration is really a major step forward, it's a major step forward for indigenous peoples because they have a document now that they can use whenever negotiating with their government, I think that's one of the important things. And the other thing is, and you asked me what in the UN processes, and of course when you have a declaration, it is also an important document within the UN system, within the UN agencies, it's useful in UN agencies to have this kind of blue stamp that they can work on, and of course for interaction between UN agencies and states. But you asked me specifically, I guess it's because I'm a Permanent Forum member, I have been so from the beginning, it has been kind of a very interesting job to set up a Permanent Forum within the UN system because it's different from all other organizations within the UN system, and for us, of course, what we will deal with in the coming years is using this in our efforts to promote indigenous rights. The UN declaration is not, so to speak, the work of the UN Permanent Forum, I mean it's the outcome of a process which is almost twenty-five years old and it has had its own process, its own life within the High Commission on Human Rights, and that is just one of the agencies that the Permanent Forum deals with. As you know we deal with, we all do, I don't know how many agencies in the UN system, but our mandate is threefold: to advise, main thing is to advise all UN agencies, and therefore the Declaration is the blue stamp on what we do. Where do we go from now, if you want specifically, you asked me for the Declaration or about the Permanent Forum work?

sv: Both.

in: For us it would be to incorporate the Declaration in our work, but I would say that we have, so to speak, done that all the time, anticipating that this was accepted, and also as we would advise the UN agencies on the indigenous peoples' rights, I mean that's kind of obvious. I think the thing that the issues that the Permanent Forum is facing now are, it would be a very interesting process from now because there has to be a major shift in my view, in the forum's work, and we first had to set up the organization, which was difficult, we didn't have funding in the beginning, we had to find the work processes, it's new in that we have all the agencies whom we advise, we have all the states, at least the closer agencies have indigenous issues, and then we have all the indigenous representatives who come as observers. Now *we have to juggle what is actually our mandate, which is to advise the agencies as experts, and then the expectations of, last time more than 2000 registered to come, [those] who consider this their international parliament and expect the right to speak [my emphasis]*, that's why we have sixty or seventy side events, God knows, more. So we have to juggle this, you think it's a detour, but I don't think this is a detour ...

sv: No, no.

Venkateswar

IN: It means the expectations from indigenous peoples to be listened to were all there, problems that they have from wherever they live, and all the various problems, very different kind of situations they are living in, therefore somewhat different interests and problems, so we have to take that in and that of course is the stuff that you work from, but they expect us also to come up with recommendations on their specific issues, and there being an enormous pressure on the forum to continuously come up with recommendations to agencies. Now in six years we have already come up with six hundred, I don't know, but we have come up with an enormous amount of recommendations to the agencies, we come up with so many in fact that they can't cope with them. The key thing for the forum in the future, in my view, will be to reduce the number of recommendations, that will be politically difficult with the activism of the indigenous peoples because *each group, if you come from Peru or if you come from Siberia, if you come from New Zealand, you want to see, you want to justify also to your group that you represent, that you made a difference, and there is an imprint of what comes out of the forum's work that reflects the concerns your particular group have* [*my emphasis*]. And then what the forum should do is that all these recommendations funnel into workable avenues for the agencies, that they have the manpower and keep on the interest to work for indigenous peoples, and that means that it has to be manageable for them. It's not that we don't have people that want to do these things, you may or you may not, there are actually a lot of good people in the UN system, but there is limit to what they can do because they have a lot of other concerns, each agency has many other concerns, for the indigenous people, and that will be the really hard thing, to focus, *so the key thing is to focus, on the monitoring, on the recommendation that we have and in that respect also the Declaration ...* [*my emphasis*]. And how that can be done, a main part to the forum is that if we had funds available, I think that we should work much more on a regional level, we have talked about that from day one, you know, one possibility was that the forum kind of rotates, it has a backdrop that a number of agencies wouldn't turn up, that other regions would feel slighted, all that kind of thing, but what we have had is professional, so far in Greenland and in China, and that's one way where we have a presence, but *if we had funding we could do much more, on pushing issues at a regional and national level, which we don't, so the thing is we can only advise agencies to start implementing and monitoring the things that we have recommended, that they follow up* [*my emphasis*]. Does that explain some of the, some of what ...?

sv: What seems to emerge from here, what seems very clear, is the issue of funding. Can you talk a little bit about how the Permanent Forum is funded and why its funding is so constrained?

IN: Funding is constrained to the whole UN system, I mean you all have this idea of why don't the UN do this and that and the other. Funding is a permanent problem for all UN agencies, and one of the things is of course it is costly to run a UN system because you have to have the collaboration between so many states, the things like all documents have to be translated into six languages, so that kind of thing makes it expensive, but it's definitely underfunded, and *indigenous issues is just one little corner of the big world* [*my emphasis*], peacekeeping and general development and Millennium Development Goals and all the other things ... so we are underfunded, we have a budget that allows us to have a small secretariat, I think now with five people.

sv: In Geneva?

IN: No, it's in the UN.

sv: OK, it's in New York.

IN: It's in New York, and we have funds for a small secretariat, and we have funds for an annual session, which is incidentally the biggest meeting that is held in the UN – you have participated?

sv: No, I have a friend who does, who went once.

IN: It's the biggest meeting ever in the UN history.

sv: My goal is maybe next year, after the Declaration comes out.

IN: So, that is basically what we have, then we have within the UN system the voluntary funds, which means the friendly governments can give us extra contributions and a few governments have, including the Danish, I have to say, and a few other governments, the Norwegians, we have a few governments, and they give us a little bit of money, and that is the only money we have, for instance to allow our chair or others of us to travel for meetings with agencies or states during and between sessions. It's a very small budget we ... there isn't enough money in it for us to have a workshop, we can't even fund a workshop, we get special funding for one technical workshop every year specifically from the general budget in the socio-economic council, which leads up to the topics we are discussing, so we started out particularly on data collection, we had technical workshops, but that's all that we have.

sv: In an ideal world, if the Permanent Forum did receive the funds it needed, and since we are in the business of making dreams, what would it be able to do that it's not able to do now?

IN: Well, I would think, like I said before, it would be extremely useful if we had more regional and national presence, you know, that we would be able to travel and have meetings with agencies, states and with indigenous peoples in various parts of the world. Now, there are a number of conferences, that kind of thing, which is convened by the agencies, special agencies can do so, say world intellectual property or UNDP or FAO, it's mainly been some agencies that have been specifically interested in indigenous issues, the UN Habitat has done that, then some NGOs are well funded, you are familiar with IWGIA who are funded with Danish money, who have run workshops, it's been mainly capacity-building workshops for indigenous peoples. But I think *it would be immensely useful if the forum could bring together at a regional/national level the UN agencies with indigenous peoples and state representatives and say, here we are in Malaysia, in Peru, wherever, let us see what are the issues, how is the Declaration implemented, how is it with mother tongue, education, how is it with, you know, are indigenous people treated in a equal way with citizens, what are the special needs, and that is where one could push things* [my emphasis], the polished halls in New York or Geneva are very far away from reality in the Amazon rainforest, or you are living up on the top of the gas drums, of oilfields in Siberia or wherever you are ...

SV: Thank you.

The convening of UNPFII in 2002 has been perceived as a major political milestone in the history of international indigenous activism. The brief interview with Ida offers a somewhat different perspective on what UN agencies can achieve, despite the many expectations regarding its role, as well as the constraints and limitations under which they operate.

Commentary

Editor's note: Teanau Tuiono, a Māori activist and a participant in the Aotearoa/New Zealand section, was chosen as a commentator for this chapter to add an indigenous perspective on the preceding discussions derived from a location within a settler nation combined with his own ongoing familiarity as a participant at numerous international forums. Emma Hughes, on the other hand, responds to Teanau's comments and engages with the preceding discussions by drawing on her experience of the Nubian situation within the very different post-colonial context of North Africa. Both sets of commentaries augment our understanding of the role of INGOs like SI and IWGIA as perceived through other lenses.

Teanau Tuiono

One of the things I try to do when I meet other indigenous peoples is to see what kind of connection we have between us. We call this *whanaungatanga* here, which means in English 'to make like family', we like to look for *whakapapa* (geneaology) links, and if possible to do it *kanohi ki te kanohi* (face to face). Because by and large I won't have close *whakapapa* connections to, say, an indigenous Masai from Africa I would look for other ways that my situation, my people, are connected to that person and to their people.

I looked at the transcripts with IWGIA, Survival International and Ida Nicolaison from the UNPFII. I think all of them raise some valid points. When talking about indigenous organizations, for me, the organization has to be run by and for indigenous organizations. So although both Survival International and IWGIA do extremely crucial work, I would not classify them as indigenous organizations. Why make this distinction? There are probably many theses out there about self-determining spaces and the need to empower the authentic indigenous voice, etc. I think it's important because I like to hear it from the horse's mouth if possible. When it is not possible that is where the non-indigenous indigenous advocacy organizations play a crucial role, and here I'm drawing from my own limited experience of working in the international arena.

1 Connecting indigenous peoples across the language divide One of the things that I have noticed is that indigenous peoples, when working in the international arena, gravitate towards others who speak the same language, more so if you are, for example, in the Commonwealth countries. So peoples living in Canada, the USA, Australia and New Zealand tend to be drawn together, and then outside of that those whom we can communicate with in English. You can see this, for example, in the organizing of WIPCE,[2] at least the last one I went too. It is predominantly English-speaking indigenous peoples. Although over the years I have met dozens of indigenous peoples from Latin America, I keep in close contact only with those who can also speak English. Indigenous peoples who are bilingual or multilingual in the four common languages of communication (English, French, Spanish and Russian) are crucial bridges and links between peoples. Non-indigenous groups who have this capability are crucial in enabling us to connect the dots, and I'm thinking about groups like DOCIP[3] (Indigenous Peoples' Centre for Documentation, Research and Information), a non-indigenous organization which does support work for indigenous peoples at the UN.

2 Dominance of English-speaking indigenous peoples in the international arena There are historical reasons why the international dialogue is dominated by North American indigenous peoples and by peoples such as us. The simple reason is because we've been there the longest. The North American indigenous peoples were there about the same time as we were.[4] In the international arena indigenous delegates are showing up with very local and national concerns; this idea of global indigeneity takes a back seat. In the interview with Ida she points out the huge numbers of indigenous delegates who show up at the UNPFII; it is a real problem.

3 Speaking for people when they can't speak for themselves I take Stephen Corry's point about how some indigenous peoples are worse off than others and their need to focus on the most vulnerable tribes. I could see that when I was in the Borneo jungle and met some Penan people. The tribal versus indigenous peoples distinction, however, doesn't work for me. Here in Aotearoa we are tribal peoples, we get it drummed into us at a young age, you are from this tribe. We have tribal gatherings, cultural competitions and all of those things. But we are in the well-off Western country of New Zealand and are not like, for example, the Penan people. So I think there needs to be another way to distinguish the privilege that some indigenous peoples have by being resident in Western countries, and I also think this distinction needs to extend (or maybe it requires its own distinction) to address the privilege of non-indigenous advocates in the context of indigenous issues. Having said all of that I think it is more important that people get out and support vulnerable peoples, which is real *whanaungatanga*, which is where organizations like Survival are crucial.

4 Resources I think organizations like IWGIA do a lot of points 1 and 3, providing an overview of where indigenous peoples are at. There is an idea that if indigenous peoples were resourced enough to do the things that IWGIA does, then possibly we could do these things for ourselves. The reality is that I am not sure that an indigenous organization would receive funding to do those sorts of things for political reasons.

Emma Hughes

Organizations such as Survival, IWGIA and UNPFII I see as able to take a broad, overarching view of indigenous concerns, while most local NGOs are not in a position to encompass the kind of holistic approach they take. Jens at IWGIA refers to four elements: human rights, documentation, project support and lobbying. Local indigenous organizations would probably be able to focus effectively on only one of these without losing the support of their constituency and, as Teanau points out, this would almost certainly also affect their ability to attract funding. Lobbying and human rights activities, for example, will assume the adoption of a political position and will often be working in conflict with the state, whereas other organizations may be able to progress concerns by taking an apolitical approach. Three examples detailed further in Chapter 4 illustrate how very different approaches function to advance similar goals for Nubia.

In terms of documentation, I am thinking here of the Nubian Museum, opened by UNESCO in 1997 as a repository of artefacts rescued by UNESCO's campaign after the flooding of Nubia by the Aswan High Dam, which also serves to preserve the cultural heritage, language and traditions of its people. The museum's education programme works closely with schools and the community to raise awareness of Nubian history, culture and traditions. While the director, Osama Abdel Meguid, and other key staff are Nubian, the museum is Egyptian (it was only on UNESCO's insistence that the museum is called 'the Nubian Museum'; the government wished to name it the 'Museum of Egyptian Civilization') and as such content must remain strictly apolitical.

At the other end of the spectrum is the political lobby group known as 'the follow-up committee', which was formed in April 2007. They have no meeting place, communicate only by mobile phone, don't receive any funding, and don't openly identify their members. Nor is their existence openly acknowledged by the government. They are generally not supportive of the type of documentation showcased by the museum because of their distrust of the government and scepticism regarding the cautious 'softly softly' approach which has resulted in limited progress.

In terms of non-indigenous NGOs, a small human rights NGO, the

Egyptian Centre for Housing Rights, recently adopted the Nubian cause, hosting a conference in 2007 to address Nubian rights. Many Nubians were discouraged from attending, owing partly to security issues and threats that they would be arrested, and partly to the fact that they are not accustomed to working with a non-Nubian organization or receiving external assistance. A good deal of suspicion surrounded the conference, which received predominantly negative attention from the press, but it did succeed in bringing together 200 politically active Nubians who have since continued to advocate for change.

Can all these approaches be said to have advanced the Nubian cause? In actual fact, they probably achieve more by virtue of the others' existence.

Reflections and analysis

Early in the new millennium, Andrea Muehlebach (2001) looked closely at the ways in which international indigenous activism has been situated within the UN Working Group on Indigenous Populations (WGIP), functioning as a 'vital nodal point in the global "indigeno-scape"' (Beckett 1996). She identifies with insight the ways in which the 'politics of morality' and the tropes of 'knowledge, culture and biodiversity' were harnessed towards 'international indigenous activism as a transnational cultural political movement involved in a number of battles on a number of fronts' (p. 416). It is not insignificant that Fred, the Batwa man whom Chris Kidd interviews earlier in this book, had participated at an international conservation and biodiversity conference, one of the grounds on which indigenous political claims are being advanced. Claims around knowledge and biodiversity as articulated at other international indigenous activist gatherings can also be heard by following these links:

www.indigenousportal.com/Biological-Diversity/

www.indigenousportal.com/Human-Rights/Interview-with-Kenneth-Deer.html

www.indigenousportal.com/Health/Jessca-Yee-Interview-at-the-UNPFII-2009.html

www.indigenousportal.com/Africa/UNPFII-2009-Interview-with-Ibrahim-Njobdi.html.[5]

Muehlebach also reveals how the terms of these tropes were being appropriated by the democratic, liberal politics of the advanced, industrialized nations of the global North, thus brilliantly presaging the developments at the end of the first decade of the new millennium, so clearly manifested during the debacle of the much-hyped climate change conference in Copenhagen at the end of 2009. This event visibly highlighted the conflicts between emergent 'relational ontologies' and the entrenched 'dualist ontologies' (Escobar 2010), so that accredited indigenous activists were evicted from the proceedings.[6] Francesca Merlan's (2009) paper, on the other hand, looks at the politics of indigeneity as it has played out in various forums and the 'constraints and opportunities' of democratic liberal politics within the current 'double conjuncture' (Escobar 2010) in the global North, to explain the position on the Declaration on the Rights of Indigenous Peoples of the four major settler nations.

Set at the two ends of the current decade, these papers frame many of the issues raised during the preceding discussions and commentaries, while also comprehensively pulling together the contentious history of indigenous political activism and its many achievements since the movement exploded on to the international scene during the seventies. Teanau Tuiono's subsequent comments highlight yet again the disparity and distinctive contexts of indigenous activism within the settler nations, especially those that have been signatories to treaties, when compared to the post-colonial turmoil of indigenous politics in Africa and Asia. Emma's rejoinder speaks to the cautious praxis of Nubian activism in Egypt as it struggles to assert and maintain an identity within the Egyptian polity.

Against this backdrop, I want to extend the rejoinders to the preceding dialogues by reflecting on the situation of one indigenous group that has lurked in my interpolations throughout this book. I will do this by focusing on the period subsequent to the tsunami of 26 December 2004. The situation of the indigenous groups of the Andaman Islands provides a sobering reminder of the fact that, despite the momentum of the Declaration and the excitement generated by that significant milestone, there is a yawning gulf between those who can reach and have their voices heard at forums such as the UNPFII or the WGIP and the quotidian lives of other indigenous groups such as the Andaman Islanders.[7]

Simron Singh's discussion earlier in this book highlights just how devastating the tsunami of 2004 was for the inhabitants of the Nicobar Islands, the islands just south of the Andamans, so close to the epi-

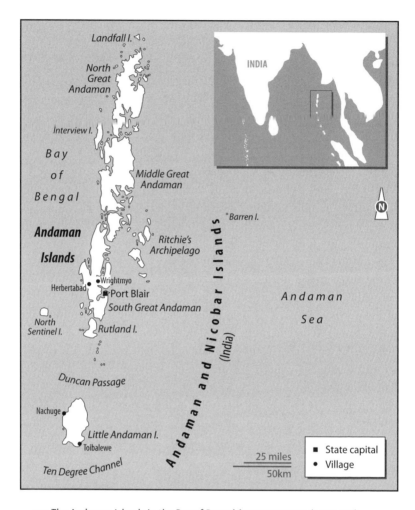

7.1 The Andaman Islands in the Bay of Bengal (*source*: www.andaman.org)

centre that the raging seas engulfed the islands with nowhere left to escape. But, strangely enough, it was not calamitous for the indigenous groups of the Andaman Islands, all of whom survived the earthquake and the subsequent onslaught from the sea. Instead, in this context, the event presented an unforeseen opening to make things right, to learn from the errors of the past, and put in place measures and processes that were truly innovative. As the marauding seas destroyed every material trace of colonial, administrative intervention in their lives, the space was cleared to envision a different kind of future.

What is the context that fosters the emergence of grassroots activism with the political acumen to engage with state structures? Simron Singh's discussion points to another area of difference between the indigenous groups of the Andaman and Nicobar Islands, the presence of indigenous leadership as manifested by the far-sighted vision of Chupon or the outspoken activism of Rashid, whom Simron writes about elsewhere (Singh 2003). It is not merely incidental that the Nicobar Islands were the sites of missionary activity, both Christianity and Islam flourishing in these islands since they were colonized, existing side by side with other more traditional animistic beliefs and practices. It is such 'enabling violations' (Spivak 2008) which have prepared the ground for the emergence of literacy and political consciousness, both crucial to the emergence of indigenous activism wherever they have occurred across the world. Violations of other sorts[8] have been the basis for the political acumen that is visible among many of the Great Andamanese women, but this has been harnessed only to survive the vicissitudes of petty, quotidian battles with the Andaman administration, and their own lives as women within the embattled indigenous community.

In the immediate aftermath of the tsunami, within the newly created space for more radical thinking and practices, however, neither Survival International nor IWGIA understood the opportunities that the post-tsunami context presented for fostering leadership and political 'know-how' among the Great Andamanese and Onge towards augmenting the long-term well-being of the indigenous Andaman groups. In their inability to interpret the situation correctly, in my view, they both failed the islanders. It is this failure of thinking outside of established procedures which will, over the ensuing years, go on to further the destructive processes under way that have led to severe consequences for the islanders.

These failures on the international front emerge from the kinds of roles that SI and IWGIA have prescribed for themselves. In the case of SI, although they are not averse to acting on behalf of indigenous groups, drawing attention to their plight through their various interventions and media, they have to be *seen* to be doing what they are, because they too, like the NGOs in Botswana that Stephen Corry is critical of, have to be *noticeable* in their efforts because their funding hinges on that visibility.

The tsunami occurred in the wake of quite dramatic activism[9] in the Andaman Islands. It brought about a coalition of activists, NGOs, academics, writers, journalists, policy analysts and local citizens, bringing collective energy, enthusiasm and innovative thinking into negotiating with the government to address the situation of the indigenous groups. One of the strategies that was identified as crucial to altering the mindset of non-indigenous settler inhabitants in the islands towards bringing about long-term change, something that Stephen Corry identifies as an important component of SI efforts, was to work with local schools in the islands, training teachers and students to learn more about indigenous peoples, their rights and their place in the overall scheme of things. This was to be achieved using materials that SI had developed for schools in the UK, which were to be translated into the local languages. Through the schoolchildren, the parents were also to be reached, thus imparting and reinforcing the message. Initially, SI was very interested in such an intervention, but backed away when it became evident that for the initiative to succeed, it was necessary that they remain behind the scenes and did not derive any publicity from the support that they provided. The initiative never got off the ground!

In the case of IWGIA during the post-tsunami phase, despite Jens Dahl's avowal of support, it never actually materialized. It should also be mentioned that during this period, IWGIA was also engaged in the process of reassessing its priorities in South Asia. And yet, any focused interventions in the form of efforts towards capacity-building with the Great Andamanese or the Onge at that crucial juncture could have actually assisted in developing political awareness leading to the emergence of conscientization and activism among some of the indigenous Andaman groups. Had they been far sighted enough, IWGIA could have been the harbinger of indigenous political activism in the islands, and the 2007 UN Declaration on the Rights of Indigenous Peoples would have had a significant presence in the islands.

India was one of the abstaining countries at that event on the grounds that all its inhabitants are indigenous, hence that Declaration was not pertinent to the Indian context. However, in contrast to mainland India, the Andaman and Nicobar Islands are a location where the distinction between those who are indigenous and all the rest can be clearly demarcated. If SI and IWGIA had seized the day during the momentous turn of events at the end of 2004, the seeds could have been sown for the Declaration to become a charter towards the realization of a very different future for the Andaman Islanders.

Conclusion

I want now to look to the future as well as track developments in the intervening years since the UN Declaration on the Rights of Indigenous Peoples, and situate the two INGOs within the spectrum of emergent post-Declaration trends. It is clear that concerns around vulnerability to climate change and the mitigation of these impacts are at the forefront of UN processes, with IWGIA taking a leading role in seeking 'entry points' to respond to these directions, while also providing the relevant documentation to support its initiatives with indigenous groups. SI, too, continues its 'watchdog' role, alerting the global public regarding precarious tribes facing the threat of extinction or extermination as multinational corporations or governments extend their reach to extract resources despite the cost to indigenous peoples' lives, livelihoods and well-being.

Related but disturbing developments within the UN Permanent Forum revolve around carbon offsets and REDD (Reducing Emissions from Deforestation and Forest Degradation). A spokesperson at the forum who prefers to remain unnamed has the following pithy comments to make regarding the polarized positions that indigenous groups have taken on this matter. I quote this individual at length below to detail the basis of the rifts under way:

> One grouping hopes that they will be able to control Wall Street,
> national forestry departments and police departments, the UN,
> the legal system, etc. enough so that indigenous communities and
> indigenous leaders will be able to get some benefits from REDD, such
> as money for communities, local forest conservation, etc. This group
> stresses the right to self-determination, pointing out that it is every
> indigenous community's right to decide for itself whether it wants to
> make a deal with carbon traders or forestry consultants or the UN or
> whatever. Some in this grouping have already made deals with com-
> panies, Big Green organisations in Washington, DC, the World Bank
> or other UN agencies (some indigenous leaders are also being tempted
> by the prospect of high positions in the UN REDD apparatus).
>
> Some of the people in this grouping have had long experience
> negotiating in the UN process, which has moved to the centre of
> their consciousness somewhat. One of the peculiarities of indigenous
> politics is that while local indigenous groups are sometimes quite
> powerful in being able to defend their local territories and ways of

life, the record of success in bargaining with national governments is usually not good. Instead, indigenous groups have often tried to 'leapfrog' reactionary national governments and take their issues to the UN, where various indigenous niches have successfully been carved out that many groups believe will enable them to turn around and apply pressure on their obdurate national governments to, for instance, [introduce] the principle of free prior informed consent into various instruments. All this naturally tends to make for a situation in which some international indigenous leaders become 'addicted' to UN processes.

The other grouping also affirms the right to self-determination, but suggests that communities and alliances considering REDD could find it useful to share more information about the possible implications of REDD beforehand so that they know what they are getting into. They point out that REDD carbon trading projects not only affect the indigenous community that is accepting the project, but also other indigenous communities, often on the other side of the world, who may suffer because the carbon credits provided will allow extraction or pollution to continue somewhere else. Those communities also have the right to self-determination, and their rights might be interfered with by the first community's accepting a REDD project. This grouping also points to the precedent of previous REDD-like schemes (including the Tropical Forest Action Plan), which have resulted in violations of indigenous rights and loss of sovereignty, as well as rampant forest degradation. How, they ask, does any indigenous group think they will be able to control this?

> Indigenous groups' rights are already being trampled by REDD, and the process has hardly begun. Inequalities are likely only to be exacerbated, and forests taken over and destroyed. This grouping tends to feel that the whole debate in the indigenous world has been corrupted by the enormous sums of money, billions of dollars, that are being waved around by REDD advocates. Trust has broken down in an unprecedented way within the indigenous world because of this. They also tend to be more concerned about the violation of the sacred implied in REDD than are the first grouping. Some of them may also be more concerned about climate change than the first group.

This provocative analysis suggests that IWGIA and others are likely to have their work cut out in responding to the kinds of divisions voiced above. They could potentially undermine the hard-won achievements of the Declaration, as indigenous groups become embroiled in the wheeling and dealing around climate change and its spin-offs which currently dominates the global political landscape.

Acknowledgements

I want to acknowledge here with gratitude the generosity of Survival International, IWGIA and Ida Nicolaison in making available the time and space amid their busy schedules to engage in extended discussions with me.

Venkateswar

Conclusion. Naming and claiming second-wave indigeneity: a dialogue and reflections

SITA VENKATESWAR, HINE WAITERE, CHRISTOPHER KIDD, AVRIL BELL, BENNO GLAUSER, KATHARINE MCKINNON, EMMA HUGHES, SIMRON JIT SINGH

This concluding chapter seeks to explore the concept of second-wave indigeneity through the defining mode of engagement that has been characteristic of this collection, namely through dialogue and reflections. The first part of this chapter is a dialogue between Hine Waitere, a Māori academic and one of the contributors to the Aotearoa/New Zealand chapter, and Sita Venkateswar, who is the interlocutor in the discussion. The conversation is followed by a series of reflections on second-wave indigeneity by the other contributors, who respond to a question that was posed to them as we reached the final stages of the project.

Naming and claiming: a dialogue on second-wave indigeneity

SITA: As interlocutor to this discussion, I want to first locate myself as a 'non-indigenous ally'[1] who has a 'response-ability' to the indigenous context and equal stakes within that political terrain as regards any future outcomes. But in the interests of a decolonizing discourse, naming and claiming is not my prerogative, although I can work alongside you in charting the contours of that concept or assessing its relevance.

HINE: Yes, I think it is important to remember that we are all located and locatable as we enter these conversations. Of course, that does not mean that we cannot work to understand those who enter the discussion from other locations but rather that we do nevertheless engage from different commencement points, socio-political histories and contingencies, even if the articulation of aspirational spaces may converge. This places us within a political sphere of necessary and productive discomfort, exposing existing orthodoxies and entrenched normative entry points as indigenous peoples move into the complex discussions about the differentiated response-abilities you allude to.

Locating me as indigenous, while differently located to Sita, does not give me the mandate to speak for all indigenous peoples; we are not homogeneous. So I want to remind myself as much as anyone else that as I join this conversation I am *a*, not *the*, indigenous voice.

Thinking about the notion of a second wave (just as with the word indigenous) would evoke interesting and intense debate by indigenous peoples but probably provide little consensus. This is likely to be because we are talking about 300–500 million people who embody and nurture eighty per cent of the cultural and biological diversity and occupy twenty per cent of the land surface (UN Declaration on the Rights of Indigenous Peoples); it's a lot to subsume within one wave. I am not attempting to be glib but want to signal that the most unifying tenet of indigenous debates is to honour the localized diversities collapsed within.

SITA: To refer to a second-wave indigeneity is, admittedly, drawing on the legacy of the international feminist movement, including the interventions of 'Third World' feminists, its strengths and achievements, which have influenced and left traces on all subsequent social and political movements globally. If you were to insist on a chronology for such a characterization, to my mind a 'first-wave indigeneity' was roughly concurrent with the feminist movement in the early seventies when indigenous rights as a political issue made their presence felt internationally and were mostly led by indigenous groups in the settler nations. However, within individual nation-states across the globe, indigenous struggles continued apace without necessarily connecting with the international political movement and were responsive to their own domestic situations. Through the nineties, with the convening of the UN Working Group on Indigenous Populations and culminating in the UN Permanent Forum in the early years of the new millennium, there has been a shift in the global political scene, signalled by the WTO protests and the World Social Forums and the emergence of a visible wave of indigenous mobilization and activism that has extended beyond the Fourth World settler nations.

HINE: I hear what you are saying and can understand how the centre might want to make sense of the periphery through some movement (such as feminism) associated with its own socio-political activism. And while I understand the progressive intent by numerous critically oriented movements in the academy, many of which have seriously looked at their own structuring frameworks and found them wanting, I am not sure that that is enough to co-locate feminism and indigeniety within the same political orb. In fact I wonder in this context whether second-wave indigeneity marks the shifting terrains of colonial consciousness of indigenous realities rather than of internal indigenous movements.

In terms of a chronology, if that is what is signalled by second wave, the first must surely mark pre-colonial contact, not to overly romanticize the past, but to assert that our political, social, cultural existence and awareness of self did not commence at the point of contact. Nor did it come into being at the point at which we gained international recognition or had our plight 'discovered' by the non-indigenous masses. While the shifts evoked by critically oriented social commentators identify the ways in which the academy has been part of the problem, they provide a detectable Freudian slip. Ironically, professing the shortcomings of the centre, in spite of its self-conscious recognition that it has been the problematic to the very viability of indigenous peoples (physiologically and culturally), is very much predicated on the unwavering belief that in spite of its historic blunders it remains the ultimate source of the rectifying answer(s). The very liberal project of inclusion then begins to unravel because if one creates space within its own canon to hear and engage with indigenous peoples and then fills those very same fissures, these social movements then become part of the very pathology they are attempting to speak back to.

So I guess if *second wave* is to have any salience for indigenous peoples it is likely to be best marked by the shift indicated by Radhakrishnan (2003) when he hints at the distinction between talking *for-oneself* and doing so *in-oneself*. That is marking the shift from talking on behalf of oneself but through the frameworks of our dominant counterparts, to the shift to talking about ourselves within the epistemic and ontological frameworks of origin. One of the detectable shifts in Aotearoa/New Zealand is the movement into post-treaty settlement discussions in our conversations earlier in the book. The sentiment underpinning these conversations is best summarized by Audre Lorde's commonly quoted adage 'the master's tools will never dismantle the master's house' (Lorde 1984: 111).

SITA: Considering the very disparate contexts of indigenous lives as highlighted in the varied discussions convened by the contributors, the unevenness of the global indigenous situation is what appears most evident to me. But two recent developments, one academic and the other political, offer ways to think through some of these differences. First, the academic: the recent special issue of the journal *interventions*[2] interrogates the intersections of indigeneity and subalternity, and the overlaps and tensions between the colonial and post-colonial constructs. For me, these two intellectual and political traditions provide the conceptual bridge not only *between* the Fourth World settler contexts and the post-colonial contexts of Africa and Asia but also *within* each of those blocs, in the attentiveness to the ways in which privilege and deprivation manifest themselves. Through the situated common ground of experienced oppression, suffering and marginalization, those constructs engage with the kinds of unevenness that I have remarked on earlier, as differentiating the diverse contexts of indigenous lives across the globe.

The second, more political set of developments, such as those that are currently under way across the Middle East and parts of Africa, with the naming and claiming of democracy and its associated rights and freedoms, in parts of the world where these were perceived as foreclosed, augurs a new set of possibilities that can provide the momentum for mobilization and activism on a range of fronts. Perhaps the responsibilities that are integral to the claiming of democratic rights will also become more widely comprehended through the shifts and turns of the political terrain.

HINE: The modes and sites of engagements are diverse not only across but also within indigenous groups, and certainly with the number of international movements and the availability of the internet, the range of possibilities for collective activism grows. As in the conversations arising out of the interviews with those in Aotearoa/New Zealand, the power of conversations held with other indigenous groups in international forums, although never simple, is valued. Not only does the ability to mobilize from our living rooms happen as we bear witness to the shifts alluded to, they also become the site of political activism and critical engagement.

A current focus of preference for those spoken to in Aotearoa/New Zealand is associated with embracing variances within collapsed collectives mediated by the specificities of place, and a self-expression based in in-itself concepts of *Tino Rangatiratanga*. This of course requires a shift both nationally and internationally from paternalistic modes of engagement to honouring ones based on social justice.

Reflections on second-wave indigeneity

The question that was posed to the contributors of this volume as we approached the end of the project is as framed below:

Reflecting on the international indigenous rights movement and situating the context that you have worked with against that backdrop, is it possible to discern an emergent, but uneven 'second-wave' indigeneity? Is this a pertinent concept or merely a mirage or wishful thinking? If not, what are the ways in which such a concept can be given shape and form?

CHRIS: In the Ugandan context the Batwa are entering into the international indigenous rights movement without much of the history other indigenous groups have had and therefore without much of the experience others have formed over the last thirty years. While the international movement spent many years fighting to define what indigenous rights were at the global level and to have them recognized, the Batwa today enter the movement with their rights already laid out for them. While this is useful in many ways it also inhibits the Batwa in embarking on their own journey of self-determination and understanding fully how they would like their rights to be defined in their own contexts. Despite any reservations it is already clear that the gains of the international movement will be readily utilized by the Batwa in their own contexts.

However, while the journey of the Batwa has been short on the international level, they have nonetheless been forced to confront their place in Ugandan society and their position as indigenous people. And while this took place largely uninfluenced by the international movement, it ultimately showed similar steps and advances. If there is a second-wave indigeneity for the Batwa it might be that such a wave is based on the successes of the first wave in having the rights of the Batwa and indigenous peoples in general acknowledged at many levels. The next stage for the Batwa is to have those rights, so widely recognized in policy, put into practice on the ground, where individual Batwa families can experience the benefits of the rights they have so desperately demanded.

AVRIL: What immediately comes to mind for me is whether this concept refers to the idea of a second era among the groups and in the societies (largely settler societies) out of which the 'first wave' of indigenous politics developed and led to the global movement, or to the expansion of indigenous rights struggles beyond those initiating contexts to encompass other struggles for survival and rights being undertaken by minority, tribal groups in non-settler societies. I'm going to consider the impact of the second of these possibilities.

It does seem that the global indigenous movement – and now the international level of visibility and acceptance represented by the UN Declaration on the Rights of Indigenous Peoples – has been an important support for the struggles of groups in Africa, Asia and South America. Chris's comments on the Batwa situation are interesting – the global movement has been helpful to them, but also has meant they haven't had the space (or need) to work through their own 'journey to self-determination' and to work out exactly 'how they would like their rights to be defined'. The template for indigenous rights already exists.

This flipside of the gains made that Chris points to links to my own concern about the globalizing of the politics of indigeneity, and that is that it is important that the concept doesn't get stretched so broadly as to lose its specificity. Within the category of 'indigenous', important differences need to be remembered and marked in various ways. The term usually encompasses 'tribal and/or colonized' peoples, so is already diverse. Within the sphere of political action carved out by that definition, I think it is crucial that 'indigeneity' doesn't homogenize the diversity of interests and contexts that exists – for example, the differences in politics between, say, groups struggling against settler states and those that are tribal minorities within larger states of neighbouring ethnic/national groups, the differences between those in 'developed' and 'developing' states, the differences between those struggling for sheer survival and those seeking forms of cultural, economic and political equality, recognition and restitution.

BENNO: *Second-wave indigeneity: one* Speaking about Latin America, a favourable, less self-centred concern for the situation of indigenous peoples and for indigeneity has been expressed and translated into actions by non-indigenous circles especially since the time of the Barbados Declaration (1972), but has been worded and increasingly promoted also by the indigenous peoples' own organizations and indigenous movements in their own right, in recent decades. The explicit aim of this concern was a favourable change in the life conditions of indigenous peoples, affected in many and deep ways by the impacts of the century-long and still ongoing colonial process.

In the present time and complementarily, I see indigeneity gradually emerging in a new way, in part of the global mainstream, as a concept and a concern considered important not just for the indigenous peoples themselves, but for the future of all. Within the mainstream, it is an emerging time-spirit, though presently represented and expressed still only by minorities (the progressive, the innovative, those who seek alternatives to their own life situation and/or to society, the dissatisfied, etc.).

It is our (the non-indigenous') own indigeneity which is coming alive after having been declared obsolete and suppressed for a long time. As it comes alive, we are in need of defining it. It comes alive as a place in ourselves which starts echoing and exchanging signals with the indigenous worlds and values. The 'we' is clearly a minority of people privileged by the possibility of being in touch, sensitive to the messages coming from the indigenous worlds, and of receiving them and deciphering them.

As a new movement within humanity, it could certainly be seen as a 'new wave of indigeneity' ('second-wave indigeneity'?). This time, the concern is for our own indigeneity, not any more for 'the other's' as had always been the case within the colonial process, from the time of conquest, passing through the different historical roles of anthropology, to a modern – but still external – concern on the part of action anthropologists and grassroots militants for the indigenous peoples.

Second-wave indigeneity: two As to the indigenous' own organizations and movements themselves, although there was and is a sympathetic affinity with other movements like the feminists' or, more recently, the ecologists', I also note an increasing need to keep apart and to differentiate themselves from such movements. This will be a necessity until the non-indigenous societies – today a majority – decide and start to live diversity – cultural diversity. To live human diversity means to put at stake and forsake one's own culture and way of being, in order to create a 'wider, new world' in which the diverse have as much room and space as oneself. Acceptance of cultural diversity until now has normally been understood as an attitude which will not affect oneself, but which consists in conceding part of one's own space to the other, diverse, who is invited to share one's own space, in an integrative process which, however, is asymmetrical.

As long as indigenous peoples don't keep the necessary distance but instead fall prey to a process of mere integration into the other's world, their own way of being, collective identity and culture are under threat. As a consequence, indigenous interests – and those of indigeneity – have to be defended in ways that do not seek integration in a globally merged, culturally uniform humanity or global society (the struggle for recognition of rights is one of the ways seeking integration!), but rather seek autonomy, independence and sovereignty. In present times, such a quest is visible in the Zapatistas movement in Mexico, but also elsewhere, where indigenous peoples, after decades or centuries of asking and struggling for spaces and recognition of externally defined rights without any success, grow wary and realize that they are vastly on their own, and end up turning around to look at the culture of their fathers and ancestors as a source of force and stability. It increasingly happens with the Ayoreo, but there are also such tendencies visible in eastern Paraguay, where among the Païtavyterä there occurs a revaluation of traditional cultural concepts, or the Mbyá of Itapúa, where there are groups that have withdrawn after decades or centuries of contact to a state of voluntary isolation.

KATHARINE: It is clear that the (collective) victim of an imposed, invasive and destructive colonial process, which moreover still continues, will first of all be in need of reaffirming themselves in their own right, before being able to relate to a radically diverse other without risk of losing themselves. This is even more so, considering the 'other' here is no tame lamb and has not precisely set aside yet his colonial voracity.

The indigeneity sought here is associated with diversity, locality and a self-expression based in culturally endogenous concepts. I believe personally that this is the only position compatible with the notion of authentic human respect.

I think it could be a useful way to think about international indigenous politics – especially in terms of how groups like the highlanders of Thailand are engaging. I remember a conversation with a friend of mine who is a highlander activist who spoke about the first time he met a Māori rights activist at an international meeting. He was astounded by the force with which the activist laid claim to Māori rights to land and to sovereignty. This friend of mine could see no similarity between the position of highlanders and the position of Māori – there was no desire or ability to claim a right to the land in the way first peoples in settler societies have. And there are no foundations for claiming sovereignty or mimicking in any way the ideas of property or state that dominate. This was a good decade ago now, and I think the movement in Thailand has changed, but nevertheless, if highlanders are to be accommodated in an indigenous rights movement (as I believe they

Venkateswar et al.

should be), then there needs to be room in it for very different ways of claiming rights. So much of it has been about territory in the past. And for highlanders, territory, in terms of long-term claims to land and to belonging, is really an alien idea. But of course, they live in a world where they need title to land, and so that too has changed. If there is a second wave I guess it's a second wave that incorporates a much wider range of ways of being in which indigeneity is not just about indigenous peoples in settler societies, and the kind of politics that comes with it is able to incorporate ways of seeing land and power that are starkly different to ideas of nations, territories or states. Highlanders, I think, are using indigeneity very strategically, and this too might characterize a second wave – perhaps it's a little savvier and a little more rhizomatic. Hopefully it's a good thing!

EMMA: Second-wave indigeneity for Nubians would inevitably be differently defined either side of the Egyptian–Sudanese border. For the increasing number of Nubians in the diaspora it would probably centre around cultural revival as a key element of giving shape and form to this indigeneity; this is visible in Cairo, Khartoum and beyond. For many Nubians closer to home it is reflected in the continuing reclamation of the right to choose to live on ancestral lands in Nubia itself. This is a refrain heard from each continent represented in this book and is likely to continue to be highly contested. If indigeneity is seen as a relational term, as Kidd and Kendrick and Glauser suggest, then we can surmise that this will experience significant change in a situation of dramatically evolving relationship dynamics with the state. Both Egypt and Sudan are experiencing a time of flux as the very nature of the state changes around them – a redefining of the nation-state they inhabit via the 2011 referendum in Sudan and revolution in Egypt will lead to a rewriting of the political landscape. How will these questions of democracy and national identity be inclusive of the rights of indigenous peoples and minorities in each country?

SIMRON: In the context of the Nicobar Islanders, I can relate to the concept of second-wave indigeneity, albeit as an academic observer. Since the tsunami I have often been surprised by how the Nicobarese are now more conscious of being 'indigenous' in a political sense. This is in sharp contrast to the situation before the tsunami, when it was enough to distinguish themselves from those from outside. But with increasing contact with outsiders in the form of aid workers, increased inflow of government officials and academics, they begin to reflect on their own identity as indigenous people in relation to the non-indigenous in a political sense. The term is now often used to negotiate for favours, subsidies, special conditions, welfare programmes, and also to evoke a sense of emotion in terms of their vulnerability. At the same time, the term is also used as a political lever to demand rights as a minority and marginalized population within a nation. As far as I understand it, this expression does not play a powerful role when it comes to their sense of identity among themselves, which is not in any way different from what it was prior to the tsunami.

Gathering the threads to weave a mutual future

The dialogue and reflections above offer a diversity of positions that highlight the opportunities provided to us through this project to become aware of the intersections between us rather than a single point of entry or departure.

As depicted by Waitere and Allen, Glauser, Kidd and Kendrick, McKinnon, Hughes and Singh, the engagement of indigenous peoples with the state, other nationals and indigenous peoples worldwide is an ongoing process, a continuing and evolving journey which will continue into the future grounded in the *in-itself* collective sense of self. Within this process, engagement at an international, intercontinental level provides us with a sense of the shared experiences, the alliances created, and the recognition of commonality in the face of oppression, as articulated by the contributors and spokespeople in this volume, alongside a glimpse of the ongoing conversations that will foreground the mobilizations to come, for both indigenous and non-indigenous.

Notes

Introduction

1 This phrase is placed within quotes within the text the first time it is used and subsequently discontinued. The same protocol is observed with other neologisms and conceptualizations.

2 See also Christie (2011: 329) for what he terms 'a second form of resistance', in the Arctic.

3 Exemplified by the performative indigeneity of Māori of Aotearoa/New Zealand.

4 A poem written by Elizabeth Allen in response to the 'State Terror Raids' (October 2007) refers to state power manifested through its naming and claiming of Māori as 'noble savages' or 'global terrorists' (see p. 48). See also Waitere and Johnston (2009: 15) for a discussion on the power of naming, claiming, defining and theorizing. These references highlight the typically colonial practices of naming and claiming, while here the term marks the shift to the 'in-itself' mode of engagement as elaborated on p. 61.

5 See Charters et al. (2010).

6 See discussions on New Zealand's position by Charters 2010 and Jones 2010. For more wide-ranging implications of the Declaration see Charters and Stavenhagen 2010.

7 See Bibliography, p. 264, for example Byrd and Rothberg (2011), de la Cadena and Starn (2007), Merlan (2009) and Trigger and Dalley (2010).

8 www.docip.org/ (accessed 3 June 2011).

9 The disciplinary affiliations of the contributing authors are social anthropology, development studies, geography, human ecology, women's studies, education and philosophy.

10 These questions are not meant to serve as a straitjacket but to provide a thematic umbrella which is also nuanced by context. See the chapter on Aotearoa/New Zealand for a discussion of the reframing of the questions (p. 49). Other chapters, such as the one on the Nicobar Islands (p. 172), are responsive to the key issues that emerged from that context and the discussion is framed accordingly.

11 The Aotearoa/New Zealand component in Section 1 included a large number of participants, both Māori and non-Māori, in various and sometimes separate capacities, indigenous activists, non-indigenous allies, contributing authors, or commentators. It includes the presence of two commentators who have not authored a chapter but were involved in the Aotearoa/New Zealand component of the project. Avril Bell has published on settler concerns, while Teanau Tuiono was also a spokesperson involved in convening and participating in the discussions with other Māori activists.

12 The tsunami referred to here is the Boxing Day tsunami of 2004.

13 See Kidd and Kenrick's chapter for an extended discussion on indigeneity as a tool of accommodation.

14 Benno Glauser's commentary in Chapter 6 explicitly refers to the necessity of advancing indigenous and global mainstream concerns in parallel, to ensure that 'at least their worlds and realms are safe, and have opportunities for a survival we are uncertain to still have for ourselves' (p. 185), reflecting the deep-running anxiety for the foundation of the non-indigenous world and the global crisis that it has perpetuated.

15 Indigenous, or literally 'people of the land'.

16 Tribal affiliation.

17 Loosely translates as 'self-determination'.

18 'We want to get our land back,' asserts legal activist Moana Jackson, in 'agentic mode, and in the spirit of speaking both *"for-himself and in-himself"'* (p. 63).

19 This highlights the intersection of indigeneity and subalternity – see also the special issue of *interventions* (Byrd and Rothberg 2011) for a more extended discussion of such a nexus.

20 These are the group of islands that lie north of the Nicobar Islands in the Bay of Bengal.

Invocation

1 Also: 'song of Ibegua' ... Among the Ayoreo (Paraguay and Bolivia), visions are sung when waking up, sometimes in the night, sometimes at daybreak.

2 The subject does not appear in the text; she refers to the spirit which entered her dream and asked her to wake up.

3 Ibegua refers to 'what we know exists, it has no form ... something which is there ...'. The Ayoreo understand what is meant, and they depict it as dust, or very dense smoke; they even talk about ashes. It is a foggy cloud.

4 Ibegua uses a formulation which depicts an exam-like situation, when one is being asked a question one is expected to answer but is unable to do so. Thus, she expresses the idea that the task of proclaiming her dream is an enormous one, implying that she may not get to satisfy what the spirit asked of her, to deliver the message to the Ayoreo.

5 Asunción is the capital of modern Paraguay, the country where Ibegua lives; here, it symbolizes the places of the non-indigenous people as well as their non-indigenous way of life.

6 The parents worry as the children adopt foreign, non-indigenous ways; the young girls paint their faces in the fashion of non-indigenous women, and as a result, *the Ayoreo face underneath becomes invisible.*

7 There is an analogy used here with a situation in which one is dealing with a vice: something which will not turn out well if one continues, but in spite of this one continues with what one is doing, and in doing so, one damages oneself.

I Being indigenous

1 The interviews were held in Spanish; expressions in the Ayoreo language Zamuco (part of the Zamuco language family), whenever used in the course of the interviews, were translated and expressed in Spanish by the two interviewed leaders themselves.

2 Union of Native Ayoreo of Paraguay.

3 Comparable to the size of Italy, or Norway.

4 In the psychological sense.

5 Fragmenting and isolating the nuclear 'essential' part of a discourse, or connecting elements in a linear sequence, etc.

6 *Weltsicht* – also 'their theory about how the world functions'.

7 Although the definition 'indigenous peoples in voluntary isolation' sometimes also includes already contacted peoples who preferred to retire again from our civilization.

8 Ayoreo word for non-indigenous (will be defined below).

9 Aquino mentions thermos flasks as an example of being seen like objects ... thermos flasks are very common in Paraguay; they are much used to drink the daily ('*yerba*') maté tea, a habit also adopted by the contacted Ayoreo.

10 Chicori (*Jacarantia corumbensis*): a water-holding root vital for the survival of the nomadic Ayoreo in the forests, where water is scarce.

11 For instance, they take the possibility of sensual perception out of the generalized whole ... presumably a precondition for being able to overlook diversity and for multiple schemes of massive domination.

12 Emblematic tree species common in the northern Gran Chaco and the Ayoreo territory; Lat. *Bulnesia sarmientoi.*

13 Another widespread tree species; Lat. *Schinopsis balanseae.*

14 Spanish word for small, non-indigenous subsistence peasants in Latin America.

15 I thought this question was interesting, as Paraguayan '*criollo*' *campesinos* are the racial result of intimacy over many generations between non-indigenous colonial settlers from Europe and the indigenous population, and their main cultural traits and patterns still reflect nowadays the Guaraní culture as we know it from the Guaraní indigenous peoples, such as the Mbyá, the Ava Guaraní or the Paï-Tavytëra, even though the cultural system of the campesinos underwent a process of incisive semantic changes. Nowadays, the campesinos themselves normally deny strongly any close cultural relation with indigenous cultures or people.

16 Region of the Ayoreo territory, where Mateo was born; his present settlement, Campo Loro, lies outside and far away from his local groups' territory.

17 The original term used by Aquino literally means 'heavy'.

18 Mateo refers to one of the consequences of contact and being forced to adopt a new, unknown life model with its inherent new world-view. Many concepts of the original world-view left behind lose their semantic support both as concepts as well as a part of, and with a role in, a belief system or world-view. Thus, the myth about Namochai, if still told, will be perceived as vastly meaningless, or 'pointless'.

19 Likewise, in non-indigenous use of modern language, a specific quality appears sometimes as an adjective to describe another person or object of the same context. Example: when we speak about a 'happy coincidence', it is not the coincidence which is happy, but ourselves.

20 Thus, the Ayoreo had only a fleeting contact with the Jesuits. Apparently a significant number of Ayoreo – but by no means all of them – lived for about twenty years in a Jesuit mission called San Ignacio Zamuco. Its location is a cause of

speculation: it may have been near Cerro León or in the Ingávi area of what is now Paraguay. No tangible trace has been found of their contact with the Jesuits, other than a few myths – like the present one – and words in the vocabulary.

21 In the sense of epistemology.

2 Beyond indigenous civilities

1 This Māori proverb from Waikato highlights how multiple voices may be woven together to achieve a common goal. The translation reads, 'the needle has one eye, through which, the white red and black threads must pass'.

2 What follows is a *pepeha*, a formulaic expression that grounds the speaker within the collective of the tribe. Reference is commonly made to geographic locations through mountains and rivers and the sites of ancestral houses. In Māori contexts it is common to introduce yourself in this way. In fact, traditionally, it would have been considered forward to name yourself individually; you are known because your people are known as is the land you are a part of. On p. 48, when Hine first speaks, she also commences with a *pepeha*, as does Teanau later in the chapter when he commences his commentary.

3 Standing tall and proud is my mountain Hikurangi, flowing by is my river Waiapu a living energy for the people of Ngati Porou. The people of Te Awemapara Ngai Te Aowera call from below the roof of Kapohanga a Rangi standing at Hiruharama. We welcome the crowds into the *wharekai* of Tamatoa. Those who have passed lay at Huria. Kati, writing to you now is a descendant of the Hiroki family.

4 In 1852 the government passed the Constitution Act, allowing freehold landowners to vote and enter parliament. Māori landowners were excluded owing to the communal nature of their landownership; thus they were denied the rights to any decision-making. In 1862 the Native Lands Act was created to break up the communal ownership of Māori land, and this was supplemented in 1863 by the Suppression of Rebellion Act. This Act removed various rights for Māori, including the right to trial before imprisonment, established military courts and promised to punish 'certain aboriginal tribes of the colony'. Any Māori who resisted the incursion of Pākehā 'settlers', supported by the military, were labelled 'rebels' and their land was forfeit. It was through this Act that more than three million acres of Māori land was stolen through confiscation.

Another Act that was instrumental in the confiscation of Māori land was the New Zealand Settlements Act 1863. Furthermore, in July 1863, a proclamation was created that threatened further land confiscation if Māori in Waikato resisted the installation of military posts on their land. In fact resistance to military invasion was regarded as sufficient cause for confiscating land, as was the case in both Taranaki and Waikato, and the threat of confiscation was made after military invasions or occupations had begun. Land was also confiscated on the ground in both places before its taking was made legal.

5 Including a monumental land march in 1974, led by Dame Whina Cooper, as well as Waitangi

Day protests from 1971 (to the present), the occupation of Bastion Point (1978) and of Raglan Golf Course (1978), the disruption of the Springbok tour (1981), the development of Kōhanga Reo (1982), the Māori Education Development Conference (1984), the Māori Economic Development Conference (1985) and the establishment of Kura Kaupapa (1986). It was through this greater visibility and awareness of Māori that in 1987 the Māori language was finally recognized as an official language of Aotearoa/New Zealand.

6 On Monday, 15 October 2007, more than three hundred police, many wearing full riot gear, wielding machine guns, handguns and knives, carried out dawn raids on approximately sixty houses throughout the country. These houses were the homes of Māori, anti-war activists, environmental activists and anarchists, as well as elders and children. Equipped with warrants issued under the 2002 Terrorism Suppression Act, the police claimed that they were acting in response to 'concrete terrorist threats' from indigenous activists. The majority of those targeted were indigenous peoples from the *iwi* of Tūhoe, Te Atiawa, Maniapoto and Ngā Puhi.

7 In fact, the police set up a road-block (preventing anybody from leaving and entering the Rūātoki Valley) along the Autaki line. This is a line marked out by the people of Tūhoe to show the boundaries of hundreds of acres confiscated in the 1860s.

8 An excerpt from a poem written by Elizabeth Allen in response to the 'State Terror Raids' (October 2007).

9 This is Hine's *pepeha*:

As I return to the belly of the fish of Maui (the centre of the North Island)
I climb the sacred mountain Tauhara
To the sub-tribe Tute Mohuta
There lie the dancing waters of Taupo nui a Tia
As I turn my face to the east there lie the ashes of the canoe Te Arawa
May your spirit be well.

10 The *Timaru Herald* of 4 April 2009 was to say this about Paul Holmes (a well-known newscaster after making comments about the UN secretary-general): 'A colourful broadcaster coming unstuck is not a new phenomenon. Back in 2003, broadcaster Paul Holmes hit the bottom when he referred to former United Nations Secretary General Kofi Annan as a "cheeky darkie". He also incensed the female population by suggesting that newspapers might be more judgemental at certain times of the month because of the high number of women working in print. His career stalled after that.' www.stuff.co.nz/timaru-herald/opinion/2314164/Bottom-of-the-barrel (accessed 26 February 2010).

11 With your food basket, and my food basket, the people will thrive.

12 Ngai Takoto, Ngapuhi, Ngati Toki, Ngati Ingatu are the tribes, Areaora and Poroti are the ancestral homes, Enuamanu and Te Tai-tokerau are the ancestral lands.

13 Accessed 9 June 2011.

14 Accessed 9 June 2011.

15 A prominent statement made by Prophet Tohu Kakahi, Pai Marire, Taranaki. Figuratively it is used to say no matter what people place on the outside, fundamentally they remain Māori.

4 Displacement and indigenous rights

1 See Adams (1977), Fernea and Kennedy (1966: 354) and Fernea and Gerster (1973).

2 President Nasser first used the term 'Nubians' to refer collectively to the tribes living in Nubia; Fernea et al. (1991: 187).

3 A road between Kostol and Wadi Halfa is under construction. This would not permit border crossing for individuals, but would form a trade link between the two towns.

4 Nubians in Egypt estimate a shortfall of 5,000 houses, which the government has promised to build, but for which they are still waiting.

5 See, for example, Fahim (1972: 5), who notes that the Sudanese government aimed to double each family's income over a five-year period, and Poeschke (1996: 36), who quotes President Nasser's speech promising that 'the benefits that the Nubian people will enjoy are very great'.

6 *Daily News*, Egypt, 19 March 2008.

7 Old Nubia stretched from the first cataract in the River Nile, just south of Aswan, to the fourth cataract, south of Dongola in Sudan.

8 Among other similar reports, *Al-Nabaa al-Watany* reported on 11 June 2006 that 'Nubians want to pull down the high dam'.

9 Personal communication, Mohamed Abdel Azim, Egyptian Centre for Housing Rights, March 2008.

10 In February 2010, ECHR, along with the Cairo Institute for Human Rights Studies, petitioned the United Nations High Commissioner for Human Rights. The resulting summary report can be accessed at ap.ohchr.org/documents/alldocs.aspx?doc_id=16440.

11 Wadi Halfa became an official settlement once more in March 1967; Fahim (1981: 96–7).

12 This discussion resulted from a 1982 symposium convened by Maybury-Lewis. See Maybury-Lewis (1984).

13 This led to media accusations that Nubians constituted a threat to national unity. See Tito Eman (1997: 80).

14 Personal communication, Suad Siamy and Mohamed Mahmoud, Mahafaza Club, 14 May 2008.

15 Kajbar Resistance Committee Nubian Alliance, Renewed Appeal, 28 July 2007.

16 Chinese companies have been contracted to build the dams.

17 Oddoul spoke at the Second International Coptic Conference, held in Washington, DC, in November 2005. *Al-Ahram* weekly, 30 March–5 April 2006, weekly.ahram.org.eg/2006/788/eg9.htm.

18 Ahmed Ishaq, president of the Tomas Social Club, Abdin. Personal communication, 5 March 2008.

5 Being indigenous in northern Thailand

1 Except for the presentation I made to the group, which was given in English and translated by one of the workshop attendees, the presentations and the majority of the discussions on the day took place in Thai. The discussions were recorded and then later translated into English by a research assistant who had also attended the workshops. I also kept notes and asked colleagues for translation when I couldn't keep up with the discussion. Much of the discussion during the workshop was

around the intricacies of language, and in the translation of these discussions into English many of the subtleties of meaning have undoubtedly been lost, both as I struggled to follow the discussion on the day with my rather rusty language skills and as the recordings were translated. I have tried to add in some of the complexities through consultation with colleagues in Thailand as I conducted my analysis and by inserting explanations through the workshop text below.

2 All names of participants have been changed.

6 Chupon's dilemma

1 The impact of humanitarian aid on the social structure and on the local ecology has been termed a 'complex disaster' and has been dealt with in great detail elsewhere (Singh 2009).

2 The dialogue took place using a mix of Hindi and English, which are languages in which both Chupon and the author are quite well versed.

3 In ancient India, the only way to receive knowledge or skills was to be accepted by a guru (teacher), invariably a holy man, a sage. The student would then go and live in the ashram (hermitage) of the guru (somewhere in the forest). Students stayed for years with the guru and served him (cooking, cleaning, fetching water, etc. – there were no fees, only services) in return for which they received training in all forms of knowledge and skills. At the end of the studies, before leaving, the student offered a gift to the guru as a token of appreciation – known as *guru-dakshina*. Sometimes, the guru can also ask for something specific from the student as *guru-dakshina*.

4 The author withdrew from active engagement in the islands at the end of 2009. In the two years that followed, the Sustainable Indigenous Futures (SIF) fund, co-founded by the author in Austria, was wholly committed to the Tata Institute of Social Sciences (TISS) for promoting a cooperative marketing structure and for strengthening a network of (government-initiated) Rural Knowledge Centres (RKCs) across the archipelago. In addition, the viability of virgin coconut oil was explored, and a community newspaper – *Hamara Nicobar* – with large contributions from the Nicobarese themselves, was initiated to rebuild a sense of community and indigenous identity.

7 Indigeneity and international indigenous rights organizations

1 'On 16 December 2010, in an address to the White House Tribal Nations Conference, USA President Barack Obama announced that the United States supports the UN Declaration on the Rights of Indigenous Peoples. Following Australia's endorsement in 2009, and New Zealand's and Canada's endorsement in 2010, all four countries who initially voted against the Declaration at the time of adoption by the UN General Assembly in 2007 have now reversed their position' (22 December 2010, tkbulletin.wordpress.com/2010/12/22/this-week-in-review-%E2%80%A6-us-endorses-undrip/, accessed 20 April 2011).

2 www.wipce2008.com/ (accessed 11 June 2011).

3 www.docip.org/ (accessed 3 June 2011).

4 www.nzhistory.net.nz/people/tahupotiki-wiremu-ratana (accessed 11 June 2011).

5 Accessed 11 June 2011.

6 It is instructive to ponder the role of a government like Denmark's, supportive of the efforts of IWGIA, but then also playing a leading role in controlling, excluding and muzzling dissenting voices whose demands would have required a more equitable distribution of 'global space' and a curtailment of that already occupied by the advanced, capitalist nations of the North.

7 For more information on the Andaman Islanders, go to George Weber's site: www.andaman.org (accessed 10 May 2011), which is an extensive resource and archive of current and historical material.

8 See Venkateswar (2004 or 2001) for more details on these violations.

9 This has been discussed in 'Manifesto for a public anthropologist: insights from fieldwork', *India Review*, 5(3/4), 2006, pp. 268–93, and 'Of cyclones, tsunamis and the engaged anthropologist: some musings on colonial politics in the Andaman Islands', CIGAD Working Paper Series, Working Paper no. 2/2007.

Conclusion

1 This term was used by Eva Mackey, a Canadian scholar, who visited Massey University in March 2011 during a workshop entitled '(Un)reconciled differences: a dialogue about decolonising settler relations in Canada and New Zealand', convened by Avril Bell, a commentator in this volume.

2 *interventions*, 13(1), 2011.

Bibliography

Abdel Meguid, O. A. W. (2005) 'The role of the Nubia Museum in the community', *Museum International*, 57(1/2): 225–6, UNESCO.

ACHPR and IWGIA (2005) *Report of the African Commission's Working Group of Experts on Indigenous Populations/Communities*, Banjul/Copenhagen: ACHPR and IWGIA.

Adamczyk, C. (2011) '"Today, I am no Mutwa anymore": facets of national unity discourse in present day Rwanda', *Social Anthropology*, forthcoming.

Adams, W. Y. (1977) *Nubia. Corridor to Africa*, London: Allen Lane.

All Africa (2009) 'Barack Obama's address to Ghanaian parliament', allafrica.com/stories/200907110013.html, accessed 20 April 2011.

Appiah, K. A. (1991) 'Is the post- in postmodernism the post- in postcolonial?', *Critical Inquiry*, 17(2): 336–57.

Argyrou, V. (2005) *The Logic of Environmentalism: Anthropology, ecology, and postcoloniality*, New York and Oxford: Berghahn Books.

Asch, M. and C. Samson (2004) 'Discussion: on the return of the native', *Current Anthropology*, 45(2): 263.

— (2006) 'More on the return of the native', *Current Anthropology*, 47(1): 146–9.

Barnard, A. (2002) 'The foraging mode of thought', *Senri Ethnological Studies*, 60: 5–24.

— (2004) 'Comment: indigenous peoples: a response to Justin Kenrick and Jerome Lewis', *Anthropology Today*, 20(5): 19.

— (2006a) 'Discussion: the concept of indigeneity', *Social Anthropology*, 14(1): 17–32.

— (2006b) 'Kalahari revisionism, Vienna and the "indigenous peoples" debate', *Social Anthropology*, 14(1): 1–16.

Baviskar, A. (2007) 'Indian indigeneities: Adivasi engagements with Hindu nationalism in India', in M. de la Cadena and O. Starn (eds), *Indigenous Experience Today*, Oxford: Berg, pp. 275–304.

BBC News (2009a) 'Aborigines angry a year after "sorry"', news.bbc.co.uk/2/hi/asia-pacific/7909649.stm, accessed 26 April 2011.

— (2009b) 'Indigenous people descend on NYC', news.bbc.co.uk/2/hi/americas/8058689.stm, accessed 26 April 2011.

Beckett, J. (1996) 'Introduction. Contested images: perspectives on the indigenous terrain in the late 20th century', *Identities: Global Studies in Culture and Power*, 3(1/2): 1–13.

Berg, J. and K. Biesbrouck (2000) *The Social Dimension of Rainforest Management in Cameroon: Issues for co-management*, Kribi, Cameroon: Tropenbos-Cameroon Programme.

Bhabha, H. (1994) *The Location of Culture*, New York: Routledge.

Bowen, J. R. (2000) 'Should we have a universal concept of "indigenous peoples' rights"? Ethnicity and essentialism in the twenty-first century', *Anthropology Today*, 16(4): 12–16.

Buchan, B. and M. Heath (2006) 'Savagery and civilization: from Terra Nullius to the "tide of history"', *Ethnicities*, 6(1): 5–26.

Butcher, M. (2003) 'What is Maori? Who is Pakeha?', *North and South*, August, pp. 36–47.

Butler, J. and J. Scott (eds) (1992) *Feminists Theorize the Political*, New York and London: Routledge.

Byrd, J. A. and M. Rothberg (2011) 'Between subalternity and indigeneity: critical categories for postcolonial studies', *interventions*, 13(1): 1–12.

Castaneda, T. (2009) 'American Indian lives and voices: the promise and problematics of life narratives', *Reviews in Anthropology*, 38(2): 132–65.

Chainarong, S. and J. Suppachai (1999) *Citizenship, Ethnic Identity and State Policy: Thai or Non-Thai for Hilltribe People?*, Paper presented at the 7th International Thai Studies Conference, Special Round Table, Amsterdam.

Chakrabarty, D. (2007) *Provincializing Europe: Postcolonial Thought and Historical Difference*, Princeton, NJ: Princeton University Press.

Charters, C. (2010) 15lambtonquay. blogspot.com/2010/04/un-declaration-on-rights-of-indigenous.html, accessed 29 April 2011.

Charters, C. and R. Stavenhagen (2010) *Making the Declaration Work: The United Nations Declaration on the Rights of Indigenous Peoples*, Copenhagen: IWGIA.

Charters, C., L. Malezer and V. Tauli-Corpuz (eds) (2010) *Indigenous Voices. The UN Declaration on the Rights of Indigenous Peoples*, Oxford: Hart Publishing.

Christie, G. (2011) *South Atlantic Quarterly*, 110(2): 329–46.

Clay, J. W. (1985) 'Nation, tribe and ethnic group in Africa', *Cultural Survival Quarterly*, 9(3): 2–4.

Clech Lâm, M. (2000) *At the Edge of the State: Indigenous Peoples and Self-Determination*, New York: Transnational Publishers.

Clifford, J. (2001) 'Indigenous articulations', *Contemporary Pacific*, 13(2): 468–90.

Cockburn, C. and L. Hunter (1999) 'Transversal politics and translating practices', *Soundings. A Journal of Politics and Culture*, 12 (Summer), special issue on Transversal Politics, 89(4).

Colchester, M. (2002a) 'Indigenous rights and the collective conscious', *Anthropology Today*, 18(1): 1–3.

Collins (2009) *Collins Dictionary*, www.collinslanguage.com/, accessed 19 August 2009.

Conklin, B. A. (2002) 'Shamans versus pirates in the Amazonian treasure chest', *American Anthropologist*, 104(4): 1050–61.

De la Cadena, M. and O. Starn (2007) *Indigenous Experience Today*, New York: Berg.

Department of Labour (1985) *Immigrants and Ethnic Minorities – What words should I use?*, Immigration Division Department of Labour, prepared by the Resettlement Unit for the Interdepartmental Committee on Resettlement.

Dombrowski, K. (2002) 'The praxis of indigenism and Alaska native timber politics', *American Anthropologist*, 104(4): 1062–73.

Dove, M. R. (2006) 'Indigenous

people and environmental politics', *Annual Review of Anthropology*, 35(1): 191–208.

Durie, M. (1995) *Nga Matatini Maori: Diverse Maori Realities*, Paper prepared for the Ministry of Health, Wellington.

— (1998) *Te Mana, Te Kawanatanga: The Politics of Maori Self Determination*, Auckland: Oxford University Press.

Escobar, A. (2010) 'Latin America at crossroads: alternative modernizations, post-liberalism or post-development?', *Cultural Studies*, 24(1): 1–65.

Fahim, H. M. (1972) *Nubian Resettlement in the Sudan*, Florida: Field Research Projects.

— (1973) 'Nubia after resettlement', *Current Anthropology*, 14(4), October.

— (1981) *Dams, People and Development. The Aswan High Dam Case*, New York: Pergamon Press.

Feit, H. A. (1995) 'Hunting and the quest for power: the James Bay Cree and Whitemen in the 20th century', in R. B. Morrison and C. R. Wilson (eds), *Native Peoples: The Canadian experience*, 2nd edn, Toronto: McClelland & Stewart.

Fernea, R. (2004) 'Putting a stone in the middle: the Nubians of northern Africa', in G. Kemp and D. P. Fry (eds), *Keeping the Peace. Conflict Resolution and Peaceful Societies around the World*, New York and London: Routledge.

Fernea, R. A. and G. Gerster (1973) *Nubians in Egypt: Peaceful People*, Texas: University of Texas Press.

Fernea, R. A. and J. Kennedy (1966) 'Initial adaptations to resettlement: a new life for Egyptian Nubians', *Current Anthropology*, 7(3): 349–54.

Fernea, R., E. Warnock Fernea and A. Rouchdy (1991) *Nubian Ethnographies*, California: Waveland Press.

Fischer-Kowalski, M., S. J. Singh, L. Ringhofer, C. M. Grünbühel, C. Lauk and A. Remesch (2011) 'Socio-metabolic transitions in subsistence communities. Boserup revisted', *Human Ecology Review*, 18(2).

Fischermann, B. (forthcoming) *La Cosmovisión de los Ayoréode del Chaco Boreal*, Translation of B. Fischermann (1988), *Zur Weltsicht der Ayoréode Ostboliviens*, Bonn: Rheinische Friedrich-Wilhelms-Universität.

Flower, L. (2003) 'Talking across difference: intercultural rhetoric and the search for situated knowledge', *College Composition and Communication*, 55(1): 38–68.

— (2008) *Community Literacy and the Rhetoric of Public Engagement*, Carbondale: Southern Illinois University Press.

Forsyth, T. and A. Walker (2008) *Forest Guardians, Forest Destroyers: The Politics of Environmental Knowledge in Northern Thailand*, Chiang Mai: Silkworm Books.

Fox, J. (2000) 'How blaming "slash and burn" farmers is deforesting mainland Southeast Asia', *Analysis from the East-West Center*, 47: 35–42.

Friedman, J. (2002) 'From roots to routes: tropes for trippers', *Anthropological Theory*, 2(1): 21–36.

Garroutte, E. M. (2004) *Real Indians: Identity and the Survival of Native America*, Berkeley, Los Angeles and London: University of California Press.

Geschiere, P. (2005) 'Autochthony and citizenship', *Quest: An African Journal of Philosophy*, XVIII: 9–24.

Giles, J. (2006) 'Tide of censure for African dams', *Nature*, 440, 23 March.

Gomes, A. G. (2004) 'The Orang Asli of Malaysia', *International Institute for Asian Studies Newsletter*, 33: 10.

Gramsci, A. (1971) *Selection from the Prison Notebooks of Antonio Gramsci*, ed. and trans. Q. Hoare and G. Smith, New York: International Publishers.

Grandstaff, T. (1980) *Shifting Cultivation in Northern Thailand*, United Nations University Resource Systems Theory and Methods Series no. 3.

Guardian (2009) 'Nubian fury at "monkey" lyric of Arab pop star Haifa Wehbe', 17 November, www.guardian.co.uk/world/2009/nov/17/nubian-fury-haifa-wehbe?INTCMP=SRCH, accessed 17 November 2009.

Hale, C. R. (2006) 'Activist research v. cultural critique: indigenous land rights and the contradictions of politically engaged anthropology', *Cultural Anthropology*, 21(1): 96–120.

Hale, S. (1979) *The Changing Ethnic Identity of Nubians in an Urban Milieu: Khartoum, Sudan*, PhD dissertation, Los Angeles: University of California.

— (1989) 'The impact of immigration on women: the Sudanese Nubian case', *Women's Studies*, 17: 53–6.

— (2001) 'Testimonies in exile: Sudanese gender politics', *Northeast African Studies*, 8(2): 83–128.

Hassan, F. A. (2007) 'The Aswan High Dam and the international Rescue Nubia Campaign', *African Archaeological Review*, 24(3/4), December.

Hinton, P. (1983) 'Do the Karen re-ally exist?', in J. McKinnon and W. Bhuksasri (eds), *Highlanders of Thailand*, Kuala Lumpur: Oxford University Press, pp. 155–68.

Hirsch, P. (ed.) (1997) *Seeing Forests for Trees: Environment and environmentalism in Thailand*, Chiang Mai: Silkworm Books.

Hodgson, D. L. (2002a) 'Introduction: comparative perspectives on the indigenous rights movement in Africa and the Americas', *American Anthropologist*, 104(4): 1037–49.

— (2002b) 'Precarious alliances: the cultural politics and structural predicaments of the indigenous rights movement in Tanzania', *American Anthropologist*, 104(4): 1086–97.

Indigenous Peoples Caucus (2006) *UN Thumps Indigenous Peoples*, www.ipcaucus.net/, accessed 25 May 2007.

International Crisis Group (2007) 'A strategy for comprehensive peace in Sudan', *Africa Report*, 130, 26 July.

International Rivers (2011) *New Chinese Dam Project Fuels Ethnic Conflict in Sudan*, 20 January, www.internationalrivers.org/en/node/6121, accessed 20 March 2011.

Jeffreys, M. D. W. (1946) 'The wanderers', *African Affairs*, 45(178): 37–41.

— (1953) 'The Batwa: who are they?', *Africa*, 23(1): 45–54.

Jones, A. and K. Jenkins (2004) *Journal of Intercultural Studies*, 25(2): 143–59.

Jones, C. (2010) ahi-ka-roa.blogspot.com/2010/04/new-zealands-support-for-undrip.html, accessed 29 April 2011.

Jonsson, H. (2005) *Mien Relations: Mountain People and State Control in Thailand*, Ithaca, NY, and London: Cornell University Press.

Kennedy, J. G. (1966) 'Occupational adjustment in a previously resettled Nubian village', in R. Fernea (ed.), *Contemporary Egyptian Nubia. A Symposium of the Social Research Centre, American University in Cairo*, Connecticut: Human Relations Area Files.

Kenrick, J. (2005) 'Equalising processes, processes of discrimination and the Forest People of Central Africa', in T. Widlock and W. G. Tadesse (eds), *Property and Equality*, vol. 2: *Encapsulation, Commercialization, Discrimination*, Oxford: Berghahn.

— (2006) 'Discussion: the concept of indigeneity', *Social Anthropology*, 14(1): 17–32.

— (2009) 'The paradox of indigenous peoples' rights', *World Anthropologies Journal*, 4.

Kenrick, J. and J. Lewis (2004a) 'Discussion: on the return of the native', *Current Anthropology*, 45(2): 263.

— (2004b) 'Indigenous peoples' rights and the politics of the term "indigenous"', *Anthropology Today*, 20(2): 4–9.

Keyes, C. (1993) 'Who are the Lue? Revisited ethnic identity in Laos, Thailand and China', in *Conference on the State of Thai Cultural Studies*, Bangkok: Office of the National Commission on Culture.

King, M. (2004) *Being Pakeha Now. Reflections and Recollections of a White Native*, Auckland: Penguin.

Kronenberg, A. (1987) 'Nubian culture in the Sudan in the 20th century: state of research', in T. Hägg (ed.), *Nubian Culture Past and Present*, Papers presented at the 6th international conference for Nubian Studies in Uppsala, 11–16 August 1986, Stockholm: Konferenser A.

Kunstadter, P. (1979) 'Ethnic group, category and identity: Karen in northern Thailand', in C. Keyes (ed.), *Ethnic Adaptation and Identity: The Karen on the Thai frontier with Burma*, Philadelphia, PA: Institute for the Study of Human Issues, pp. 119–63.

Kunstadter, P. and E. C. Chapman (1978) 'Introduction: problems of shifting cultivation and economic development in northern Thailand', in P. Kunstadter, E. C. Chapman and S. Sabhasri (ed.), *Farmers in the Forest: Economic Development and Marginal Agriculture in Northern Thailand*, Honolulu: University Press of Hawaii, pp. 1–23.

Kuper, A. (2003) 'The return of the native', *Current Anthropology*, 44(3): 389–402.

— (2004) 'Discussion: on the return of the native', *Current Anthropology*, 45(2): 261–7.

— (2006) 'Discussion: the concept of indigeneity', *Social Anthropology*, 14(1): 17–32.

Lawrence, B. (2004) *'Real' Indians and Others: Mixed-Blood Urban Native Peoples and Indigenous Nationhood*, Lincoln and London: University of Nebraska Press.

Leach, E. (1954) *Political Systems of Highland Burma: A Study of Kachin Social Structure*, London: London School of Economics and Political Science.

Lee, R. B. (2006) 'Twenty-first century indigenism', *Anthropological Theory*, 6(4): 455–79.

Leonhardt, A. (2006) 'Baka and the magic of the state: between autochtony and the citizenship', *African Studies Review*, 49(2): 69–94.

Lesch, A. M. (1998) *The Sudan:*

Contested National Identities, Bloomington and Indianapolis: Indiana University Press/Oxford: James Currey.

Lewis, J. (2005) 'Whose forest is it anyway? Mbendjele Yaka Pygmies, the Ndoki Forest and the wider world', in T. Widlock and W. G. Tadesse (eds), *Property and Equality*, vol. 2: *Encapsulation, Commercialization, Discrimination*, New York and Oxford: Berghahn.

Lorde, A. (1984) 'The master's tools will never dismantle the master's house', in A. Lorde and C. Clarke, *Sister Outsider: Essays and Speeches*, Berkeley, CA: Crossing Press Feminist Series.

Mackey, E. (2005) 'Universal rights in conflict: backlash and benevolent resistance to indigenous land rights', *Anthropology Today*, 21(2): 14–20.

Maybury-Lewis, D. (ed.) (1984) *The Prospects for Plural Societies. 1982 Proceedings of the American Ethnological Society*, Washington, DC: American Ethnological Society.

McIntosh, I., M. Colchester and J. Bowen (2002) 'Comment: defining oneself, and being defined as, indigenous', *Anthropology Today*, 18(3): 23–4.

McKinnon, K. (2006) 'An orthodoxy of "the local": post-colonialism, participation and professionalism in northern Thailand', *Geographical Journal*, 172(1): 22–34.

— (2007) 'Post-development, professionalism and the political', *Annals of the Association of American Geographers*, 97(4): 772–85.

— (2011) *Development Professionals in Northern Thailand: Hope, Politics and Power*, Singapore: Singapore University Press, forthcoming.

Merlan, F. (2009) 'Indigeneity: global and local', *Current Anthropology*, 50(3): 303–33.

Mohamed Salih, M. A. (1993) 'Indigenous peoples and the state', in H. Veber, J. Dahl, F. Wilson and E. Waehle (eds), *'Never drink from the same cup': Proceedings of the Conference on Indigenous Peoples in Africa, Tune, Denmark, 1993*, Copenhagen: IWGIA & the Centre for Development Research.

Moon, P. and P. Biggs (2004) *The Treaty and Its Times – the Illustrated History*, Auckland: Resource Books.

Morton, J. (1989) 'Ethnicity and politics in Red Sea Province Sudan', *African Affairs*, 88(350): 63–76.

Muehlebach, A. (2001) '"Making place" at the United Nations: indigenous cultural politics at the U.N. Working Group on Indigenous Populations', *Cultural Anthropology*, 16(3): 415–48.

Namara, A. (2007) *GEF Evaluation Case Study: Impacts of creation and implementation of national parks and of support to Batwa on their livelihoods, well-being and use of forest products*, Washington, DC: GEF Evaluation Office.

Omura, K. (2003) 'Comment: the return of the native', *Current Anthropology*, 44(3): 395–6.

Paul Oldham, M. A. F. (2008) '"We the peoples." The United Nations Declaration on the Rights of Indigenous Peoples', *Anthropology Today*, 24(2): 5–9.

Pelican, M. (2009) 'Complexities of indigeneity and autochthony: an African example', *American Ethnologist*, 36(1): 52–65.

Plaice, E. (2003) 'Comment: the return of the native', *Current Anthropology*, 44(3): 396–7.

Poeschke, R. (1996) *Nubians in Egypt and Sudan. Constraints and Coping Strategies*, Saarbrücken.

Poirier, S. (2010) 'Change, resistance, accommodation and engagement in indigenous contexts comparative (Canada–Australia) perspective', *Anthropological Forum*, 20(1): 41–60.

Pratt, M. L. (2007) 'Afterword: indigeneity today', in M. D. L. Cadena and O. Starn (eds), *Indigenous Experience Today*, Oxford and New York: Berg.

Radhakrishnan, R. (2003) 'Postcoloniality and the boundaries of identity', in L. Martín Alcoff and E. Mendietta (eds), *Identities: Race, Class, Gender and Nationality*, Oxford: Blackwell, pp. 312–33.

Rangihau, J. (1975) 'Being Maori', in M. King (ed.), *Te Ao Hurihuri: The World Moves On, Aspects of Maoritanga*, Wellington: Hicks Smith and Son.

Republic of Uganda (1995) *Constitution of the Republic of Uganda*, Kampala: Law Development Centre.

Reuters Africa (2010) 'Sudan's Bashir sees Islamic law, defends flogging', 19 December, af.reuters.com/article/topNews/idAFJOE6BIo4I20101219, accessed 20 April 2011.

Rist, G. (2008) *The History of Development: From Western origins to global faith*, London and New York: Zed Books.

Rose, D. B. (2009 [1992]) *Dingo Makes Us Human: Life and land in an Aboriginal Australian culture*, Cambridge: Cambridge University Press.

Rosengren, D. (2002) 'On "indigenous" identities: reflections on a debate', *Anthropology Today*, 18(3): 25.

Saugestad, S. (2000) *Dilemmas in Norwegian Development Assistance to Indigenous Peoples: A Case-Study from Botswana*, se1.isn.ch/serviceengine/FileContent?serviceID=7&fileid=895F0E0D OOₓO-ᴜᴦʙᴜ-ᴄᴇᴜ 8-3 FC5432051A9&lng=en, accessed 3 April 2008.

— (2001a) 'Contested images: "First Peoples" or "marginalized minorities" in Africa?', in A. Barnard and J. Kenrick (eds), *Africa's Indigenous People: 'First Peoples' or 'Marginalized Minorities' in Africa?*, Edinburgh: Centre of African Studies, University of Edinburgh.

— (2001b) *The Inconvenient Indigenous: Remote Area Development in Botswana, Donor Assistance, and the First Peoples of the Kalahari*, Boras: Nordic Africa Institute.

Schadeberg, T. C. (1999) 'Batwa: the Bantu name for the invisible people', in K. Biesbrouck, S. Elders and G. Rossel (eds), *Central African Hunter-gatherers in a Multidisciplinary Perspective: Challenging elusiveness*, Leiden: Research School for Asian African and Amerindian Studies (CNWS), University of Leiden.

Scott, J. C. (2000) *Hill and Valley in Southeast Asia ... Or Why the State is the Enemy of People Who Move Around ... Or ... Why Civilizations Can't Climb Hills*, Paper presented at the conference Development and the Nation-State, Washington University.

— (2010) *The Art of Not Being Governed: An Anarchist History of Upland Southeast Asia*, Singapore: National University of Singapore Press.

Sharif Saeed, M. (1993) *The Changing Role of Nubian Women in Khasm*

El-Girba, Eastern Sudan, Unpublished master's thesis, American University in Cairo.

Singh, S. J. (2003) *In the Sea of Influence: A World System Perspective of the Nicobar Islands*, Lund Studies in Human Ecology 6, Lund: Lund University Press.

— (2006) *The Nicobar Islands – cultural choices in the aftermath of the tsunami*, Vienna: Czernin Verlag.

— (2009) 'Complex disasters: the Nicobar Islands in the grip of humanitarian aid', *Geographische Rundschau*, international edn, 5(3): 48–56.

Smith, G. H. (1992) 'Education: biculturalism or separatism', in D. Novitz and B. Willmontt (eds), *New Zealand in Crisis*, Wellington: Government Printers.

Smith, L. (1992) 'Maori women: discourses, projects and Mana Wahine', in S. Middleton and A. Jones (eds), *Women and Education in Aotearoa* 2, Wellington: Bridget Williams Books Ltd.

— (1999) *Decolonizing Methodologies: Research and Indigenous Peoples*, London: Zed Books.

— (2005a) 'On tricky ground: researching the native in the age of uncertainty', in N. Denzin and Y. Lincoln (eds), *Handbook of Qualitative Research*, 3rd edn, London: Sage, pp. 85–107.

— (2005b) 'Imperialism, history, writing, and theory', in G. Desai and S. Nair (eds), *Postcolonialisms: An Anthology of Cultural Theory and Criticism*, New Brunswick, NJ: Rutgers University Press, p. 102. Reprinted in *Decolonizing Methodologies: Research and Indigenous Peoples* (1999), London: Zed Books, pp. 19–41.

Spivak, G. C. (2008) 'Righting wrongs – 2002: accessing democracy among the Aboriginals', in *Other Asias*, Oxford: Blackwell, pp. 14–57.

Suppachai, J. (1999) *Citizenship and State Policy: How We Can Move Beyond the Crisis*, Chiang Mai; Legal Aid for Marginalized People (LAMP) Project.

Suzman, J. (2001) 'Indigenous wrongs and human rights: national policy international resolutions and the status of the San in southern Africa', in A. Barnard and J. Kenrick (eds), *Africa's Indigenous People: 'First Peoples' or 'Marginalised Minorities' in Africa?*, Edinburgh: Centre of African Studies, University of Edinburgh.

— (2002) 'Kalahari conundrums: relocation, resistance and international support in the Central Kalahari Botswana', *Before Farming*, Online version, 3/4(12): 1–10.

— (2003) 'Reply: the return of the native', *Current Anthropology*, 44(3): 399–400.

Sylvain, R. (2002) 'Land, water, and truth: San identity and global indigenism', *American Anthropologist*, 104(4): 1074–85.

— (2005) 'Disorderly development: globalization and the idea of "culture" in the Kalahari', *American Ethnologist*, 32(3): 354–70.

— (2006) 'Class, culture, and recognition: San farm workers and indigenous identities', in J. S. Solway (ed.), *The Politics of Egalitarianism: Theory and practice*, New York and Oxford: Berghahn Books.

Thongchai, W. (1994) *Siam Mapped: The History of the Geo Body of a Nation*, Chiang Mai: University of Hawaii Press.

Tito Eman, L. (1997) *Nubians in the Urban Diaspora: Change and*

Revival of Ethnic Identity, Unpublished master's thesis, American University in Cairo.

Toyota, M. (1998) 'Urban migration and cross borer networks: a deconstruction of the Akha identity in Chiang Mai', *Southeast Asian Studies*, 35(4): 197–223.

Trigger, D. S. and C. Dalley (2010) 'Negotiating indigeneity: culture, identity and politics', *Reviews in Anthropology*, 39(1): 46–65.

UNDF (United Nations Democracy Fund) (2008) *News from the Field: Promoting and protecting the rights of Indigenous and Highland Ethnic Peoples in Thailand*, www.un.org/democracyfund/XNewsIndigenousPPLThailand.htm, accessed 20 February 2008.

United Nations (2006) *General Assembly GA/SHC/3871*, www.un.org/News/Press/docs/2006/gashc3871.doc.htm, accessed 25 May 2007.

Venkateswar, S. (2001) 'Gender/power: some perspectives from the "outside"', in I. Keen and T. Yamada (eds), *Gender and the Dynamics of Culture*, Senri Ethnological Series 56, Japan: National Museum of Ethnology, pp. 207–26.

— (2004) *Development and Ethnocide: Colonial Practices in the Andaman Islands*, IWGIA Monograph Series, Copenhagen: International Work Group for Indigenous Affairs (IWGIA).

Waitere, H. (2008) 'Cultural leadership: creating futures our ancestors can walk in with our

children', *Journal of Educational Leadership, Policy and Practice*, 23(2): 3–47.

Waitere, H. and P. Johnston (2009) 'Echoed silences: in absentia, Mana Wahine in institutional contexts', *Women's Studies Journal*, special issue: 'Feminisms in practice', 23(2): 14–31.

Waitere-Ang, H. (1998) *Te kete, the Briefcase, Te Tuara, the Balancing Act – Maori Women in the Primary Sector*, Unpublished Master of Educational Administration thesis, Massey University.

Waitere-Ang, H. and P. M. Johnston (1999) 'If all inclusion in research means is the addition of researchers that look different, have you really included me at all?', Te Uru Maraurau, Palmerston North: Department of Maori and Multicultural Education, Massey University.

Walker, A. (2007) 'Will the community forest act be good for farmers?', New Mandala blog, asiapacific.anu.edu.au/newmandala/2007/11/23/will-the-community-forest-act-be-good-for-farmers, accessed 20 April 2011.

Wanat, B. (1989) 'Government policy: highland ethnic minorities', in J. McKinnon and B. Vienne (eds), *Hill Tribes Today*, Bangkok: White Lotus, pp. 5–31.

Woodburn, J. (1982) 'Egalitarian societies', *Man*, 17(3): 431–51.

Wyatt, D. (1984) *Thailand: A Short History*, Chiang Mai: Silkworm Books.

About the contributors

Elizabeth Allen (Ngati Porou/Te Aowera) received her BA in criminology, and her BA (Hons) in women's studies, at Victoria University, Wellington, New Zealand. As an activist, Elizabeth is concerned with the rights of *tāngata whenua* throughout the world. Her research interests are feminist, post-colonial, queer and cultural studies. Email: wahinearts@gmail.com

Avril Bell is a senior lecturer in sociology at Massey University in Palmerston North, New Zealand. Her main research interests are in settler–indigene relations, settler nationalisms and the cultural politics of immigration, with a particular focus on Aotearoa/New Zealand. She is the author of a number of chapters and journal articles on these topics. Email: s.a.bell@massey.ac.nz

Benno Glauser was born in Switzerland and graduated in philosophy of science from the universities of Fribourg (Switzerland) and Cambridge (UK). He has lived in Latin America since 1974. After working in several countries with political prisoners in the context of dictatorial governments and repression, from 1977 he settled in Paraguay and has directed his work since then towards social minorities and marginalized, voiceless and 'invisible' social groups, and particularly towards indigenous peoples, combining grassroots work with social research aimed at their empowerment and at creating space for an active presence and role in today's world. From 1993, he explored the situation of isolated (uncontacted) indigenous groups in Paraguay. In 2002 he was a co-founder of Iniciativa Amotocodie, an NGO concerned with monitoring and protecting isolated indigenous groups in the northern Paraguayan Chaco whose work he directed until 2009. He has also worked as a teacher at Paraguayan universities, and is the author of books and articles on topics related to his social work. E-mail: bennoglauser@gmail.com

Justin Kenrick received a BA in social anthropology at the University of Cambridge and his PhD in social anthropology at the University of Edinburgh. He lectured in social anthropology at the University of Glasgow until 2009, when he returned to working with the Forest Peoples

Programme to support Central African forest peoples, and to working on parallel processes of community resilience in Scotland (e.g. www. pedal-porty.org.uk and www.holyrood350.org). He is a member of the St Andrews Sustainability Institute, and a research fellow in social anthropology at the University of Edinburgh. Email: justin@forestpeoples.org or justinkenrick@yahoo.co.uk

Christopher Kidd received his MA in anthropology at the University of Glasgow and his PhD in social anthropology at the same university. His research and work among the Batwa of south-west Uganda focus on the impact of development and conservation initiatives on Batwa livelihoods and futures. Chris works for the Forest Peoples Programme, an indigenous rights group that works to secure the rights of forest peoples globally. Email: drchriskidd@gmail.com

Katharine McKinnon is a lecturer in human geography at Macquarie University, Sydney. She is a cultural geographer working on the geopolitics of development with a particular interest in how dominant social and political discourses come into being and how they are challenged and altered through the everyday actions of ordinary people. Much of her research is based in the northern borderlands of Thailand, exploring development professionalism, the practice of community development and the indigenous rights movement. Email: katharine.mckinnon@ mq.edu.au

Simron Jit Singh (PhD, human ecology) is engaged in field-based sustainability studies in Asia, primarily among non-industrial societies on their way to integrating fully into the market economy. His main empirical interests are examining the altering patterns of society–nature interactions within the framework of sustainability science, humanitarian aid and the environment, and sustainability transitions. His books are: *In the Sea of Influence: A World System Perspective of the Nicobar Islands* (2003), *The Nicobar Islands: Cultural Choices in the Aftermath of the Tsunami* (2006), *Humanitarian Aid and Sustainable Development: The Nicobar Islands as a Case for Complex Disaster* (forthcoming). He has been awarded an International Fellowship from the Austrian Ministry of Education, Science and Culture, a START Fellowship within the framework of the IHDP-IT global environmental change research and, more recently, the RAI Fellowship in Urgent Anthropology attached to Kent University, UK. Email: simron.singh@aau.at

Teanau Tuiono (Ngai Takoto/Ngapuhi/Atiu) is a Māori activist from Aotearoa/New Zealand. He is a key contributor to Indigenous Portal, an initiative of IITF: International Indigenous ICT Task Force. He currently works with UNESCO and is involved in a capacity-building project in the Solomon Islands. Email: teanau.tuiono@gmail.com

Hine Waitere (Nagti Tuwharetoa/Kahungunu/Tuhoe me Tainui) is the director of the newly established Centre for Indigenous Leadership at Te Whare Wananga-o-Awanuiarangi, an indigenous university on the east coast of the North Island. She is concurrently the Professional Development Director of He kakano, a project working to develop culturally responsive leadership in a third of all secondary schools in Aotearoa/New Zealand. Her research interests are grounded in Kaupapa Māori, Mana Wahine (equated to Māori feminism), educational leadership and critically self-reflective practice(s). Email: Hine.Waitere@wananga.ac.nz

Index

new view of, 105–6); definition of, 49, 193–5; first-wave, 247, 250; mapping of, 77; politics of, 49, 50, 51, 239; resistance to, 107 (in Africa, 96); second-wave, 1, 7, 8, 14, 246–55 (among Nubians, 254); use of term, 53–4 (tensions in, 93)

indigenous: as relational term, 26, 108; meaning of term, 13; use of term, 43, 154, 157, 162, 168, 170 (as tool for enablement, 56–7; by Maori people, 56; contested, 12–13; in Africa, 98; in political sense, 254); usefulness of term, 167

indigenous activism, 1, 9, 51, 194

indigenous culture: as tourist curiosity, 98; understanding of, 175

Indigenous Futures Workshop, 153

indigenous identity, assertion of, 94, 96, 103

indigenous peoples: concept of, discarding of, 4; connecting of, 235–6; distinct from tribal peoples, 193; existence of, denied, 199; ILO definition of, 147–8; in Northern Thailand, 149–53; in voluntary isolation, 25, 30; interchangeable with tribal people, 194, 197; modes of production of, 112; names of, 69; relationship with nature, 111; stereotypes of, 80; struggles of, 45–8; treatment of, 29; use of term, 57, 93, 158, 163; used as scapegoats, 95

Indigenous Peoples' Centre for Documentation, Research and Information (DOCIP), 4, 236

Indigenous Peoples' Decades, 153, 154, 155, 160, 161

indigenous rights: denial of, 95; organizations, 191–245

infanticide, of twins, 202

influenza, epidemics of, 192

integration, option of, 202

International Indigenous Day, 169

Internationa Labour Organization, 168; Convention 107, 198; Convention 169, 198, 229; definition of indigenous peoples, 147

international non governmental organizations (INGOs), 14, 192, 216

International Work Group for Indigenous Affairs (IWGIA), 7, 14, 153, 168, 191, 192, 203, 206–30, 234, 237, 241, 242, 243, 244

interviews, methodology of, 23–4

Intra-American Commission, 219

intuition, 25; as a cognitive device, 24

Inuit People Circumpolar Conference, 228

iwi, 64; English translation of, 55

Jackson, Moana, 55, 56, 57, 63–5, 143

Jarawa people, 201; resettlement of, 191–2

Kahnawake Mohawk reserve (Canada), 72

Kajbar Resistance Committee (Sudan), 137–8

Kamol, an activist, 163

Karne, use of term, 155

Kasem, an activist, 160, 161

kawa, 64–5

Khamkhaeng, an activist, 163, 165

Khamu peoples, 145

khonmuang, use of term, 158–9

Kidd, Christopher, 140–1, 238

King, Michael, 54

Klahan, an activist, 158

knowledge: internal and silent, 35; traditional, 161 (seen as less relevant, 152)

Kuna peoples, 89

Kuper, Adam, 4, 199

KURU organization (Botswana), 205

Lachmi, Rani, 177

Lahu peoples, 145

land: ancestral lands, return to, 135, 254; and mining companies,